The Comedy of Manners

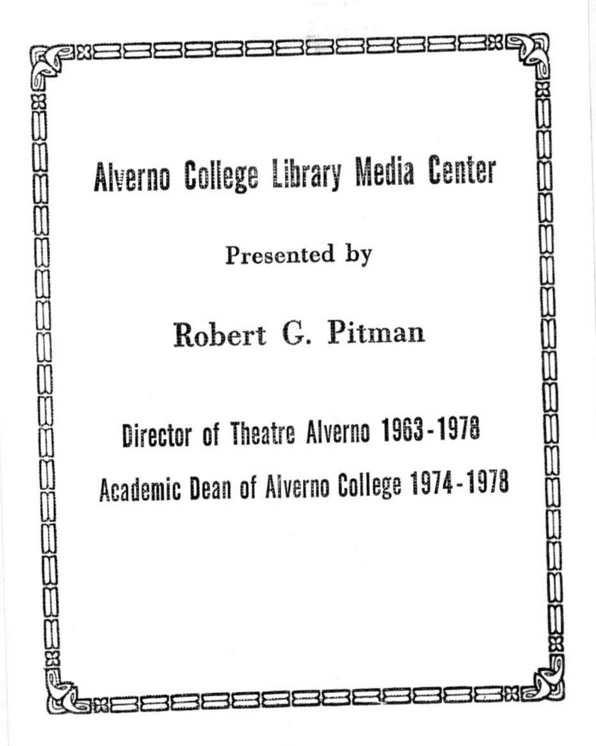

The COMEDY of MANNERS from SHERIDAN to MAUGHAM

by Newell W. Sawyer

A Perpetua Book

A. S. Barnes & Company, Inc.

New York

Printed in the United States of America

PERPETUA EDITION 1961

TO MY MOTHER

IN LOVING APPRECIATION
OF HER INVALUABLE HELP

CONTENTS

I

THE DECLINE OF A TRADITION

1730–1800

IT has been often attested that one gets close to the real soul of a man or a people through observing what that man or that people finds to laugh at. Without entering into the philosophy of the matter, however, we may at least be sure that the term "comedy" connotes larger possibilities than those of mere entertainment, and as a form of drama, for instance, affords a vehicle for the criticism of life. The purpose of our present discussion is to note the character and performance of a particular type of comedy, the comedy of manners, in England from the time of Sheridan's *The School for Scandal* to the beginning of the World War in 1914. When we contrast this type in its flourishing in 1700 and in its languishing in 1800 we are confronted with more than the vicissitudes of stage history: we glimpse in reflection significant changes in English society.

For a moment let us call to mind the nature of comedy in general and of the comedy of manners in particular.

Comedy may be said to direct its emphasis upon incident, manners or character, though of course these elements cannot be exclusive of each other. The first entertains by its complications, the second by its exposure of a social scene and the third by its depiction of human nature. The last two, often merged indistinguishably, take us into the realm where true or high comedy prevails. High comedy views man as a social animal in the midst of his fellows, with customs, conventions, and traditions of his own devising, and prods him gently or mockingly, as he stands confounded by that which he has made. It catches him red-handed in folly or stupidity, in inconsistency or errors of taste or of judgment, or in self-pity or sentimentality, and administers the lash on his bare back or thumps him playfully over the head with the blown bladder. According to the extent of his obliquity is the severity of the castigation, whereby the soul is cleansed by laughter as by a fresh, sweet wind.

Furthermore, incongruity being at the heart of the comic, and man, as a bundle of disparities and contradictions, being the supreme incongruity, it follows that the higher types of comedy will concern themselves primarily with people rather than with incident, except as incidents grow out of what the people are. The glory of comedy, as of drama in general, has been its portraiture, based on observation, subject to the transmuting power of the imagination. In the apprehension of such characters the intellect functions more than the emotions. The judgment is stimulated more than sympathy. As Walpole said, "Life is a comedy to him who thinks." Hence high comedy is for the few, though it may contain surface elements that suffice for the amusement of the many.

It is upon characters, thus responsibly conceived, that the thoughtful Meredithian laughter is directed, by which comedy is lifted above the plane of sensation and amusement and becomes an intellectual experience. One laughs, but, having detachment of mind, he sees his potential self in the object of his laughter; and thereby, as it were, he is laughed at as well as laughing. Thus laughter must be finely tempered, searching, corrective, yet always humane, if it is to rise to the noble pretensions of a spiritual therapeutic and comedy be realized to its highest. If it be tinctured with sentiment, it loses its silvery peal and becomes conscious of itself, breeding self-pity. Only when an individual or a society has become emancipated morally and intellectually can he or it withstand the fusillade of that laughter with remedial effect. Yet high comedy does not purport to be satire. To reflect sincerely the social scene suffices. Satire is rather a matter of mood or flavor as the writer may dispose. Neither is a moral implication necessary to nor conformable to the highest reaches of comedy. What of ethical significance the reader or beholder elects to gather from a play is his own; that which a too zealous author elects to do for him will probably be nobody's. Setting up standards and passing judgment upon the people of a play as their conduct betrays a departure from those standards is a posture the Englishman with his endowment of moral earnestness is prone to assume. But here a danger lurks—the engrossment of the writer may cloud that high disinterestedness which art should display.

The phrase " comedy of manners " refers to a comedy form reflecting the life, thought, and manners of upper-class society, faithful to its traditions and philosophy.

It is intellectually and dispassionately conceived, in the nature of a detached commentary, in which the only moral considerations are sincerity and fidelity to the facts of the society represented. The attitude of the playwright is, at least theoretically, unpartisan, although it is difficult for a latent flavor of satire to be kept out entirely. Characters may emerge into complete individuality, but more often universal traits give way to those types into which the world of fashion inclines to reproduce itself. Dialogue is naturally of more than ordinary importance, for the leisure of this world promotes the cultivation of verbal smartness, and this smartness dialogue must display, even if at the expense of naturalness. And lastly, one feels a certain idealization of the whole picture—a heightening of values, a seasoning of effects, an acceleration of tempo.

By the end of the third decade of the eighteenth century the last of that group of talented playwrights who had caught into their comedies of manners the wit, the *raillerie* and the glamor of the world of fashion had passed from the earthly scene. Commencing with George Etherege and ending with Vanbrugh and Farquhar they had for all time achieved the comedy of high life. Cibber's *The Provoked Husband* (1728), a reworking of Vanbrugh's *A Journey to London,* and one of the very last full echoes of the Restoration, still adhered essentially to the traditions of the type, though the protecting cynicism and unmoral nonchalance of that type were beginning to crumble before the rising tides of a moral awakening. A momentum had been created, however, which continued until well past the mid-century, with very appreciable acceleration from the pens of George Colman the elder, particularly in *The Jealous Wife* (1761) and *The Clandestine Marriage* (1766), and of Arthur Murphy, e.g., in his *The Way To Keep Him* (1760) and *Know Your Own Mind* (1778).

And yet the comedy of manners as a type was becoming ineffectual as the second generation since its apogee arrived. Mr. Nicoll says[1] the phenomenon was due to a degeneration of taste, a complexity of standards and aims, a confusion of sentiment with purely artistic purposes in a play, lapsing into burlesque and farce, whereas the decay of the drama of 1610–1642 was symptomatic of a great age going to seed in its social and moral ideals. Even the comedies of George Colman the elder marked a drift from the manners school, which may be glimpsed in an occasional character, phrase or scene. Satire was gone. Dialogue was no longer paramount, but incident. We are in a world of squires and middle-class folk. The gentry appeared now as decadents in their dotage, to be laughed at or made occasions for preachments on democracy. Melodramatic situations began to appear, as is inevitable when playwrights have lost the art of dialogue. Sensibility was everywhere. Harriot in *The Jealous Wife* is so shocked and hurt that Charles, the romantic hero, should have been tipsy the night before, that she is blinded to his unmistakable devotion and manly remorse and orders him out of her life with an imperious

[1] Allardyce Nicoll, *History of Early Eighteenth Century Drama*, 1700–1750.

gesture. (Of course she orders him back later.) How many hundreds of years have elapsed from 1661 to 1761! In Harriot we have entered a new world—the world of Clarissa and Evelina, of Amelia and Lydia Bennet.

Just when it seemed that the English comedy of manners was to die out altogether, Sheridan penned his *School for Scandal,* which with all the defects that critics have essayed to lay at its door is a brilliant *tour de force* of comic writing, a gem of artifice and scintillant cleverness. Yet we see it to have sprung from Sheridan and not from his age. Its very remarkable vogue of popularity extending well into the next century was but a tribute to its intrinsic capacity to entertain; it was powerless to stem the tides of popular taste drifting toward the didactic, the sentimental, and the sensational upon the stage.

The quarter century elapsing between *The School for Scandal* and the close of the century found the London theatres dispensing a liberal fare of comedy, some of which established a faint kinship with comedy of manners; but only faint, because of the impregnation of sentiment and of moral consciousness. Hugh Kelly's *School for Wives* (1773) presents surface features of the comedy of fashion, but the chief use by the author of the Irish servant, Connolly, is to point some wholesome apothegms against dueling. Though a happy, roistering sort of fellow such as Farquhar knew so well to draw, he can burst into tears when it seems his master is to marry for money, and exclaims, "I am sure nobody's eye ever looks half so well as when it is disfigured by a tear of humanity." The last lines of the play are worth quoting as showing how a moral can be dragged willy-nilly into a play by the heels.

Miss Walsingham: The modern critics say that the only business of comedy is to make people laugh.

Belville: That is degrading the dignity of letters exceedingly, as well as lessening the utility of the stage. A good comedy is a capital effort of genius, and should therefore be directed to the noblest purposes.

Miss Walsingham: Very true; and unless we learn something while we chuckle, the carpenter who nails a pantomime together will be entitled to more applause than the best comic poet in the kingdom.

Mrs. Hannah Cowley's *The Belle's Stratagem* (1780) is quite a lively play, full of amusing situations and of neatly turned, satirically flavored dialogue. Mrs. Inchbald in *I'll Tell You What* (1785) and *Everyone Has His Fault* (1793)—containing a serious minor plot—espouses the spirit of meliorism unmistakably. Situations in the hard, clear, unemotional manner of the Restoration she shows herself capable of devising, only to turn away from the invitation at the beck of feeling. The temper of her dramatic instinct is exemplified in her typically eighteenth-century attitude toward the comedy of Shakespeare. Frequently his exuberant naturalism offended her sense of decorum. Of the Falstaff of *Merry Wives of Windsor* she naturally disapproved. Dryden's version of *The Tempest* she preferred to Shakespeare's. Caliban repulsed her; Ariel was evanescent.[2] In *Everyone Has His Fault* and in *Wives as They Were and Maids as They Are* (1797) characters pursue the follies and vices of fashionable life; intrigue abounds; and yet we strive in vain to succumb to the illusion of old comedy. Libertinism, which abounded as profusely during the Regency as in the days of Charles and of Anne, suffered a timely redemption; gayety was dissolved in a saccharine solution of sentiment. We are conscious of the presence of a thesis just out of sight. Already comedy was turning to domestic scenes and themes. Nicoll justly senses the atmosphere of Dickens fifty years before the *Pickwick Papers.* Like most of her confreres Mrs. Inchbald borrowed liberally from the French—from Molière or from lesser lights that followed him—but as is normally found in such English practice she failed to catch the *élan* of the original.

Other references to comedies of the eighties and nineties will but deepen our impression that comedy of manners cannot breathe an air too freighted with the urge to exalt virtue; to weep with apprehension when it is under the cloud and weep with tremors of relief when it at last emerges triumphant. These things were but symptomatic of the moral consciousness of the age of the English doctrinaire novel and of Rousseau's *Nouvelle Heloise.* A solemn, persevering sense of reform was remote indeed from the light, acid touches of corrective satire that comedies of manners were wont to employ. Thomas Holcroft was caught up in the sweep of humanitarian ideas, in the political and philo-

[2] S. R. Littlewood, *Elizabeth Inchbald and Her Circle,* p. 112.

sophic speculation emanating from the struggle for liberty in France. Even his lighter comedies did not escape a too pronounced intentionalism. Sir Frederick Fashion in *Seduction* (1787), a not unworthy successor of the long line of fashion-worshipping old rakes throughout the eighteenth century, like Sir Fopling and Lord Foppington, not only does not succeed in his amours but is held up to open repudiation as an object lesson of depravity. Count Villars in *The School for Arrogance,* Covent Garden (1791), a prosy borrowing from the French, exchanges sensibilities with the nobly born Lucy as if he were not to the manner born. *Duplicity* (1781), in both briskness of dialogue and in fresh, natural presentation of men and women, is distinctly the nearest to genuine comedy of the three.

Frederick Reynolds in the nineties, connected with the Della Cruscans of sentimental memory, wrote such reasonably actable comedies as *The Dramatist* (1789) and *The Rage* (1794), retaining something of the conduct and characterization of the Restoration—but only something. Among the people of the play are "Sirs" and "Lords" and "Ladies," but the titles are worn with a difference. In *The Rage* Sir George Gauntlet, the not very convincing rake of the *beau monde,* is defeated in his designs by Gingham, who represents the honest, outspoken merchant class, proud of its common origins. The folk of fashion are now made stupid, the butts for ridicule. And the way they are drawn, they undoubtedly deserve it. From this time on for decades one finds practically never the world of society represented as sufficient to itself; whether one calls it immoral or unmoral, it had at least been represented in earlier years as superbly unconscious of any obligations or allegiances save to itself. It wore life upon its breast only as a bauble perhaps, but at least it wore the toy exquisitely. But in *The Rage* the Honorable Mr. Savage is a boor, consorting with touts and gamblers, and his sister is a loud, horsy woman, arrogant, mannish, of atrocious tastes. Mrs. Darnley in Act II, Scene 2 somewhat smugly voices not only herself but Mr. Reynolds and his London public when she remarks, "I find that good breeding is confined to no rank or situation; it consists in good sense and good humour; and I believe we may see as large a share of it under the roof of the cottage as in the splendid mansions of the great." A very proper note in itself but a discord to the ear of worldly comedy. And characteristically enough, the play ends with protestations of virtuous conduct as the characters see the curtain, like the coming of the final Judgment, descending upon them. Here as elsewhere the surface earmarks of genteel comedy are illusive. The voice is Jacob's voice, but the hands are the hands of Esau.

In much the same general category fell the erstwhile popular comedies of Thomas Morton, such as *A Cure for the Heartache* (1797) and *The School of Reform or How to Rule a Husband* (1805). Here, too, the touch of gentility, of breeding in so-called polite society, is gone. Behavior is shoddy and uncouth. Folly and knavery no longer attract because done with a flourish of aplomb. Sinning has ceased to be a fine art. The scene characteristically shifts from town to country.

Beaus and roués give way to country squires.[3] Our entertainment depends now not so much upon cleverness of language and of plot manipulation as upon strong contrasts, strong flavor, broad humor. With the advent of rural and domestic scenes came a new ardor in lifelike imitation of sights and sounds upon the stage. The curtain of *The School of Reform* went up on such a scene—"Farmyard: house on one side; neat flower-garden on the other; the bells of a team jingling." Little by little stage effect came to be an absorbing end in itself. The integrity of art was being sacrificed to the temporary and local achievement of actor and scene-painter. Adroit yet honest play construction fell into disuse. Plays we feel to be built arbitrarily from the outside in, not from the inside out. The old comedy with its ingenious involution and evolution and neat correlation of character and plot became a rarity. Furthermore, the plays of Morton illustrate the ever-growing trend toward language of the theatre rather than language of life. This tendency is but another indication of a waning dramatic instinct. Such passages as the following from *The School of Reform* (by no means exceptional) will illustrate for Morton and for others this indulgence in theatricalism:

Frederick: 'Tis true, I think of my birth with grief, but till vice can be proved hereditary, I will not think of it with shame: if virtue be an inmate in this breast, shall I basely scorn the foster-

[3] It is almost symbolic of this shifting emphasis that the wearing of court dress and swords as Parliamentary attire is changed by the innovation of Mr. Fox and that the plebeian umbrella begins to supplant the more patrician cane in the hands of the gentleman pedestrian. Traill and Mann, *Social England,* V, 600.

ing hands that placed it there? . . . O generous imperial Britain! Look proudly round; and while other nations boast their Pantheons of gods, do thou display thy princely endowments for calamity—thy palaces for poverty. I've talked too long—pray pardon me; but, oh! this heart—this grateful heart—was bursting! (I: 2).

Sir Hubert Stanley: But away with care—this is a moment devoted to ecstasy—this is the hour a doating father is to clasp an only child, who, after combating with disease and death, returns triumphant to his arms, in lusty health and manhood. (I: 3).

Among other comedies of these latter years of the eighteenth century, worthy at least of mention for their partial adherence to the manners genre, were Richard Griffith's *Variety* (1782), in which the characters hold up rather well the patrician manner, speech, and philosophy; Charles Macklin's *Man of the World* (1781), a robust and assertive play, devoid of taste and finesse, of a hackneyed plot but popular through its satirically treated Scotch caricature of Sir Pertinax Macsycophant; General Burgoyne's *The Heiress,* first played in Drury Lane in January, 1786, a near approach to the true spirit of comedy, praised by Walpole for its gentility and, despite its sentimental propensities, an easy and pleasant, if not smart treatment of polite society;[4] and Edward Jerningham's *The Welsh Heiress* (1795), a talented play by one who knew the world of fashion at first hand, if he did not entirely know the secret of writing a stage play. One is forced to believe that these, as

[4] Lady Emily's words in Act II might be used to describe the play: " A light, airy sketch of genteel manners as they are; with a little endeavor at what they ought to be, rather entertaining than instructive, not without art, but sparing in the use of it."

other comedies of the time, were in large measure given vitality by the talented way in which they were interpreted by the actors of the London theatres.

While these plays were in a measure continuing the manners tradition, the tastes of the day were being subscribed to by the unqualifiedly sentimental and decorous plays of George Colman the younger and of Richard Cumberland, both of whom possessed theatrical sense in considerable degree though but little dramatic power. *The Heir at Law* (1797) and *John Bull* (1803) of the former held the boards consistently with their ample effusions of humor and sympathetic treatment of everyday people. The aristocracy when introduced is confirmedly unprincipled or stupid. A romantic atmosphere, obviously foreign to comedy of manners, prevails. But Richard Cumberland is the arch-sentimentalist. If manners engage him, they are those of the lower classes. He is rectitude itself. Reconciliation and moral adjudication stamp themselves deeply on his endings, whatever violence may have been done meanwhile to the facts of life and human nature. Cumberland's words applied to his five-act comedy, *A Hint to Husbands* (1806), betoken his general practice:

> This play has been published, and they, who are pleased to patronize it in their closets, will perceive that I have persisted in making no sacrifice to the ruling fashion of the times, nor studied to contrive any situations which the favorers of farce are likely to be amused with; if it may aspire to any merit, it will be found where I would wish to place it, in the moral.[5]

[5] *Memoirs of Richard Cumberland*, p. 395.

We see comedy following two divergent courses: irresponsible, hilarious farce or a sentimentalized, morally intentioned comedy that nearly loses touch with laughter. Hear Cumberland again in the same book:

> I thereupon looked into society for the purpose of discovering such as were the victims of its national, professional, or religious prejudices; in short, for those suffering characters which stood in need of an advocate, and out of these I meditated to select and form heroes for my future dramas, of which I would study to make such favorable and reconciliatory delineations, as might incline the spectators to look upon them with pity, and receive them into their good opinion and esteem.[6]

It must be confessed that the author of *The Jew* and *The West Indian* wrote plays sincerely, according to the light as he saw it; the following decades were to show work less worthily conceived. Already the drift was setting in, as when he says: [7]

> I . . . never disgraced my colors by abandoning the cause of the *legitimate Comedy,* to whose service I am sworn, and in whose defence I have kept the field for nearly half a century—till at last I have survived all true national taste, and lived to see buffoonery, spectacle and puerility so effectually triumph, that now to be repulsed from the stage is to be recommended to the closet, and to be applauded by the theatre is little else than a passport to the puppet show—I only say what everybody knows to be true.

This last quotation from Cumberland voices in part at least the grievance of all types of legitimate comedy. Certain it is that drama of the theatre and drama as a form of letters had gone divergent ways—always a

[6] *Ibid.,* p. 142.

[7] John Genest, *Some Account of the English Stage,* VIII, 397.

parlous situation—and in the realm of comedy such a thing as literary standards may be dismissed as negligible. Even a high degree of structural skill and a talent for assemblage and manipulation of material with a maximum of effect was wanting. With occasional scenes of gayety and smartness and with occasional instances of vivid characterization we must rest content. Unity of action and effect were little sought after. Incidents were thrown together unconnectedly and without a sense of proportion. Writers played fast and loose with dramatic probability. Instead of ease and elegance were fustian and strained rhetorical effects; instead of wit and humor were cheap joking and buffoonery. As to the people of the play, they were man-made, not nature-made, and as such became absolute embodiments without shading. Leigh Hunt, a sympathetic playgoer, affirmed that he laughed at the actors in the comedies of Dibdin and Reynolds but could not recall the dialogue.

The comedy of manners that had flourished in the middle-eighteenth century soil of leisurely courtesy and good breeding found itself an anomaly in the new day of vision and revolt incident to and following the French Revolution. Paine and Godwin provoked a philosophy of mankind. Humble life was dignified. With such theories and such controversy the comedy of manners could have little traffic, nor was it amenable to such phrases as "the rights of man" and "the triumph of nature over artificial civilization." When Cumberland says[8] that he made a special search for those characters

[8] S. T. Williams, *Richard Cumberland, His Life and Dramatic Works*, pp. 103, 104.

that are usually exhibited upon the stage as butts for ridicule and abuse, that he might, as their advocate, so present them to an audience as to awaken its good opinion and esteem, his humanitarianism at once betrays his affiliations. Moreover, the years of the Napoleonic Wars were years of discipline and denial. Amusements were curtailed. Promenades and masquerades by the *beau monde* ceased. Ranelagh and Almack's were suffering a sea-change. Bishop Wilberforce inaugurated a society for the reformation of manners. The externals of good breeding gave way before a compelling decorum. Of course all joy was not dead. The regency and monarchy of the fourth George was an epoch of fashion, like that of the first, though with more of glitter and less of *politesse* and taste. The routs and fêtes and balls of the Duke of Devonshire, the Marquis of Hertford, and the Duchess of St. Albans were almost national events, but somehow there was a pronounced decadence in it all. Beneath the laughter and the music was the ominous muttering of the discontented. We have already hinted at the new fashion to ridicule the aristocrat, to laugh at him rather than with him, to relegate him in a play to a rôle of villainy or senility and to exalt instead the worth and virtue of the true-born, common-bred Englishman. Yet in large measure the aristocrat was treated no worse than he had a right to expect; he was no longer a sympathetic part of the theatrical world as he had been a hundred years before. Indeed, he was vanishing from the drawing-room as he was from the stage. The modern beau, says *Blackwood's* for June, 1818,[9] has not the wit and the mischief

[9] *Blackwood's,* III (1818), 330.

of his ancestors. He is harmless but not innocent, unprepossessing in his naughtiness, too obvious by far. If he is still a beau, he is most positively no beau ideal.

> They would not injure a lady's honor if they could, if it required any trouble;—and they could not if they would, if it required any wit. . . . Damages have taken the place of duels—horses of mistresses—and boxing of intrigue. Or if they do fight now and then, it is not to defend a woman's honor,—for they would scorn to own a woman who had any; or to prove that they possess it themselves: but merely to show that they have nerves and impudence enough to do without it.

Hence it was quite inevitable that comedies of manners should have all but ceased to exist and that audience and play alike should have become bourgeois and parochial. The possibilities for a sympathetic or at least for a satirical treatment of high life in comic vein were not being realized. Perhaps a Sheridan could have compassed the task, but it would have been another labor of Hercules.

It is interesting to note that *The School for Scandal,* as the last great comedy of manners down to our time, continued to hold the audiences of a day foreign in spirit to its own, and that by reason of its unmatched brilliance of dialogue and situation. If the public seventy-five years after its advent were unused to and unfriendly toward the derision of affectation and sentimentality on the stage and found Sheridan's deft, complacent handling of the lancet of satire upon the world of the Surfaces and the Teazles not so derogatory as their palates would fancy, yet their continued patronage of the play testified to the power with which the psychology of high life was presented, to their delight in conversation raised to the level of an art, to the inherent capacity of wit and gayety at their best to triumph over sentiment, maudlin and diffuse. Walter Sichel in his work on Sheridan[10] states that *The School for Scandal* was played in London seventy-three times in the three seasons of 1777–1779 and nearly succeeded in making the American War of Revolution forgotten. Nor in the early seventeen-eighties did it lose its appeal, for according to the Theatrical Register of the *Gentleman's Magazine* it was performed at Drury Lane eighteen times in 1780, nineteen times in 1781, thirteen in 1782. In the years 1783–1790 it appeared in the neighborhood of fifty times and in the year of 1791 alone, twelve times. All this while it retained its popularity in the provincial theatres, which evaded the Licensing Act of 1737, when necessary, by "changing" the play into a burletta by the introduction of casual music

During the first seven years of the nineteenth century the Sheridan play appeared in the Theatrical Register twenty-four times, along with continued revival of the most popular comedies of manners, especially those of Colman the elder, Hannah Cowley and Arthur Murphy. From 1808, in which *The School for Scandal* was listed but once, there seems to be a marked falling off in the presentation of the manners genre of comedy, although revivals appeared at sporadic intervals on past the mid-century mark. Sheridan's comedy, for example, was revived in 1810, 1813, 1818, 1823, 1825, 1837, and 1839 (during this last season it played sixteen times). The

[10] Walter Sichel, *Sheridan from New and Original Material,* I, 580.

next year its stellar brightness was temporarily overshadowed by a comedy of far less magnitude, which had caught the public taste, i.e., the *London Assurance* of Dion Boucicault, playing sixty-nine times to a modest three by the older comedy. But the eternal gayety of the latter is evidenced by its occasional but persistent and successful revivals up to our own day. That it was repeatedly reprinted in England and upon the Continent and that it was translated into most of the languages of Europe and was reproduced variously on the Continental stage are corroborative evidences beyond the field of this paper. *The School for Scandal* put fresh lifeblood into the anæmic form of comedy by holding up in frequent revivals an example before the British theatre, but the transfusion of blood was ultimately futile. It was the last of a dramatic dynasty, not the precursor of a new. It was revived much but imitated seldom and in vain. Genest lists in the index to his *Some Account of the English Stage* twenty titles of plays beginning with "School for" or "School of," exclusive of *The School for Scandal.* Of these, fourteen appeared after 1777. The influence here of a very successful play upon the titles of other plays and possibly through the title upon the character of the work itself is to be expected but goes little beyond a verbal echo.

The consensus of critical reaction to the Sheridan play was what we should anticipate from the prevailingly Puritan attitude toward the theatre and the drama. Once again the *Gentleman's Magazine* affords us evidence. In January, 1778, appeared an article[11] deploring its immorality and reminding the theatres of

[11] *Gentleman's Magazine,* XLVIII (1778), 57, 58.

their commanding duty to combat vice and support the cause of virtue. The comedy is "as defective in morality as abundant in wit." "More dangerous to the manners of society than it can possibly tend to promote its pleasure." Referring presumably to Joseph Surface the writer remarks that "however odious hypocrisy may be, it is for the interests of virtue that some attention should be paid to appearances," and further says that Charles is more dangerous to morality than his brother because he is made attractive. He concludes by saying that Sheridan probably wrote the play to assist in destroying a taste for the sentimental comedy of Cumberland, but the latter "has judiciously exerted the whole duty of an author, which is, not only to paint nature, but to paint such parts of it as every good man would wish to see imitated." The judicial type of criticism with a vengeance! Again in 1799 the reviewer of a satirical poem[12] of passing interest takes occasion to cite *The School for Scandal* as making gambling, libertinism and debauchery amiable and attractive. Finally, in a critical and biographical article[13] running in the July and August numbers of 1816 and occasioned by Sheridan's death in July (hence certainly as adulatory as the circumstance would permit) we read that "it is to be lamented that the author did not apply himself with more care to improve the heart and stimulate the public mind to the cultivation of morality," and that "Mr. Sheridan on this occasion appears in a great measure to have forgotten the legitimate end of dramatic composition and not to have been sufficiently

[12] *Gentleman's Magazine,* LXIX (1799), 682.

[13] *Ibid.,* LXXXVI (1816), 178 ff.

sensible that whatever is intended for the amusement of society at large should also be capable of communicating solid instruction and producing real amendment."

In such clouding of values one wonders if the insouciance and *gaieté de coeur* of old comedy could ever return. In the whirligig of time, however, it did. To the mind of Macaulay, well ordered but frequently lacking in perspective and balance, robust but not subtle or adroit, and imbued with the thought of its generation, the comic dramatists of the Restoration were only the profligate spokesmen of a profligate age.[14] To meet their plays on a neutral, amoral ground, effecting the fine gesture of detachment, as Charles Lamb invites, is too exacting for a genius notably partisan and insular. Furthermore, though he commends the comedies of Sheridan (and of Congreve) for their correct and vigorous delineation of human nature, he believes that he has injured the cause of English comedy, for comedy is corrupted by wit. Sheridan's prodigality of wit is especially reprehended. "Flowers and fruits of the intellect abound; but it is the abundance of a jungle, not of a garden, unwholesome, bewildering, unprofitable from its very plenty, rank from its very fragrance." The eminent Macaulay does not apprehend the character and function of manners comedy when he compares Sheridan to Shakespeare to the detriment of the former. He finds no place for the confessedly artificial, confessedly over-wrought presentment of high life, its series of coruscating pictures drawn together by a plot into a lightly affected unity.

[14] T. B. Macaulay, "Comic Dramatists of the Restoration," *Edinburgh Review,* LXXII (1841), 490–528.

II

THE REIGN OF BAD TASTE

THE unequivocally reprimanding criticism of *The School for Scandal* on grounds of immorality (to which reference was made in the last chapter) was but one specific instance of excessive punctiliousness. Other illustrations of this moral "sensitivism" are not far to seek as the new century advanced. In 1809 Theodore E. Hook's farce, *Killing No Murder,* was refused a license by Mr. Larpent, the reader of plays, on the ground that Act II contained lines prejudicial to the Methodists (to which sect incidentally Mr. Larpent belonged). The following are the lines excised, as printed by Genest:

Apollo Belvi: I ordained myself and preached in a field, but I couldn't get a living by it . . .

Buskin: You a preacher!

Apollo Belvi: Yes and a teacher—now—I'll tell you how it was—over against my master's office—right opposite—lived an old dissenting gentleman—by trade a tailor and by calling a minister—dear man he used to discourse delightfully to be sure—and he—he Mr. Buskin—had a daughter—so to get favor in her eyes, I turned to and fell a preaching like anything myself.

Buskin: What a queer gig you must have looked in a pulpit . . .

Apollo Belvi: A tub—as I hope to be saved it was no better—so I preached and preached—la, how I did preach! till at last I preached myself plump into the heart of my young saint, ...[1]

[1] Genest, VIII, 148.

While George Colman, the younger, was censor of plays about the year 1825, he found occasion to strike out of a one-act farce at Covent Garden a topical joke relative to macadamized roads, just then coming into public notice: "They call the road muck-Adamed, but I call them damn'd muck."[2] Had the lines been extirpated because of their insipidity we could have applauded. (Some wag commented at the time that Colman always said "Maca - - -'s" roads, as he could never bring himself to pronounce the last syllable.) And still more squeamish was his ukase in 1832[3] that such phrases as these parenthesized be excised from *The Rent Day* of Mr. Douglas Jerrold: "(God) bless 'em;" "I can't (damn) business—it's (profane);" "isn't that an (angel)? (I can't tell, I've not been used to such company);" "(heaven) help us." But it would seem that the meticulous Colman must have achieved the apotheosis of seemliness when he affirmed, in answer to a query, that if *The Merchant of Venice* had never been acted and being suddenly brought to light should be submitted to censorship he would have to omit "It is an attribute of God himself" as a derogatory reference to Deity upon the stage.[4]

This "Victorian" attitude was still in continuance after the mid-century, when we still find all oaths and such words as "Lord" and "God" being expunged before production. In a footnote to one of a series of articles in the *Gentleman's Magazine* for 1827[5] on the

[2] C. E. Pearce, *Madame Vestris and Her Times,* p. 114.

[3] W. Blanchard Jerrold, *Life and Works of Douglas Jerrold,* V, 108.

[4] R. B. Peake, *Memoirs of the Colman Family,* pp. 432, 433.

[5] *Gentleman's Magazine,* XCVII (1827), 529.

London theatres and in connection with what he terms the estimable service to society of Jeremy Collier's early strictures upon the stage, the writer expresses his gratification at the propriety of plays of the early nineteenth century by noting that the Reverend James Plumptre, B.D., Vicar of Great Gransden, is able to deliver in 1808 a series of four sermons at Great St. Mary's Church, Cambridge, upon the "Lawfulness of the Stage." One feels from the trend of the times that the vicar probably saw a play as "lawful" if it enforced the proprieties of conduct rather than viewed it in that larger sense in which any sincere attempt to show mankind its own image in the glass of drama is a "lawful" thing.

In the midst of such profusion of propriety regarding things of the stage it is refreshing to re-encounter a sense of the abiding values in one who writes for the *Edinburgh Review*, June, 1829.[6] He says in substance that

> fastidiousness and hypocrisy have grown for many years, slowly but surely, and have at last arrived at such a pitch that there is hardly a line in the works of our old comic writers, which is not reprobated as immoral, or at least vulgar. The excessive squeamishness of taste of the present day is very unfavorable to the genius of comedy, which demands a certain liberty and a freedom from restraints.

During the years 1802–1804, a certain German, Herr Goede, sojourned in England and later set down his rather penetrating observations upon what he saw and heard. He has this to say of Cumberland's *West Indian*, one of the most popular comedies of its day:[7]

[6] *Edinburgh Review*, XLIX (1829), 317–351.

[7] C. A. G. Goede, *A Foreigner's Opinion of England*, p. 418.

I have seen it performed in Drury Lane before a very large audience; and have witnessed to my no small astonishment, the tumultuous applause bestowed upon the trivial sentences interwoven in the body of the piece. Whenever the actor, with a solemn accent, pronounced one of those choice scraps of morality, all the bystanders began to clap their hands; as if the goddess of Wisdom herself were promulgating her oracles for the illumination of mankind.

The whole question of the audiences of this time as one of the vital factors in explaining its drama is a vastly interesting one. Their degree of responsiveness is to us astounding. Their taste was doubtless vitiated, their sense of their own integrity as arbiters and critics was of course ill founded; yet, like all crowds drawn from the common levels, they could be considerate and charitable if they felt so prompted. The mention of true British hearts, British homes, British love of country or the strains of "Rule Britannia," enkindled audiences then as now. Vocal demonstrations from the galleries of approval or condemnation of a play were more or less patiently endured by the pit, itself a scene of frequent inattention or confusion. The meaner elements in society could be riotous and unreasonably dogmatic as during the famous O. P. (old price) riots, 1809, which lasted for sixty-seven days, at the opening of the newly rebuilt Covent Garden Theatre. In 1825 the actor, Young, while playing the part of Sir Pertinax Macsycophant at Covent Garden, was forced to stop and appeal in person to two critics whose collocations had become so loud and insistent as to drown out the play. Plays were often interrupted, sometimes forced to discontinue, because the smugly respectable crowd had discovered that some one upon the stage had been guilty of unconventional conduct in his private life. Thus Boaden recounts[8] that when the popular actress, Mrs. H. Johnston, who had violated her marriage vows and was at the time, 1807, a mother, attempted to return to the stage, she was greeted with a storm of boos and hisses that all but wrecked the performance. Reynolds remarks in 1826[9] that the incident in the epilogue to his *How to Grow Rich* of the actor pulling from under his coat at a certain juncture in his recital a lady's pad as a trophy of conquest was received with tolerance back in 1793, but in 1826, "what actor would have the temerity to do so and thus risk not only his loss of profession but actually his life?" One may be very sure the typical theatre audience craved sensation, novelty, declamatory delivery. With it the actor loomed very large or became indeed of sole importance. One can imagine the difficulty confronting a sensible actor in making the finesse and subtlety of a comedy of manners appreciated before such a crowd, for instance, as that which in 1804 carried its noisy adulation of the acting of young Master Betty to the point of actually hissing the work of far more reputable performers in the cast.[10]

As one scans the lists of stage performances in London from 1800 to 1850 he notices, early in that period, the rapid decline (begun years before, as already noted) in legitimate comedy forms, even in adaptation and revival, and in their stead an even more rank harvest of sensations and novelties. England's three great thea-

[8] James Boaden, *Memoirs of the Life of John Philip Kemble,* II, 446.
[9] Genest, VII, 105.
[10] *Memoirs of Joseph Shepherd Munden,* p. 118.

tres, the only three at that time receiving the sanction of the Crown, took on the nature of overgrown vaudeville houses and dance halls. Comedy had sunk to the level of mere entertainment. Mechanical stage tricks, lavish scenic display, extravaganza, pageantry were what theatre-goers wanted. Music became a stage feature: as a full-course repast in the form of opera for the élite, as a *hors d'oeuvre* in comic plays, and a sweet sauce of vocal numbers in romantic, sentimental plays. Such illegitimate intrusions of music upon the fields of drama are of course a sign of distress and decay. From about 1830 one notes a steady influx of foreign opera and foreign singers, the popularity of the mode having far surpassed the modest capacity of English composers and performers to supply. From 1847 Covent Garden became entirely a grand-opera house.

A dramatic critic in the *London Magazine* (1822)[11] goes to print in the lugubrious note he must have used so many times before: "This month has brought with it the usual quantum of what in the language of playbills is called novelty but still not that which would be the greatest of novelties—a sterling drama." Three months before, the same magazine had commented on the very pronounced vogue for processions in and for themselves[12]—not at the lowly minor theatres, as might be supposed, but two at Drury Lane and three at Covent Garden. The delightfully trenchant *John Bull* vents its disgust continuously at the parlous state of drama in the twenties. In 1820 not one good comedy ap-

[11] *London Magazine,* VI (1822), 373.
[12] *Ibid.,* VI (1822), 39.

peared, but sparring exhibitions were held on the stage of Drury Lane where Siddons and Kemble had blended their art with Shakespeare's. We note at Covent Garden in 1811–1812 the appearance of an elephant upon the stage in the pantomime *Harlequin and Padmanaba*[13] and in the opera, *The Virgin of the Sun* (libretto derived from Kotzebue, whose over-indulged, turgid romanticism was still exerting so marked an influence on English drama), an earthquake was introduced into the first act.[14] Again, at Drury Lane in 1823 we note the production of the romantic melodrama by Moncrieff, *The Cataract of the Ganges or The Rajah's Daughter.* Genest[15] says it was the finest spectacle ever exhibited, horses and a waterfall being features of this *tour de force.* Of a presentation of this same play the next year at Bath he quaintly remarks that the quadrupeds acted very well, the bipeds (with one exception) but badly.[16]

Earlier in 1792 at the same theatre the audience was regaled with a fox-chase in *Harlequin's Museum.*[17] Frederick Reynolds is responsible for the statement[18] that of the years 1809–1821, the most illustrious in the whole history of Covent Garden, the season of 1810–1811 was the most memorable, at least in point of financial return, the box-office receipts being £100,000, due largely, he asserts, to the introduction of cavalry

13 Genest, VIII, 287.

14 *Ibid.,* VIII, 290.

15 *Ibid.,* IX, 229.

16 *Ibid.,* IX, 273.

17 C. E. Pearce, *The Jolly Duchess, Harriott Mellon,* . . . , p. 136.

18 Frederick Reynolds, *Life and Times,* II, 403, 404.

upon the stage. The first forty-one nights of *Blue Beard,* revived with horses, alone was responsible for over £21,000. Of this same spectacle Genest feelingly remarks[19] that the smell of the horses was so strong in the front of the pit "that one might as well have sitten in a stable." Still it was heralded as one of the "exhibitions of the drama worthy of a critical and enlightened people."[20] All of which led Sheridan to say:

> Mr. Kemble would much rather, I am sure, act on his own two legs, than call in the aid of cavalry; but the fact was, that the taste of the town was more gratified by them; that taste being perverted by the depravity of manners, and the alteration in the mode of living, which prevented people of fashion from attending and taking the lead in the theatre as formerly.[21]

Reynolds claims[22] that his play, *The Caravan,* at Drury Lane in 1803 afforded for the first time the novelty of a dog jumping from a height into real water to rescue a child. He comments with evident satisfaction upon the impression created. It was with a general situation in his mind's eye such as these illustrations expose that Lord Harcourt, the friend and patron of the young comedian, Robert Elliston, wrote him in 1802:[23] "The pure drama has but little attraction for the unhappy fancy of the day. How is success at present calculated on?—a five act farce composed of such characters as never did yet exist, intermixed occasionally, with some forced or sickly sentiment, supported by grimace or

[19] Genest, VIII, 232.

[20] *Memoirs of Joseph Shepherd Munden,* p. 190.

[21] *Ibid.,* p. 193.

[22] Frederick Reynolds, *Life and Times,* II, 350.

[23] Geo. Raymond, *Memoirs of Robert William Elliston, Comedian.* I, 148.

buffoonery, with the motley train of processions, battles, spectres, pantomimes and Scaramouch ballets." And in much the same vein Mr. Jerrold wrote to T. J. Serle in 1835:[24] "A writer who, unassisted by a troop of horse, an earthquake, a conflagration, or a cataract, trusts merely to the conduct of his fable, his words and his characters, must fail, at least in the treasury sense, at either Drury Lane or Covent Garden."

To demonstrate the dearth of true drama, the *London Magazine* presented in 1822[25] a typical theatrical menu, to which a supposedly robust British appetite must resort:

1. *Virtue's Harvest Home,* bucolic comedy in five acts by T. M. Of broad, rustic humor, excellent handling of dialect, slender characterization.

2. *Britain's Glory,* by T. D., a comic opera in three acts abounding in punning, equivoque, and alliterative dexterities rather than in wit. Sentiment is dispensed in generous doses; as in the first play the farmers are always striking their bosoms in the fervor of their emotions, so here the sailors are ever wiping the drops from their eyes.

3. *The River-Rock; or The Crimson Hermits* by —. A French-derived, blatant melodrama in two acts.

4. *La Belle Assemblée* by Lumley Skeffington. A tame, insipid comedy of the Hugh Kelly strain, affording a glimpse into the life of fashion but denatured of all spirit, satirical or other. We little wonder at its lifelessness when we learn it had been transmogrified

[24] W. Blanchard Jerrold, "Memoir of Douglas Jerrold" in *Works of D. W. Jerrold,* V, 91.

[25] *London Magazine,* V (1822), 29, 137, 253, 362, 436.

and revamped from drama to farce to opera and finally to straight comedy. The writer of the article asserts that all that is now required in genteel comedy is decent, well-behaved dialogue, which this play possesses in plenty. Truly the Achilles of comedy had donned the clothes of a woman.

5. *Don Giovanni the XVIII*—a Musico-Burlesque, Comico-Nonsensical Opera by Moncrieff, a *mélange* of song and dialogue, slang and sensibility.

Such is a sample of the dramatic fare of those years—a veritable pot-pourri of warmed-over messes. The lines between comedy, tragedy, and farce had largely vanished, together with the sense of craftsmanship which educed them. Passing flurry of interest was all that was sought—and that largely by resort to elaborate and even grandiose stage effects, their sumptuousness being in inverse ratio to the sufficiency of the piece itself. The years of relief after Waterloo, in particular, prompted a reaction toward display and ostentation throughout society, finding its reflection on the stage in lavish scenic effects and in a rage for realism, which as a mere gesture of imitation of life, substituting for imaginative acting and sound dramaturgy, indicates decadence. This tendency toward a needless verisimilitude of stage scene is the subject of alarm by a writer in *Blackwood's* in 1856,[26] who sees the futility in supposing that Byron's *Sardanapalus* can be staged only after a thorough investigation of Assyriology, that *The School for Scandal* requires a sumptuous outlay of carpets, mirrors and silver plate, all in period, and that

[26] *Blackwood's Magazine,* LXXIX (1856), 209–231.

Dick Whittington and His Cat would be any more a success because a real cat was enticed upon the stage as one of the dramatis personae. He cites cases of the audience at a new play calling before the curtain for its commendation, not the actor, certainly not the author, but the scenic artist. In a time of such perverted emphasis one must look for clear-cut, single-minded delineation of manners and all the shades and gradations of comedy, not in the theatre but in the pages of Dickens and Thackeray.

One has only to look into the theatrical literature of this early and middle nineteenth century—its memoirs and biographies, its histories of the stage and its vast, often nondescript periodical comment and counsel—to become aware of two facts: the unanimity of opinion that dramatic art was in eclipse and the utter disparity of view as to the cause and the remedy. Here there is occasion only to note, with particular reference to the comedy of manners, a few of the diagnoses at the bedside of the patient. The major fact of the vitiation of public taste in matters of entertainment has been sufficiently referred to in previous pages, as has a Puritanism inherited from the previous century and now manifesting itself in a hypersensitive moral consciousness and a deeply grounded suspicion toward the world of the theatre. This state of the theatre-going mind is sufficient explanation for the temporary decline of the comedy of manners. But other contributory causes may be noted. In 1808 and 1809 Drury Lane and Covent Garden were rebuilt into great auditoriums inviting spectacle, extravagant action, and rhetorical delivery, inimical to that intimacy of association between actor and audience which the manners type solicits. Finesse in gesture, in facial expression, and in dialogue become incongruous if not impossible, especially when lighting and acoustic effects are inadequate. Munden points out [27] that the actor Lovegrove played at the Lyceum that fine old part of Lord Ogleby in *The Clandestine Marriage* with great nicety, but when later the play was transplanted to the huge interior of Drury Lane the effect was entirely lost. The exaggeration required to make the part heard spoiled the part. Adolphus in his *Memoirs of John Bannister* [28] bewails the advent of the larger buildings where actors must spout like auctioneers and all by-play is lost, and Alfred Bunn [29] pithily speaks of the prodigious size of these theatres as making them less temples of the drama than huge mausoleums wherein it is interred.

Again it is often claimed that the cause of the dearth of all drama at this time was the monopoly enjoyed by the great patent-houses (removed in 1843) in the production of legitimate drama. Each must maintain several companies, one for each type of performance, so that no matter how successful one may be, it fails, because it must pay for the inactivity of the others. A writer suggests (*Edinburgh Review,* October, 1843) that theatres be classified, no one to be licensed for more than one or two types of play. Thus a greater quantity of plays would be available, encouraging dramatic authorship and removing the invidious compe-

[27] *Memoirs of Joseph Shepherd Munden,* p. 178.

[28] John Adolphus, *Memoirs of John Bannister, Comedian,* I, 256, 257.

[29] Alfred Bunn, *The Stage Both Before and Behind the Curtain,* I, 45.

tition that was draining the life-blood of the theatres. The absence of a copyright law discouraged the publication of plays, which fact would have tended to lift them into literary recognition. If a manager chanced upon a successful production it was at once pounced upon by others, altered into a burlesque or an otherwise cheapened version and so foisted upon the public. Certain it is that managers then, as often now, displayed no higher interest in the drama than as a means of profit, and discouraged talented play-writing by incivility and inadequate remuneration. When a play may be seized and utilized without profit to an author, latent talent in dramatic composition is nullified at its source.

This lack of protection by copyright accounts largely for the influx of French plays into the English market in these years. It was of course folly for the manager to pay for a native play, albeit one of promise, when he might appropriate a pronounced Parisian success of one, two, or three acts and deftly adapt it for London consumption. Such a play had nothing substantial for the native drama save to furnish the object lesson of clever play handling. Sentiment it could donate in abundance, but its French smartness became lost in transit. The practice of such wholesale borrowing was indeed a confession of impotence. It spelled emasculation by thwarting germinal endeavor.

Again we hear that the stage was actor ridden. The star must arrogate to himself the part in which he could shine. The play was for him, not he for the play. Pieces of greater worth without such opportunity for self-magnification were perforce pigeonholed by managers. It was not the first nor yet the last time that a vogue of great acting stultified dramatic composition. We are left at last with a sense that many factors indeed played a part in the deterioration of drama. Probably the increase in club-life in London, the fashion for late dining and the inflooding of a tide of fiction and other reading matter were contributing factors. Actor, manager, author, theatre-goer each points at the other the finger of accusation. The manager says as George Colman did:

> If we give trash, as some poor critics say,
> Why flocks an audience nightly to our play?

and the public retorts that if better things were written it would patronize them, and then the author chimes in that he has bitter reason to know the falsity of that evasion, and so it proceeds in a vicious circle. The one great deplorable fact remaining is that drama in general and comedy in particular in a richly prolific nineteenth century were sterile.

III

VESTIGIAL REMINDERS

1800–1865

CERTAIN facts and phenomena in nineteenth-century dramatic history have been pointed out to explain, in particular, the dearth of comedy of manners in an age which was primarily given over to comedy of other kinds. The farces of Poole,[1] Pocock, Moncrieff, and Morton furnished hilarity, and the burlesques of Planché and others, which gradually replaced them in popular favor, afforded a more delicate amusement with their light piquant travesties upon serious themes and their increasingly gorgeous settings. Mme. Vestris, the talented actress and singer and even more talented manager, inaugurated at the Olympic Pavilion, beginning 1830, and later at the Lyceum in 1847, an era of light comedy in the form of extravaganza, comedietta, burlesque, farce, and the like that made her playhouse the acknowledged home of comedy in London. With such co-stars as John Liston and Charles Mathews comedy could find itself once more played with taste and moderation and with an approach to sober, simple reality, except of course in those mock-heroic travesties and delicate fairy extravaganzas already alluded to.

[1] His *Married and Single* (1824) is characteristic of his smart but intemperate composition. Wm. Farren found in Beau Shatterly another opportunity to personate the old rake in love.

With these names that lent luster to comedy should be linked that of Robert William Elliston, who in the first three decades of the century stood out as its best exponent of high comedy. In him ease and elegance supplanted buffoonery; his depiction of life and character approached as closely to comedy of manners as the vehicle he employed would permit. Yet, although one finds bits of fashionable life and flashes of wit and satire in the hands of these capable actors, they are but reminiscences. To be sure, comedies are not lacking in which polite society is featured, but the savor and the philosophy are not those of our type: it becomes either the *milieu* for a plot of intrigue or it sinks into mere froth and folly. Such for example are *Smiles and Tears* by Mrs. Charles Kemble, Covent Garden (1815); *Living in London,* attributed to Jameson, Haymarket Theatre (1815); *Husbands and Wives,* acted twenty-eight times at Covent Garden (1817); *Follies of Fashion* by the Earl of Glengall, Drury Lane (1829).

Of more interest than these (more for what it might have done than for what it succeeded in doing) was the comedy, *Quid Pro Quo or The Day of Dupes,* written by Mrs. Charles Gore, a popular and prolific novelist of the life of fashion, in response to the offer in 1843 by the Haymarket of a prize of £500 for the best prose comedy illustrative of modern British manners and customs, the contest being designed to stimulate original production in comedy, which was in thraldom to French modes either by adaptation or by actual translation.[2] After twenty meetings of the committee the

[2] *Gentleman's Magazine,* XXI, n. s. (1844), 630.

award was made to Mrs. Gore from among ninety-eight contestants. The nation-wide nature of the competition, the rather generous sum offered as a prize and the specific requirement that the comedy treat of British contemporary manners afforded the most favorable auspices under which a genuine manners play might come to light. But the almost inevitable happened. The author, who had shown herself not incapable of handling high society life in her novels, was drawn down to the level of her prospective audiences.

> If, as established rule from age to age
> Hath authorised the lessons of the stage,
> With comedy the pleasant duty lies
> To paint the manners living as they rise;
> Present fair folly's face reflected here,
> School with a smile, and chasten by a sneer;
> 'Tis time to turn some newer page and show
> Life as it is, and manners as they go! [3]

As Mr. Dutton Cook says of it,[4] she dealt with high life but in a broad, bustling way, knowing that audiences would be composed of middle-class, not aristocratic folk. Too often smartness and wit become mere plebeian jocosity. The *ménage* of the Earl of Hunsdon in the country with its affectedness and exclusiveness, its search for novelty and its private theatricals, is before us. The Countess and her lady daughter are but figures; Lord Bellemont, the son, is the young blade of the "slang school," oozing superiority and sangfroid but without the maturity to sustain such a posture. After all, it is the middle-class neighbors of this titled

[3] From Prologue of *Quid Pro Quo*.

[4] *The Theatre* (London), VI, n. s. (1882), 65–74.

family who occupy the center of the stage and it is Jeremy Grigson, the retired tradesman, who repudiates effusively his former toadyism to the aristocracy. What of discomfiture the comedy dispenses at its close is confined to the courts of the nobleman. The best of which the play can boast is a moderately interesting complication. Its dialogue is uninspired, damned by consistent mediocrity. After a sporadic run of five weeks it sank into an oblivion from which it has never been retrieved to our knowledge. Once again the creation of a comedy reflecting high life with all its charm and glamor was aborted because of insufficient artistic sympathy with the subject and the tyranny of public taste.

Other comedies by playwrights of far greater repute deserve passing recognition because of their approximation to the manners type at one point or another. Such are certain of the comedies of James Sheridan Knowles, who is best remembered in his rhetorical, pseudo-classical but impressive tragedies. *The Love Chase* (1837) and *Woman's Wit or Love's Disguises* (1838) take us into titled society, some of whom fall into categories familiar from the past. In the former, Sir William Fondlove is the superannuated but still ambitious lover, but Constance, his buxom daughter, and Wildrake, her sportsman neighbor, are scarcely detectable as upper class. In the latter comedy Lord Valentine is taught the lesson in constancy that he needs, in that he had believed his intended guilty of an assignation with the libertine, Lord Athunree, with whom he had seen her dancing. In both plays the character delineation is just enough for the safe conduct of the story. These lords and ladies scarcely know themselves sufficiently to present in word and behavior more than a suggestion of the manners of their world. Moreover, the fact that these comedies are written in blank verse presents an anomaly in the treatment of manners. Many of the speeches are long, amounting to recitals. Though not ineffective upon the stage, the dialogue and the situations are devoid of that crackle and sparkle and playfulness which the more artificial and more intense manners type displays. *The Hunchback* (1832), historical comedy of the time of Charles I, despite the fresh, sturdy sincerity in treatment and language that meant so much for English drama at that time is still more foreign to our purpose. The glimpse of the world of fashion was after all for Julia only a glimpse, a disappointing mockery. *The Old Maids* (1841) is rather more soberly and studiously limned in. In all of these the atmosphere, the flavor is not that of our type. Somehow Vandenhoff's personal impression of Knowles[5] fits the man who wrote these comedies. He emphasizes his hearty, brusque manner, his boisterous personality, one with vigor but without finesse or nicety of touch, not entirely free from affectations.

Certain of the comedies of Douglas Jerrold demand scrutiny. In the main they are distinctly domestic in type. With Jerrold's plays we feel a comfortable return to the natural after the welter of theatrical monstrosities which these barren years had afforded. Of

[5] Geo. Vandenhoff, *Leaves from An Actor's Note-Book,* p. 56.

the best, *Black-eyed Susan* (1829) is a nautical play; *Time Works Wonders* (1845) is a love story; *The Golden Calf* (1832) affords some glimpse of high life but only to prove its futility and the sedulous homage paid to wealth. *The Rent Day* (1832) is particularly close to the manners genre at the start but lapses into melodrama. On the other hand, his *Beau Nash* (1825) is a carefully studied historical comedy of the picturesque life and manners, the follies and foibles of the days of Richard Nash, Esquire, and the Pump Room at Bath. A satirical flavor is pervasive, perhaps incontinently so. The dialogue is sprightly, but repartee and the *bon mot,* neatly turned though they be, affect one as having been prepared beforehand. Reviewing this very happy comedy in the *New Monthly Magazine* for August, 1834, Mr. John Forster says Jerrold did not fear to have his characters occupy that rare and dangerous ground of neutrality between vice and virtue and yet be indifferent to neither—"the happy breathing-place from the burden of a perpetual moral questioning."[6] Much water had flowed under the bridges since such a statement about an English comedy could have been accurately made. Of it we feel that it does

> Eye nature's walks; shoot Folly as she flies,
> And catch the manners living as they rise.

To be sure it catches the manners of a time that was past, and one naturally associates the comedy of manners with a treatment of contemporary life, but the fact remains that Jerrold has assembled into one play

[6] W. B. Jerrold, *Life . . . of Douglas Jerrold,* footnote, pp. 112, 113.

in appreciable degree the essential features of a manners comedy.

Masks and Faces (1852), by Tom Taylor and Charles Reade, like *Beau Nash* and Knowles's *Hunchback* and *Beggar of Bethnal Green* (1834), is a comedy which draws its characters on a background of the past. It takes us back to a time rich in associations for the comedy of manners—the day of Peg Woffington, of Kitty Clive, of Quin and other folk of the Green Room. Colley Cibber is there—an old gentleman exhaling the fragrance of post-Restoration wit and gentility. Beneath her sophisticated exterior Peg has a true woman's heart, as she shows in shaming the lordly Pomander and in restoring the amorous Vane to his good wife. This very enjoyable play reflects the manners of a bygone day, rather as an incident to a general attempt to create historical illusion than as an expression of the inherent purpose of the piece. If it is mid-eighteenth century in subject, it is mid-nineteenth in treatment. Triplet, naïve, struggling, honest-hearted writer of tragedy with his good little wife and their hungry brood of children, each labeled with a grandiose theatrical name, is a bit of sentiment and humor consistent with the spirit of a Dickens, not of a Cibber or a Sheridan.

In 1840 a talented young member of Parliament, who had already got himself talked about by two successful romantic plays, produced a comedy. Its name was *Money,* its author's Edward Bulwer-Lytton. In terms of its day only is it considerable. Dealing with the *beau monde,* some reflection of its fashion of life is inevitable, but as we read it now, we feel how completely a thing of the stage it is, how amorphous, how overloaded like a Victorian parlor with all sorts of gimcracks of humor and sentiment, how pale in characterization, how affected in its efforts to be literary. Its creator was after all only a virtuoso, facile in rhetoric and in the weaving of a complication. Though *Money* possesses a certain surface glitter, it is at the last no true coinage. It rings false in its shallow logic of motivation and spurious sensibility. The play spins upon the theme of the emptiness of avarice beside the honest virtues as a thing to live by. Sir John Vesey is a humbug, a hypocrite, worshipping money and the respect it brings. Sir Frederick Blount is a Dundreary sort of person, a typical aristocratic ass. Evelyn, the "poor but honest" cousin of Sir John, unexpectedly inherits a fortune. Whereupon he is fawned upon by his rich relatives. When he tricks them into thinking he has lost it all, he discovers their real stripe, repudiates the proud Georgine and gains the Clara who has been all the while faithfully in love with him. The lovers are little more than "stock leads" in romantic melodrama. Lady Franklin, the outspoken, middle-aged lady of the world, subscribing to but undeceived by the dictations of society approaches most closely a manners type.

The following words as applied to Sir Frederick Blount by Georgine bespeak the difference between the young gentlemen of fashion of 1850 and of the century before:

> . . . one of the new class of prudent young gentlemen, who not having spirits and constitution for the hearty excesses of their predecessors, entrench themselves in the dignity of a lady-like

languor. A man of fashion in the last century was riotous and thoughtless—in this he is tranquil and egotistical. He never does anything that is silly, or says anything that is wise.

Times and fashions change but the method and the approach to them of the comedy of manners need not change. Bulwer-Lytton senses this fact but imperfectly.

The year following *Money* a much more significant play appeared in the field of the manners comedy, the *London Assurance* of Dion Boucicault. Artificial and full of fustian as the play is, there is in it for the stage an unmistakable heartiness and vigor of movement and dialogue and a lively vein of humor that persist even in the pages of the text. Something of the life of the town-bred, titled gentleman and his household is presented in the first act as we enter the rather carelessly conducted establishment of Sir Harcourt Courtly, a practical, unsentimental Victorian version of the middle-aged gentleman of means and social position. His son, Charles, is the young blade who drinks and does not pay his bills, but is within easy hail of reform when he hears the call of love. Young blades like Charles Courtly go on their happy, unchecked way, drinking and reveling; the town is their hunting-field, life their toy, women their especial game. Burgundy is drunk before breakfast, Sir Harcourt Courtly oils and perfumes his locks, gentlemen sing rousing songs while alone after dinner. They still duel, may be arrested for debt, and travel by post-chaise; they wear jabots, turned-over cuffs, military cloaks, white beaver hats, satin waistcoats and curly wigs. The language they affect is rhapsodical, surcharged with sentiment.[7] The later acts of the play, taking place upon the estate of a country squire, present an amusing series of involvements and mistaken identities with the expected denouement. Sir Harcourt thrusts the obvious theme upon us at the close:

> Barefaced assurance is the vulgar substitute for gentlemanly ease; and there are many who, by aping the vices of the great, imagine that they elevate themselves to the rank of those, whose faults alone they copy. The title of gentleman is the only one of any monarch's gift, yet within the reach of every peasant. It should be engraved by Truth—stamped with Honour—sealed with good-feeling—signed man—and enrolled in every true young English heart.

It would be easy to demonstrate the obvious defects of the play—its proneness to punning, its rococo style, its noisiness, its lack of articulation, its Victorian sentimentalism, concerning which Dickens is quoted as saying:[8]

> Shall I ever forget Vestris, in *London Assurance,* bursting out with certain praises (they always elicited three rounds) of a—of a country morning, I think it was? The atrocity was perpetrated, I remember, on a lawn before a villa. It was led up to by flower-pots. The thing was as like any honest sympathy, or honest English, as the rose-pink on a sweep's face on May-day is to a beautiful complexion; but Harley generally appeared touched to the soul, and a man in the pit always cried out, "Beautiful!"

It was the day of sentimental, mellifluous doggerel. One thinks of such fragrant titles as "Beauty's Garland," "Friendship's Garland," and "Memory's Gar-

[7] A. B. Walkley, *Playhouse Impressions,* p. 189.

[8] T. E. Pemberton, *Sir Charles Wyndham, a Biography,* p. 266.

land." Henry Morley[9] affords us a sane appraisal of the comedy after all the evidence on both sides is in: "That play succeeds because it has a fairly managed story, a pleasant variety of well-marked stage characters, enough of sparkle in the dialogue, although it is by no means good, and an easy sense of the ridiculous everywhere paramount. Want of power in the writing does not much offend an audience that is otherwise contented." Certainly it brings us a step further from the theatre-made comedy and a step nearer the more natural, hand-made comedies of the sixties and after. Boucicault knew the public, he knew something of the ways of society, he knew how to make a play be alive, even if he had no profound knowledge of life in the large. He contributed stagecraft to comedy production. He experimented, had the courage to discard traditions, and encouraged plays on the material of his day. His skill, ingenuity, and energy go far to excuse admitted failings. Contemporary London with its multifold social stratification was thus beginning to return to the boards, and this fact is laden with promise in any study of the comedy of manners, a promise that was soon to take on further confirmation in the comedies of Tom Robertson.

When Tom Robertson's play *Society,* after seeming doomed to languish forever in its author's pocket, was at last accepted by Marie Wilton at the Prince of Wales's Theatre in 1865, an event of importance transpired in the history of the English drama and of the English stage. It was not that Robertson was a great

[9] Henry Morley, *Journal of a London Playgoer,* p. 190.

dramatist—he was but a mediocre one; it was not that Miss Wilton was a great actress—she was only a very charming one; but in the conjunction of the two a saner, quieter, truer dramatic portrayal of life was once more afforded, where before, as Bernard Shaw puts it, there were only "sham heroics and superfluous balderdash." Robertson creatively, and the Bancrofts interpretatively (Miss Wilton married Squire, later Sir Squire, Bancroft in 1867), demonstrated the artistic possibilities in a natural story acted naturally.

We have already said something of the sorry plight of the drama throughout the foregoing half century, catering to an uneducated clientele, whose tastes ran to low comedy and spinal shudders. A few great actors lifted the drama of the past—and with it themselves—into prestige. But there was no one in all those years of vigorous intellectual activity in the literary field who wrote a play that could lead the taste of the public, instead of forever conforming to it. If we skim off the thin layer of cream from those years of the forties and fifties and sixties, we find even that a very milky fluid indeed. In society comedy this fact is impressively true. It inherited sedulously from the sentimental, respectable, prolix comedy of Colman, the younger, or of Thomas Morton, in whose *The Way to Get Married,* for instance, vice is properly ridiculed and a woman's amiability and rectitude are duly rewarded with a good husband. It also tried to reflect the drawing-room life of its day, but it was a very superficial and hearsay report that it gave. If the venerable situation of the tradesman's daughter winning the nobleman's son (it is she rather than he that the play felicitates) can be dressed up in a slightly different guise, success has been achieved. In one form or another the fopperies and follies of the social world got themselves pictured on the stage, but they were not enjoyed for their own sake, but as a foil to virtue and common sense.[10]

What are the names that come most easily to mind in those mid-century decades? There was H. J. Byron, extravagantly popular for his many light comedies, farces, and burlesques, none of which ever rises above the frivolous and puerile. *Cyril's Success* (1868) he deemed his best, but to us of today its humor seems forced, its lines padded. *Our Boys* (1875) contains some real uproarious fun, to be sure, but its author is capable of nothing beyond this native exuberance—no fulfilment of characterization, no apt dialogue, no real hold on life from the humorist's viewpoint,[11] and yet this piece of froth and foam ran 1,362 consecutive nights to filled houses, as its many modern counterparts do to-

[10] Those oft-repeated lines from *Lady Clara Vere de Vere,*

> " Kind hearts are more than coronets
> And simple faith than Norman blood "

might have been taken as the sober text for two-thirds of the comedies of those years.

[11] Sir Geoffry Champneys, a County Magnate, snobbish and class-conscious, cherishes a career for his son befitting a gentleman of station. But the young man proves to be cut out of the same cloth as the son of the parvenu butterman. At the end Sir Geoffry must acknowledge his reactionary class prejudices. Youth must be served. The claims of rank are drowned out in the lusty asseverations of democracy and independence. Manners are lost to view in broad comedy. What does it matter if the characters are strained and probability violated, so long as the audience can laugh loudly and often?

day. Byron's chief penchant was punning—a dubious expedient in excess. He is said to have expressed the ambition to write a play with a pun on every word. That he did not should be a matter for general thanks. Like many of the good fellows of the theatre, Byron was personally a man of most happy and generous instincts. The taste of the joy of life was on his lips, but his plays give it a most inadequate expression. He and Francis C. Burnand, later editor of *Punch,* became exponents of the burlesque—echoing Fielding and *The Beggar's Opera*—a vogue of light comedy that was then supplanting the older farce. Its anomalies of place and time (such as the Greek gods in a modern setting) and its travesties on opera and on the sensational East-side melodrama with its rant and its stock characters furnished a new type of amusement. It had not the daintiness or the ingenuity of the earlier Planché extravaganza, but at least it was what the people wanted.

Occasionally in the voluminous work of this recorder of mirth and irresponsibility there emerges a character or an episode that adheres lightly to the manners type. Sir Simon Simple, Bart. (the habit still persists of naming characters symbolically), in *Not Such a Fool as He Looks* (1869) proclaims at once the influence of Taylor's Dundreary. In fact, the part was originally intended for Sothern. Sir Simon is a sensible fellow enough but is unfortunate in his attempts to communicate his ideas clearly to others. As a result of a series of unlikely events he is uncertain of his parentage. At one time in the play he is a nobleman, at another a washerwoman's son, at another a member of a genteel family. Such a situation, though strained, is unquestionably ludicrous in Byron's hands.

Byron was confronted continually with opportunities which he denied. *Partners for Life* (1871) deals with gentle folk in a country house, but they talk and deport themselves rather like wags than like the best families of the county. The play proved to be one long laugh and as such was amply satisfying to the London public. In a later year we find the same farcical prostitution of material. His *The Open House* (1885) takes us to the house party of a country gentleman with all its diversity of interesting society types, but all is swallowed up in the unerring Byronian propensity for nonsense.

Tom Taylor (editor of *Punch* 1874–1880), who had collaborated with Reade in *Masks and Faces* (previously noted), was a man whom knowledge of life and of the stage rendered eligible for play-writing. In the span of thirty-five years he produced twice that number of plays, largely domestic and historical in character. He wrote with a pen that was not only facile but skilful. It is substantial, uninspired work that he did—the best of which mediocrity is capable.

His plays are as conventionally moral as were Cumberland's. *Plot and Passion* (1853), *Still Waters Run Deep* (1855), and *An Unequal Match* (1857) afford varied glimpses into that domestic play which the new democratized drama in the new age of middle-class ascendancy was bringing to the fore. *New Men and Old Acres* (with Augustus Dubourg) (1869) made a contrast between a gentleman of the old school and a self-made, purse-proud tradesman. The verdict of contemporary criticism was that it amused by its lively tempo and bright dialogue. Mrs. Kendal as Lilian Vavasour lifted the play into temporary significance.

An Unequal Match exhibits Taylor at his nearest approach to high comedy. Hester Grazebrook (Lady Arncliff) is a stage character that rises above the conventions of type. Having married above her station, she finds that her social blunders are losing her the respect of the solemnly important baronet who has stooped to wed her. In due time she educates herself into the perfect modish lady of the *beau monde,* and shows him how odious the so-called behavior of polite society can be. As we anticipate, he is led to perceive how preferable is a natural sincerity to affection. Once again a play has presented people of rank only to be lessoned, but here with less sacrifice of the happy spirit of comedy.

In *A Lesson for Life* (1866) at the Haymarket is something of the polished ease of good society. What *ton* it possessed was due in considerable measure to the presence in the cast of Sothern as Harry Vivian. *A Duke of Difficulties* (1861) needed more stiffening than even the talented Mrs. Stirling could give it, and proved a fiasco.

In these plays there seems to be no direct intention to reflect middle-class manners as is the case in later domestic drama, as we shall see. Taylor's *Ticket-of-Leave Man* (1863)[12] gave his audience its first real dip into London's seamy side since the days of Egan's *Tom and Jerry*. His prolific and fertile adaptations from

[12] *Era Almanack,* 1871, reports its 619th performance.

the French and from native novelists, like Dickens, were confessions of a lack of creative capacity that was wofully typical of the time. One feels himself confronted in Taylor, as in Boucicault, with an expert workman, a man having the talent of a playwright without the genius of a dramatist. Versatile he was, but not original. Even his adaptations were mere refurbishings without improvement. He paid no interest on what he borrowed.

A word should be said in passing of *Our American Cousin* (1861), a rather trivial piece that leaped into popularity and ran four hundred nights through the acting of the elder Sothern, who made Lord Dundreary a veritable creation. To the student of the comedy of manners, it is interesting that this portrayal of an aristocratic fop at first displeased the London swells; but later they came to relish its flavor of satire as being a commingling of what a fop really was with what the average American thought him to be. Needless to say, the country folk who saw the play at the time of the Cattle Show were more than satisfied. Here was one of many instances of a play being redeemed by an actor. The part of Lord Dundreary became memorable. He is the very glorification of inanity, the fullness of vacuity, and yet he is something more than a travesty. It was Sothern as Dundreary that set young Tom Robertson thinking about what he might do with comedies of contemporary life and manners.

A handful of minor names in comedy out of these early decades may be bundled and quickly dismissed. Most of them wrote a light kind of farcical play that is perhaps in the drawing-room but certainly not of it, for they themselves were not possessed of that experience and background of gentility which would enable them to write with conviction.

J. Palgrave Simpson, who, before his death in 1887, came to be the beloved grand old man of the dramatic fraternity, may be taken as an exception, for he came of a gentle Norfolk family, and graduated from Cambridge University. Yet, despite his instinctive breeding and his cultivation of mind, enriched by travel and refined associations, he is typical of the general run of playwrights of his day. His more than sixty pieces for the stage consist more often of melodrama, farce, extravaganza, and French adaptation than of original comedy. Two of his better plays that are available for reading will illustrate the man's work. *The World and the Stage* (1859), done especially for Miss Amy Sedgewick, was written to vindicate the stage in the eyes of the public. In a rather purposeful way he attempts to do what *Masks and Faces* had achieved—to show the humanity that lurked behind the professionalism of the actor. In *The School for Coquettes* (1859) he casts a play in the world of eighteenth-century comedy but without its tone or flair. It is a tame version of intrigue in the high life of 1730.[13] A lady places herself in the hands of Lady Amaranthe, an accomplished woman of the world, to learn the art of coquetry that she may recapture her husband's affection. The husband is cured of his philandering when he finds his wife is his equal

[13] His *Ranelagh* (1854), also a French adaptation and laid in the reign of George II, is another example of light society comedy seeking an earlier English scene for its *milieu*.

in the polite game of flirtation. Meanwhile, Lady Amaranthe has profited by her own instructions, and finds that a gentleman is to be desired above a mere parvenu of fashion. This slight comedy cannot escape notice because of the rarity of its type, but it is a feeble echo of Mrs. Cowley or Colley Cibber.

Other names are worthy of mention with Simpson's. Charles Selby wrote over sixty of the frothiest farces imaginable, mostly of only one act. Of him Godfrey Turner said that he played like an author and wrote like a player. Charles Dance was a popular writer of burlesque in the palmy days of Mme. Vestris. Edmund Falconer, associated with dramatic history both as a capable actor and as the unfortunate manager of the Lyceum and of Drury Lane in the late fifties and early sixties, is worthy of note in our study of society comedy for at least two plays, *Extremes: or Men of the Day* (1858) and *Woman: or Love against the World* (1860).[14] A word about the former will suffice for both. In it a common miner, Hawthorne, has risen to affluence through success in manufacturing and has married the daughter of a poor baronet. The play is concerned with the undignified contest that arises, after Hawthorne's death, to inherit his money. Upper class snobbery and greed are arrayed against rustic Lancashire bluntness and plebeian pride. A pretense of ele-

[14] It is interesting to note that Selby, Dance, and Falconer, like Byron and many other writers for the comedy stage, were actors. As a result their work has a facility to "get itself across the footlights," but little else. The testimony of managers of the times is of a plethora of aspirants for dramatic recognition, who were notably lacking in all practical knowledge of stage technique. This asset, at least, these actor-writers may be said to have possessed.

gance masks the cupidity of the one; the cupidity of the other wears no mask but its own vulgarity. Certainly here is a play of manners that are detestable. Only the usual pair of virtuous lovers are exempt, whose integrity rebukes the class consciousness of the others. A play that offered brilliant possibilities for satiric social comedy proves to be but labored and verbose. At many points it resembles Lytton's older comedy of *Money*. Some of the pugnacious repartee is quite readable, but the verbal duels are with clubs, not rapiers. The *London Times,* August 27, 1858, comments on the delight of the audience with this gusty, four-hour comedy. Perhaps the very blatancy of the manners it portrays in such bold strokes was the cause of their approbation. James, the butler, gives the ethics of the household when he says: "We sacrifice our haffections, but we never sacrifice our worldly interests. It haint the fashion in hupper or even in middle-life. Such things are only heard of now in Heast-hend melodramas." But their manners are as deplorable as their philosophy.

Such men as Bayle Bernard (died in 1875) and Stirling Coyne (died in 1868) are of interest only in that they touch so often the purlieus of the comedy of manners without ever actually achieving it. Like J. B. Buckstone, a genuine personality in the realm of broad comedy, both as actor and writer, Bernard was immensely prolific. Both well passed the century mark in production. Bernard, however, was capable of a more thoughtful type of play, though possessed of little dramatic aptitude. Coyne's farces were favorites at the Adelphi and the Haymarket for many years. In them manners and personality are submerged in hilarity. Coyne, like Bernard and John Oxenford,[15] borrowed freely and constantly from French sources,[16] and yet these men were regarded as among the most estimable literary critics of their day. Occasionally one meets in the Lacy or Duncombe collections with a slender one- or two-act play whose title or list of characters suggests that of the comedies of an earlier vintage, but on examination they prove to be farce or burlesque; an abortive use of the old *milieu.* The fish on our line gives a promising tug, but when he is reeled in he proves to be an inedible variety. Many of them might be described as Charles Selby labeled his *The Loves of Lord Bateman:* "an Historical, Pantomimical, Melodramatical, Balletical, Burlesque Burletta."

Other plays, perhaps, should be mentioned in these mid-century years, as showing a tinge of the manners genre here and there at a time when social comedy was prevailingly domestic, with emphasis on farcical situation, rather than on character. In 1851, through the agency of the Guild of Literature and Art, appeared Bulwer-Lytton's *Not So Bad as We Seem,* an amalgam of political intrigue and of manners in the time of George I, a pallid and artificial piece of work, as was *Money* before it. In fact, in both we find the same

15 Incidentally, Oxenford and Taylor each accounted for about one hundred plays upon the boards. Had all these men of nimble pen spent the same amount of time on five comedies each, they might have left something worthy of remembrance. But conditions rather than they were responsible.

16 His *Woman of the World* (1868), based on *Les Coulisses de la Vie,* rises somewhat above farce in its sharp contrasts of society types.

social complexion, and the stage types that appear in each have been cut from the same cloth. In the later comedy we meet the aristocrat, the prosperous man of affairs in the City, and the shallow-pated ape of the rich, Shadowly Saphead. It is a world in which money is the open sesame for high and low, and although it seems to have been the author's purpose to show that we are not so bad as we seem, yet one feels this play might with equal justice have been called "Money."

How She Loves Him (1868) by the ubiquitous Boucicault contains something of the verbal pleasantries, the witty exchanges, and the piquant situations of Colman or Murphy one hundred years before. A divorced wife is wooed legitimately by a fortune-hunting adventurer and clandestinely by her former husband whom she still loves. The husband feigns illness to evoke the lady's sympathies and summons four doctors, all of different medical persuasions. There is something here of the old madcap comedy with its gay irresponsibility and lively escapade.

Robert Sullivan's *Elopements in High Life* (1853) is a title that offers material, *in posse* if not *in esse*, to the student of artificial social comedy, as he thumbs the pages of the old theatrical journals. Reports seem to agree in calling it a vivacious but crowded little play with a flair for elegant dialogue and a fresh approach to the old theme of the fortune-hunter, his machinations and reform. From Sullivan, who had been reared as the son of a titled gentleman and who had studied at Oxford and the Inner Temple, more might have been expected than the fripperies of farce.

Of greater emphasis upon contemporary manners and certainly of greater literary merit is the very substantial comedy of J. Westland Marston, *The Favourite of Fortune* (1866), deriving in part from *Le Jeune Homme Pauvre*. The plot but rings the changes on oft-employed material, but in the dialogue is a real ease, charm, and wit quite exceptional in the sixties. Mrs. Lorrington, niece of an innkeeper and now a widow, who aspires (but unsuccessfully) to bury her past and to move in polite society, and Major Price, an old beau from the days of the Regency, approach reality. The absence of buffoonery in a comedy is in itself a refreshment.

One of the many borrowings from the French is an anonymous comedy that appeared at the St. James's in 1854. It is entitled *Honour Before Titles* and is taken from *La Poissarde*. It is one of that class of plays we have met before in which aristocratic is contrasted with plebeian life to the disparagement of the former. The haughty, purse-proud heroine is humbled through the machinations of her parvenu oppressor. In fact, so common is this type of vulgarian woman in comedies of the period that one might coin the word "poissardism" as a convenient label.

The repeal of the Special Privileges Act in 1843 enabled the minor theatres which had been entertaining legitimate drama *sub rosa* to compete with the Patent Theatres on equal terms. Gradually different houses pre-empted to themselves certain types of dramatic entertainment in favor with their patrons. Thus the Adelphi came to be the home of melodrama—an ultra-sentimental melodrama of stilted language.[17] Benjamin Webster and Mme. Celeste continued this tradition in the forties. In the fifties began an era of comedy, the Irish plays of Boucicault being the most successful.

At the Olympic we have already noted a genuine interpretation of comedy at the hands of Liston, William Farren, Mme. Vestris, and particularly of Charles Mathews, whose superb polish, ease, and nonchalance would have graced drawing-room comedy.[18] The years that followed brought the usual fare of burlesque and melodrama. In 1853 Frederick Robson, a low comedian of assured talent in his field, took the town by storm in a Talfourd burlesque of Shylock, which led so sedate a journal as the *Times* to hail him as England's greatest actor since Edmund Kean. In a trifling farce, *The Wandering Minstrel,* his singing of "Villikins and His Dinah" took fashionable London by the heels for the season, so that the tune was on every lip. 1864–69 saw the management of Horace Wigan, whose production of romantic plays, such as *The Serf* and *Henry Dunbar,* gave birth to the phrase "Olympic Drama."

After a régime of notably good revivals of old comedy under William Farren at the Strand between 1848 and 1850, that theatre became the home of burlesque, the

[17] The proclivity for rhetoric on the nineteenth-century stage may be called vestigial of the platform stage of other centuries.

[18] In lieu of that, he turned to whatever flotsam and jetsam the time afforded, playing 161 parts and writing forty-three pieces for the theatre; practically all that he did was unworthy of his potential best. In his one-act comedy, *The Dowager* (1843), a commingling of intrigue and manners in the high life of 1790, he has recaptured perfectly the flourish, the jauntiness, and the madcapping of the eighteenth-century comedy of manners at its best.

burlesque of Henry Byron, which meant hilarious buffoonery and comic effect delivered with broad, robust strokes. It was here that Marie Wilton, destined to greater things, did her apprenticeship.

Of the three great Patent Houses the Haymarket alone, by 1850, was maintaining the traditions of legitimate drama, for Covent Garden had been converted into an opera house and Drury Lane was given over to spectacle and *divertissement,* and yet the story of Haymarket productions largely duplicates that of the others we have mentioned. Buckstone, for instance, assembled a talented company, but the fare dispensed (save for occasional revivals of old comedies) was the usual farce coupled with a melodrama or domestic play, a generous evening's entertainment as to quantity, for it was often one o'clock before the final curtain was rung down. Theatre-goers patronized these plays as the best the town afforded, but their support was apathetic. They drifted from show-house to show-house as the vogue of the moment attracted them. It was habit with them mainly. It is not surprising to learn that between 1841 and 1866 no new theatre was erected in the metropolis, and those in operation were often hard put to it for tenants. In the next twenty years fifteen were to be built.[19]

[19] In general it may be said that as theatres increased in numbers they decreased in size, permitting that intimacy of treatment that social comedy requires. Before the Theatres Regulation Act of 1843 we have the anomalous spectacle of theatres growing larger and larger, since they could not increase in numbers, and at the same time the new type of picture-frame stage shrinking in size. Hence the old style of rhetorical delivery persisted with ridiculous results. The introduction of a complete electric light system in the Savoy Theatre in 1881 was to be a very great advance toward

After a survey of these decades that cluster about the mid-century mark, one's only conclusion can be that drama (and comedy, as being our especial concern) was altogether out of vital touch with humanity, regarded either by classes or as individuals. Man's impulses and motives were not brought into the reckoning in play-building. The theatre seemed to exert a perverse influence over the imaginations of writers, so that characters in a play must needs be made lifeless puppets, as if the denizens of the stage were unique in speech and behavior. Between the stage and the street a great gulf was fixed. The tyranny of a long tradition had yet to be broken. Convincing portraiture in these years was conspicuously lacking. Men and women were looked at casually and were corralled into types which were passed on from hand to hand as negotiable property. Augustin Filon has tagged them for us.[20] Of plot-construction a certain dexterity and deft artifice may be admitted, employed towards the captivation of an audience by its ingenuity in leading the character through a labyrinth of intrigue to a resolution.

These essays in plot invention were more noticeable as the influence of Scribe and later of Sardou from across the Channel came to be felt. To these French-

bringing near to each other the two worlds on either side of the footlights. Hereafter, the finer, subtler shades of gesture and facial expression were to be made possible. The challenge of all this to the actor and its significance in the presentation of the drawing-room play are self-evident.

[20] The women fall into the ingénue, the bad woman, the flirt and the chaperone. The men may be generally identified as low comedian, light comedian, villain, the honest old peasant, the rich old skinflint, the old beau, and the man about town, of whose social world the author is often manifestly ignorant.

men the contemporary drama in England was largely indebted for the mechanical triumph of stagecraft. They provided a serviceable formula or pattern, and this English writers accepted, without, however, building upon it original dramatic material. In short, comedies were being built up on situation rather than on character. Surprise was worth more than recognition. It was, then, in so far as French influence is concerned, the well-made play and not the play of ideas that affected English dramatic modes in the fifties and sixties. Alexander Dumas, *fils,* and Émile Augier were making drama a criticism of life as well as an entertainment. They were looking at the superstitions and prejudices of society and their pressure upon the individual with a moral seriousness beyond the range of comedy; but if English comedy could have reflected its own social background of manners with something of the same grasp on reality, the history of that comedy could now be told with more relish. Victorian propriety refused to handle life with the French candor until the century had nearly closed; but if London refused to tackle problems in the theatre, it need not have denied itself a living picture of society such as the theatres of Paris were richly affording. Dumas was frequently borrowed by English playwrights, but he was not assimilated.

From what has been said of the character of English drama from 1840 to 1865 we may recognize at once the hopelessness of any search for the comedy of manners. The new complexion and composition of Victorian society that were inherently unsympathetic to it as a popular mode for the theatre will be discussed at a later time. The manners of the upper levels of society were still to be presented in comedy on the nineteenth-century stage, as we shall see; but such comedy will differ from our old patrician comedies in the same degree that the Victorian upper classes differ from the *beau monde* of the eighteenth century. Our definition of terms must needs be interpreted more liberally. Yet up to the time of Robertson we find little interest in portraying the manners of any social stratum, either aristocratic or middle class. Such plays as Taylor's *An Unequal Match* and *Our American Cousin,* or Edmund Falconer's *Extremes: or Men of the Day* and *Woman: or Love Against the World* were (as we have seen) of the stuff out of which manners comedies are fashioned. But in these plays the emphasis is placed upon story. They deal with certain individuals as such, rather than as members of a group or class; they are concerned with conduct, so to speak, rather than manners. Here and there a character or a scene is suggestive of some type but only faintly so. What one of these or other plays of the period may be called "a ryghte pythy, pleasant and merie comedie"?

In the *Saturday Review* for September 26, 1868, one may read the following lugubrious statement, written not altogether without justification: "We are justified in concluding that the drama has reached a lower stage in its decline than at any former period of its existence and that, as a peculiar institution, it closely approximates to utter extinction." Yet already at that moment the first plays of Tom Robertson were infusing new life into English comedy just as it seemed to be breathing its last.

IV

ROBERTSON, GILBERT, AND A NEW SOCIAL CONSCIOUSNESS

1865–1890

TOM ROBERTSON came by the theatre naturally; he inherited it from his father, who was an actor in a circuit company. Both he (the oldest child) and later his sister Madge (the twenty-second child, who was to become the talented actress, Mrs. Kendal) played children's parts upon the stage. When his father's company disbanded, he returned to London as a hack-writer, adapting plays and writing dramatic criticism of a sort. His first play to give him a vogue was *Society,* which made its London debut in November of 1865 and was the first of a group of social comedies, including *Ours* (1866), *Caste* (1867), *Play* (1868), *Home* (1868), and *School* (1869), which last comes perilously close to namby-pambyism. From the first they were hailed as something refreshingly new in the theatre, not only by such discerning critics as John Oxenford and William Archer but by the public at large. Through the sympathetic interpretation of Miss Wilton and her company at the Prince of Wales's, and later at the Haymarket, these comedies experienced a high-noon of popular favor, which their author's failing health prevented him long from enjoying. *Society* ran

150 nights in its first appearance, 100 nights in 1868, and five months in 1874. *Ours* in an 1870 revival played continuously for nine months.[1] *School,* revived in 1873, held the boards for seven months and at the Haymarket in 1880 ran for a like period, earning £10,000 between May 1 and August 1. Altogether the Bancrofts performed *Ours* 700 times and *Caste* 650 times, the two Robertson comedies in which they made their most artistic successes. *School,* a much inferior play, reached a grand total of 800 performances, probably due to its generous use of sentiment. Contrary to expectation these quietly acted plays of everyday life do not seem to have suffered when they were transferred from the intimate associations of the little playhouse in Tottenham Street to the vast auditorium of the Haymarket. In the summer of 1873 the Bancroft company played *Caste* with great success on the huge stage of the Standard Theatre in Shoreditch.

How shall we explain the popularity of these comedies? One must confess that he reads them today without any especial elation. They are not informed by ideas nor are they broadly founded on an experience of life. The humor is often thin, the dialogue oversmart and with an undue dependence upon equivoque. Sentiment prevails, not passion. The psychology is rather juvenile. Striking situations are absent. Many of the incidents are of ephemeral interest and are aligned under the feeblest of motivation. And yet in

[1] In an 1882 revival the part of Col. Shendryn was taken by the young actor Pinero and that of Blanche Haye by Lily Langtry. At that very time Pinero's *The Squire* was being staged. Thus it is that the new and old in drama often reach across and touch each other.

these plays of such gossamer texture one finds a note of reality, a sense of contact with actual people that makes them extremely significant.

Robertson's importance is relative rather than actual, and historical rather than literary. For the first time in his century he was able to bring the trinity of drama, acting, and staging into harmonious operation for a representation of natural life. If to us he smacks of the theatre, we have but to compare him with the stilted, carpenter-built, verbose plays of Lytton, Byron, and Taylor, and of the plethora of French adaptations, to sense his advance. Garrick once advised the young actor, John Bannister, "You may humbug the town as a tragedian, but comedy is a serious thing, so don't try that just yet." For the first time in his century, Robertson was regarding comedy as a "serious thing." He opened the doors and let fresh air into a theatre that had become stuffy with conventionality and affectation. Under his pen men and women of the every day take on a fresh interest, because their creator had met and known them himself and had found them deeply engrossing. They act and talk without exaggeration. They walk into the theatre from the home and the club without the transformation of their identity. In his comedies, a cosmopolitan London audience might see itself reflected in its variety of types, not profoundly, but with a deft proficiency, such as one finds in the domestic fiction of Bulwer-Lytton or Trollope. In *Trelawny of the Wells,* Pinero modeled his Tom Wrench upon Robertson and has estimated admirably the man whom he was proud to call his master, when he has Tom say: "I strive to make my people talk and behave like people, don't I? . . . To fashion heroes out of actual, dull, everyday men—the sort of men you see smoking cheroots in the club windows in St. James's Street; and heroines from simple maidens in muslin frocks."

On the appearance of *Society* the *Daily Telegraph* had these judicious words to say: "The new comedy of *Society,* which has just been produced with so much éclat, is evidently the work of a shrewd, observant writer, who has looked at life from his own point of view, and who prefers saying smart things about the weaknesses of humanity to the utterance of solemn homilies bewailing their existence. Those who demand a subtle analysis of human motives, and require an elaborate dissection of the various component parts of the social body, must seek opportunities for acquiring knowledge elsewhere; but people who care about seeing a clever, sketchy picture of modern men and manners, dashed off in a spirited style, and giving perhaps a new view of some of the gradations in the social scale, may include themselves among the throng who nightly gather round the portals of the cheerful little theatre in Tottenham Street, and make sure of not coming away disappointed. The lower as well as the upper sections of society will find some familiar features quickly to be recognized, and whilst the plebeian occupant of the gallery will readily appreciate the very intelligible humour of the comedy, the most aristocratic patron of the stalls will decidedly approve the moral lesson it enforces." The writer need not have modified his language in describing *Ours* or *Caste.*

In all three we find a graceful, charming, somewhat bland portrayal of middle-class life and manners with an occasional glimpse of the social rank above, though not so well done, because outside the Bohemian experience and personal sympathies of the dramatist. Sir Alexander Shendryn and his lady nag and rag each other in the typically aristocratic manner of Vanbrugh and Cibber, but they are not eighteenth-century aristocrats—either in gentility or in arrogance. They are Victorian editions of the nobility as Robertson's plays are Victorian editions of the comedy of manners. The old whip-cracking wit in dialogue gives way to a pleasant humor of punning and badinage. Beau Farintosh in *School,* who might have been a young buck in the days of the Regency, is now a pathetic old man, trying to repair the ravages of the years with the appliances of art. His jaunty air is pathetic. By the final curtain-fall he has learned to be content with himself as he is, and for that we can now respect him. In Lady Ptarmigant in *Society* there is something of the traditionally aristocratic reverence for rank and wealth, especially the latter. She toadies to the fashions as obsequiously as she expects others to toady to her. In a play, the theme of which reminds us that love and sensibility are worth more than riches and rank, one will at once surmise the dramatic function of the noble lady in the story. Her husband with his propensity for falling asleep at unexpected moments is almost a caricature.[2] Something the same rôle as that of Lady

[2] The part was made memorable by that great interpreter of humors, John Hare.

Ptarmigant is played in *Caste* by the Marquise de St. Maur, the very high-priestess of caste, whose evidences of ill-breeding do not well become her pretensions. She wears the title but not the distinction of the patrician. Here again we are confronted with a wholesome paradigm for Victorian consumption not unlike that in *London Assurance* years before. "*Caste* is a good thing if it's not carried too far. It shuts the door on the pretentious and the vulgar; but it should open the door very wide for exceptional merit. Let brains break through its barriers and what brains can break through love may leap over." Such sentiments come out of a new political and social regime, in which an aristocrat may be interesting but in which he is not important. They do not seek to oust him or even to reform him, but they put him in his place.[3]

In Robertson at his best is a flickering play of raillery, an acrid flavor of cynicism, which his keen perceptions and his own bitter experiences in life had engendered. With a light hand he pens a comic libel of society. The old aristocracy of rank embraces the new aristocracy of money, and the new accepts the gesture with a glad sycophancy. All down the social ladder are various kinds and degrees of snobs, dandies,[4] parve-

[3] In fact, Robertson's consistent attitude from aristocracy to proletariat is to accept the stratification of English society as a convenient and inevitable situation. All classes, having their own particular brands of folly, are grist for the satirist's mill, but no folly is so egregious as that of poaching on the preserves of a class to which one is not native. Social fences no doubt encourage man in folly, but to demolish them would be but to invite greater absurdity.

[4] Bancroft broke away from the convention of making the fop or dandy of light complexion and hair and of long whiskers. He made him funny, but human, a "heavy swell," languid, a bit cynical, a bit sentimental.

nus, Bohemians, bourgeois barbarians with shop-keeping souls, hypocrites, and bounders.[5] The standard of social behavior (of all classes) set forth in much of nineteenth-century comedy has led to the half-jesting phrase, "comedy of bad manners."

Lest he seem always sardonic he brings before us also people who are lovable in their weaknesses and oddities or in their virtue. Perhaps they are a bit too sentimental for our taste, but they have a real flesh-and-blood texture. Vivacious young minxes like Naomi Tighe and Polly Eccles could scarcely fail to please even did they not have the piquant personality of Miss Wilton for their interpretation.[6] The public gave Robertson their liberal patronage because they got a new thrill out of seeing themselves in some approach to life, and the satire was relished equally with the sentiment. The famous Owl's Roost scene in *Society* it was thought might give offense to the journalists or the clubmen of fashion, but it was hailed with delight by the members of the Savage, the Garrick, the Fielding, and the Arundel who attended the première. In Robertson's attitude to his characters is a little of the flair and

5 A man of the world like Capt. Hawtree in *Caste* represents Robertson's democratic trend. Although caste is a fetish with him, he is not a fop. He accepts the social order as it is; he is self-opinionated; there is about him a certain touch of elegance but underneath all is a sympathetic understanding of others. It is this final trait that signifies a typical nineteenth-century attitude and is a new factor to be reckoned with in the history of the comedy of manners.

6 When one recalls that the Bancroft company included, besides the Bancrofts themselves, such histrionic talent as John Hare, Mr. and Mrs. Kendal, William Terriss, young Forbes-Robertson, and Mrs. Stirling, he will recognize one reason for the Robertson vogue of the late sixties and seventies.

flavor of Thackeray—the same tendency to discount human pretensions and yet love humanity all the while, a little of the same acid quality of satire under provocation that is a welcome antidote to sentiment. Of course, Robertson is more naïve, more trivial, but the resemblance is not far to seek.[7]

Long ago the comedy of Tom Robertson and that of his followers was tagged with the derogatory phrase, "Cup and Saucer Comedy," because it took us without ostentation into the daily lives of middle-class folk where rant and bluster were not the order of the day. The cup of tea that he passes to his readers may seem a trifle weak and tepid to some, but in it is a wholesome blending of sentiment, pathos, gayety, homely wisdom, a dash of wit and of satire, and a generous flavor of genial, kindly humanity. It is not a beverage to stimulate the intellect or to satisfy any spiritual passion, but to the student of drama its friendly warmth and sapidity are a welcome change after the fiery liquor of melodrama, the riotous concoctions of burlesque or the milky potions of love-comedy. After all a cup of tea is—a cup of tea, and something more. About it cluster certain associations—courtesy, geniality, spirited conversation tempered by propriety, and with these graces Robertson had been generously bestowed. We are not surprised to learn that Goldsmith was his favorite writer of comedy.

[7] Robertson's *Caste* defends love against the pride and class consciousness of the army and of wealth much as in *Vanity Fair*. William Archer has pointed out how Sidney Daryl in *Society* reflects Arthur Pendennis; Tom Stylus, George Warrington; Maud Hetherington, Ethel Newcome; and Lady Ptarmigant, Lady Kew. Eccles, on the other hand, is distinctly Dickensian.

English drama is indebted to Robertson not only because he reintroduced a comedy of genuinely English stamp and character and did much to restore the confidence of the intelligent public in the drama, but because he was an influence toward naturalness in the staging of plays. He may be said to have been the first to catch and utilize the significance of the new picture-frame type of stage. The twenty years that followed his death in 1871 are a time of development, more especially in the acting and producing of plays than in play-writing itself. The drift toward realism in presentation, with all its ultimate excesses, owes much to Robertson, who in turn had learned the science of play-building and of stage-setting from French drama, with which he was familiar in the original. While others were slavishly imitating and adapting French plays, Robertson was concerned with the secret of their remarkable economy of material and concentration of effect. If he cannot be said to have mastered the secret, at least his contact with the French was not without its effect. With the indispensable co-operation of the Bancrofts he carried a step further the earlier efforts of Planché and Mme. Vestris toward historical and artistic accuracy in costuming and scenery.[8]

[8] Like Gilbert after him, Robertson carefully supervised rehearsals of his plays in person. Frank Archer in his *An Actor's Notebooks* speaks of Robertson being at Newcastle while his comedy, *Play,* was being staged there. He comments on the novelty of an author's going on tour with his play and of putting a company on the road with a piece that was still running in London. Let it be remembered that it is just about this time that the old stock companies were giving way before a new era of long runs, traveling companies and elaborate productions, in which lavish spectacle and a mania for naturalism often eclipsed the legitimate art of drama. J. H. Barnes in his *Forty Years on the Stage* pays tribute to the old stock

Furthermore, the revolutionary innovations toward reality in staging and acting, inaugurated by the French actor, Charles Fechter, when he assumed the lease of the Lyceum Theatre in 1861, exerted a profound influence on Robertson and those who followed.

When the old "Dust Hole" in Tottenham Street was taken over by Marie Wilton and renovated into the most charming and cozy little theatre in London, a symbolic event had taken place, for the building, which had long been the home of horrific melodrama (Hamlet with his big black dog which throttled the King in the last act), witnessed the comedies of Robertson after a brief reign of farce and burlesque. It seemed very dubious if the theatre would succeed in its undertaking. "We must not have small-talk, but plenty of blue fire and mysterious disappearances, which can alone draw anything like a paying audience." And the words of the previous lessee suggest the fortuity with which much of theatrical entertainment was presented to the people. "In my tin-pot days we were less particular. When in doubt as to how to end an act, I sent two men on in a boat dressed as sailors, with a couple of flags. They waved their Union Jacks, I lit a pan of blue fire at the wings, the band played 'Rule, Britannia' and

company as an invaluable training-school for young Thespians. As in Shakespeare's time, the older actors of the company were the teachers. Two of the best of these companies, still active in Robertson's day, were in Edinburgh and Bristol. From the former Henry Irving, J. L. Toole, Pinero, and Mrs. Scott-Siddons received their earliest training, and from the latter, Ellen Terry, Charles Coghlan, and Madge Robertson. Bancroft tells us that in his apprenticeship of a little more than four years he played 346 parts. Charles Brookfield, the actor, tells us in his *Random Reminiscences,* 1902, that in 1879 he could find no stock company in which to get his first training.

down came the curtain."[9] An excerpt from a letter from Dion Boucicault to Mrs. Bancroft in 1868 is of interest here. Boucicault had the uncanny faculty of knowing what the public wanted and how to give it to them. "The public pretend they want pure comedy; this is not so. What they want is domestic drama, treated with broad comedy character. A sentimental, pathetic play, comically rendered, such as *Ours, Caste, Colleen Bawn, Arrah-na-Pogue*. Robertson differs from me, not fundamentally, but scenically; his action takes place in lodgings or drawing-rooms—mine has a more romantic scope."[10]

Squire Bancroft and his talented little wife gave a new dignity to the art of the theatre. Sincerity and intelligence replaced what Pinero called "mouthing and tinsel." They favored plays of English life and manners in their repertory and only resorted to foreign work when home talent was not forthcoming. By endearing themselves to a considerable part of the London public they did much to remove the barriers of Puritan prejudice against the theatre, which decades of spurious writing had reared. In fact, many who were not habitual theatre-goers were attracted by the new policies of the management. For the first time, only one play was given on a program. The public were treated as guests. The greatest care was taken in choosing casts to fit the play. No individual in the cast was exalted; the maximum of artistic effect from the cast as a whole was the goal sought. The Bancrofts themselves often

[9] Marie and Squire Bancroft, *Recollections of Sixty Years*, p. 67.

[10] *Ibid.*, p. 195.

assumed minor parts as the interests of the play demanded. While they strove for a complete illusion of reality in staging,[11] they realized that such reality will avail little without that inner vitalization that comes from a sympathetic understanding of the dramatist's plan and purpose. Theatrical traditions and conventions were set at naught in the interests of dramatic truth and beauty.

The decade of 1870–1880 should be dedicated rather to the manager and the actor than to the dramatist. Stage-technique, whereby actual life may be more nearly duplicated in the theatre, developed by leaps and bounds; but the play that could justify such mechanical progress was slow in arriving. The actor-manager system had arrived with its virtues and its defects. Because of it, plays were given sumptuous as well as accurate settings, but they were obviously presented for as well as by the star of the company. Long runs became compulsory. As a result, the old-fashioned, judicial-minded habitué of the theatre, who came to a chosen playhouse to enjoy a repertory of his favorite type of plays, passed away. It was still the day of long entertainments. The liberal dramatic bill of fare usually began with a farce at seven, then the *pièce de résistance,* then a final burlesque or another farce.

[11] Such as real doors and ceilings, changes in furniture, etc. In the last act of Taylor's *The Overland Route,* a P. & O. liner crashes on a reef. Real coolies and lascars were used as attendants on the boat. Already realism seemed to be vaunting itself as an end, not a means. In the wood-scene in Robertson's *Ours* autumn leaves were dropping, and later in the play was introduced the effect of driving snow. One critic said the scenery in *School* was so natural he could have sworn he saw a cow in the distance cropping the grass, and he longed to get on the stage and roll on the sward.

Those were the days of home-living and home-loving and a relish for scenes of domestic life upon the stage. We have not yet reached the latter days of flats and apartments and restaurants, of economy and specialization and high-pressure existence. When these days arrive we shall find the play starting between eight and nine, conducted with despatch and designed for the most part as a relaxation.

London's forty theatres were generally crowded, although the number devoted to high-class drama declined. Managers, of course, were "playing safe" and giving the public what it wanted, which was a light, easily digested fare. The revival of old comedies and of Shakespeare at the Lyceum would seem to argue that the people were ready and waiting to support intelligent productions if they were supplied. And yet the popularity of the Lyceum was largely a personal triumph for Henry Irving and Ellen Terry. They were the fashion. The public has never been quick to respond to good things in the theatre, and managers, with large investments involved, must fall back on Dr. Johnson's economic principle that

> The drama's laws, the drama's patrons give,
> For we that live to please, must please to live.

The perennial discussion for a subsidized National Theatre assumed formidable proportions in the seventies, but it resulted in nothing but debate in print. As long as audiences were composed mainly of visitors from the country, the bored society men, shopkeepers, and tradesmen, nothing else could be looked for. The substantially intelligent classes were finding outlets of diversion in concerts, lectures, clubs, and novel-reading. Why should they endure at a play the defilements of their mother tongue, when they might find it used as an instrument of power and beauty in the novels and periodicals upon their parlor-tables? That the stage was not the agency of culture in civic life was a matter of concern to many thinking men such as Matthew Arnold and William Archer in the late seventies and the eighties. Occasional evidences of a more elevated public taste and of a mitigation of Puritan prejudice against the stage brighten the prospect, but on the whole the drama and especially the comedy of manners were still languishing in the doldrums of inanity and theatricalism. As long as a theatre like the Gaiety, dispensing even a broader and coarser brand of burlesque than the Strand purveyed, continued to draw to capacity houses under the management of John Hollingshead, little hope need be held out for high comedy. In his company were players of indisputable talent as Edward Terry, J. L. Toole, Nelly Farren and Fred Leslie, whose *gaieté de coeur* was worthy of a better cause than the screaming farces of Byron and the burlesques of that arch-parodist, F. C. Burnand.[12] From time to time the management put on a few of the old type of comedies, such as *Love for Love*, "deodorized" as Hollingshead put it, or a

[12] Charles Mathews joined the Gaiety company early in the seventies. These artists made their theatre memorable for a depiction not of the manners of society but of a parody on manners. And yet Mathews was capable of superb characterization of the languorous gentleman of fashion, as in his Sir Charles Coldstream in *Used Up;* John Hollingshead, in *My Lifetime,* II, 109, says of Mathews' acting, "It was theatrical champagne of a rare and probably of an extinct vintage."

bowdlerized version of Vanbrugh's *Relapse,* but with the unfortunate intent to show their inferiority to modern comedy. It is significant that in the early nineties the Lyceum closed its doors almost unnoticed, whereas the Gaiety went out in a blaze of adulation, with the public paying extra prices for seats.

One effect of the oft-berated cup-and-saucer or milk-and-water school of comedy was to promulgate upon the stage a natural ease and polish of manners such as prevails in refined society. Old traditions of staginess in speech and bearing began to give way, though very slowly. Certain plays are written and acted with a finer, quieter touch. J. P. Simpson in the *Theatre* magazine for December, 1879,[13] attempts to refute a recent article in which it was claimed that gentlemen were no longer lured to the stage as a profession and that young actors, being recruited from the lower middle class or lower, were ill-fitted to become exponents of good manners. In reply Simpson cites a number of contemporary actors of standing who were of gentle breeding, as John Hare, Arthur Cecil, W. H. Kendal, E. A. Sothern, Bancroft, young Forbes-Robertson, and others.[14] He goes on to deplore the fact that society was treated on the stage, not in the main play of the evening but in the preceding one-act skit or comedietta, which must be played to the accompaniment of all the confusion that late comers have ever been so generous in contributing. Such conditions, of course, make nearly impossible the proper rendition of drawing-room

[13] *Theatre* (London), III, n. s. (1879), 270.

[14] The same ascription applies to those two great exponents of society life in later years, Charles Wyndham and Cyril Maude.

manners and conversation. Simpson plies his explanation stoutly, but one feels that his footing is precarious. As he himself admits, the great trouble was that actors were not given lines to speak nor parts to play that required familiarity with gentility. Plays of that sort were seldom written nor was their absence decried by theatre patrons.

The student of manners-comedy finds little to detain him in the ten years following Robertson's death. Despite the slenderness of his artistry and of his psychology, he has cast a long shadow down through the century. On the side of stagecraft or of play-making itself, in one way and degree or another a great variety of men have come under that shadow—Byron, J. A. Albery, W. S. Gilbert, G. W. Godfrey, Jones, Pinero, H. V. Esmond, R. C. Carton, and many others. Of Albery it may be said that he was a milder, more idyllic but also often coarser version of Robertson. *The Two Roses* (1870) is a satisfying little play in comic invention, and the character of Digby Grant is above the average for the time.[15] Like Robertson he redeems a sentiment that is always in danger of going to sugar by the tartness of cynicism. *The Two Thorns* (1871) could have become social comedy had it been in the right hands. Charles Coghlan's *Lady Flora* (1875) is also of the Robertson tradition, but lapses readily into farce. Of the same tenuity are Bertie Vyses' *About Town* (1873), which might be ascribed to Byron were it more smartly done, and Burnand's *Our Club* (1878),

[15] Henry Irving as Digby Grant and George Honey as Our Mr. Jenkins were memories that contemporary play-goers kept ever green in their hearts.

a farce, in which a stranger in a club is led to believe that different members are persons of distinction, and treats them accordingly. G. R. Sims' satiric little piece, *Crutch and Toothpick* (1879), which achieved long runs at the Royalty and in the provinces, ridicules a type of old age in a manner faintly reminiscent of Robertson. A late piece of Byron's, *Courtship* (1879), is another attempt of his at serious comedy, but he seems never to have learned to make people interesting by what they are as well as by the funny things they say. Byron's forte is eccentric lower middle-class folk. Elsewhere he is wooden. These, then, are some of the comedies that approach but do not arrive. Looked at as a group, they are brummagem.

Somewhat nearer to our purpose is that posthumous comedy of Bulwer-Lytton's, *The House of Darnley* (1877), to which Charles Coghlan supplied a fifth act, much to the disapprobation of Lytton's son. It was at best a *succès d'estime* in the theatre. It bears a strong family resemblance to *Money;* there is the same staginess, the same artificial polished manners, the same measured, stilted dialogue, the same pallid men and women. Always one feels in Lytton the virtuoso rather than the artist. One feels the play to be a kind of relic cast up into a decade of different dramatic fashion. Darnley is a gentleman in business who has married a frivolous, extravagant wife. Sir Philip Marsden, a self-indulgent man of the world, has found it necessary to conceal a marriage for family reasons. Darnley has been lending aid to Marsden's wife, who is in great distress, and these visits Lady Juliet, his wife, has misconstrued. She demands a separation, but when he is overtaken by financial reverses she saves him out of her own personal fortune. Miss Placid's expedient of avoiding matrimonial entanglement with Mr. Fyshe by assuming the airs, now of a demure miss and now of a hoyden, is the common property of the comedy preceding and following Sheridan. Not much can be said for the play. We may call it a torso, into which the spirited acting of Ellen Terry and John Hare was able to infuse something of the rosy hue of reality.

French adaptations of Sardou and of the thesis-plays of Augier and the younger Dumas continued until the mid-eighties, when these Anglo-French hybrids began to give place in the best houses to native productions of greater merit. Managers vied with each other in being the first to bring out almost any piece that had received the Parisian imprimatur. Augier's skilful studies of the bourgeoisie and Dumas' *comédies de moeurs,* such as *Diane de Lys* and *Le Demi-Monde,* would seem at first thought to afford just that encouragement which English social comedy needed. Dumas' is the world of fashionable, pleasure-loving society, to be sure, but it is presented not for its charm but for a preachment against a mammonism and a greed for power which was vitiating the whole social body. "*Comédie de moeurs*" is a term of greater satiric and critical import than "comedy of manners." Even were this not so, the social fabric of Parisian life in Dumas' plays is too unlike that of London life to permit of successful transplanting. For instance, the word "demi-monde" denotes a social domain which defies the efforts of the English adapter.

The same may be said for the *milieu* presented in the French naturalistic plays of later years—those of Becque, Donnay, and Hervieu, for example.

Sardou's *Nos Intimes* is another case in point. In the seventies and eighties it appeared variously as *Peril, Friend and Foe,* and as *Bosom Friends.* Despoiled of all its nuances of impropriety and its native social environment, it became an amusing but inarticulate farce-comedy without significance as a reflection of English manners. Sardou's is a story of the bourgeois; in the English rage for casting plays in the nobility, the characters are given titles and the story is made innocuous. This play is but one in many which were thus prostituted in these years. The mania for French adaptation was one reason for the dearth of English social comedy. Plays are not factory-made structures that can be torn down and set up at will. Only in rare cases has a French play ever been adapted successfully on English soil.[16]

On November 19, 1870, the audience at the Haymarket witnessed a fairy-comedy called *The Palace of Truth,* the first of a series of comedies and comedy-operas that are unique in the Victorian drama for their method of approach and treatment. They have a place in our present study because back of their fantasticality is a very pronounced modicum of criticism of society morals and manners. Through the medium of fairy-land and mythology, W. S. Gilbert cuts and thrusts at

[16] In 1882 there appeared at the Odeon in Paris a French play, *Rotten Row,* which purported to be a comedy of manners. From all London accounts it seems to have been as amusingly maladroit as French plays about the English and English plays about the French so often are.

the frailties of mankind with a satiric vigor not to be found in contemporary comedies of real life. In comedy and in opera his method is the freakish, prankish one of the jester or the magician, who stands on his head to get an untrammeled view of life, and finding, when he does so, that much of the world is topsy-turvy likewise, he is really seeing things right-side up for the first time. As Walter Sichel says, he was the apostle, not of nonsense, but of sense upside down. With this madcap in him walks the Puritan moralizer who arrays his conscience in cap and bells that it may claim the immunity of motley to speak embarrassing truths for the soul's good. "It was the core of the Gilbertian paradox that he could be serious only when he was funny."[17] Though a Victorian sentimentalist and moralist, he was an artist in the burlesque; though a Tory, he assailed its stodgy, moribund habits of thought.

In *The Palace of Truth* (1870), *Pygmalion and Galatea* (1871), and *The Wicked World* (1873), we find beneath the somewhat intractable verse-medium, the didacticism and the inflated rhetoric, a mordant, trenchant humor and a social criticism that was to find later a fuller and freer expression in Jones, Shaw and Galsworthy. He is an important conduit for the transmission of all the casual, transient ironies and humors that invest the pages of *Punch,* of the *Cornhill* under Thackeray and of *Fun* under the editorship of Tom Hood.

In the enchanted Palace of Truth, where people have to tell the truth, but unconsciously, all forms of sham

[17] Isaac Goldberg, *The Story of Gilbert and Sullivan,* p. 473.

are shown in their true light and honest motives are made believable. King Phanor and his subjects find that truth-telling, if laudable, is an uncomfortable business, with a strange propensity for stirring up a ferment. Our modern social life is a veritable tissue of lies and hypocrisies. What would happen to its house of cards should truth become its standard of word and deed? Out of the myth of Pygmalion and the statue which warmed into life under his touch we hear the same disturbing, inquiring voice of truth. Into the mouth of naïve Galatea, as she looks for the first time at the world in the audacity of innocence, Gilbert puts comments that startle because of their naked candor. The story may be clumsily motivated, but it is the vehicle for a fresh note of criticism. Again, in *The Wicked World,* the author draws very real truths from fantastic premises. When mortals invade the Arcadia of fairy-land above the clouds, where all is untainted goodness, they bring with them love which is both the cause of misery and the means whereby it is endurable. The elves succumb to its infection and straightway dissension follows in its wake. They who had known only the serenity of bliss now are torn by jealousy, inconstancy and slander. Only when the mortals go back to their wicked world, taking with them their priceless gift, does peace reign again in fairy-land.

Gilbert's prose-farce, *Engaged* (1877), this time taking its scenes and characters from ordinary life, comes face to face with human nature in the same astounding fashion as do the plays just cited. Unabashed egoism runs riot. The characters are stripped of all subterfuges and conventions, and made to act according to their real impulses, as in a kind of mundane Palace of Truth. All the polite deceptions of social practice give way to instinctive desire and selfish interest. This pungent little Aristophanic satire in mock-heroic vein might be called a burlesque on the romantic. The worn-out machinery of romance and melodrama creaks to the tune of an ironic laughter. All the modesty and selfless devotion which are traditionally associated with young lovers are made an hypocrisy. The characters are entirely without moral compunctions. They confess themselves modest or beautiful with perfect sangfroid. Their vows of constancy are subject to the size of bank accounts. The conventional idealism of love becomes a travesty and the most egregious self-seeking replaces it. What we always supposed was artlessness in those in life's springtime turns out to be a mask disguising the shrewdest designing. The old language of sentiment is there, to be sure, in extravagant degree, but beneath it is the cold philosophy of the utilitarian. It is natural to suppose that a play in which the illusions of engagements and marriages are stripped away would have to be delicately handled on the boards, or it would lapse into the merest trifling. Gilbert prefixes this admonition to his printed version: "It is absolutely essential to the success of this piece that it should be played with the most perfect earnestness and gravity throughout. There should be no exaggeration in costume, make-up or demeanor, and the characters, one and all, should appear to believe, throughout, in the perfect sincerity of their words and actions. Directly the actors show that they are conscious of the absurdity of their utterances the piece begins to drag."

The same under-current of social criticism pervades the Gilbert comic operas of the seventies and eighties. Indeed, their continued popularity into our day is due not only to their vivacity and tunefulness but to those satiric slaps at human nature which are applicable today as when they were written. In his robust, masculine way Gilbert launches out against all that was prim and stuffy and hidebound in Victorian society. He is the implacable foe of the complacent, self-righteous type of Englishman who worships convention as a thing not made with hands. He is British himself to the core in all his instincts, and he employs British common sense and breezy humor as instruments not for reform but for deft ridicule. If his countrymen are democratic at heart, they often act like opinionated snobs; if they are really very sentimental, they would be horrified to admit the fact; if they have the instincts of gentlemen, they are prone to act like bears or monkeys in their social relations. With such bundles of anomalies Gilbert found his method of topsy-turvydom the only consistent approach. Hence his operas are congeries of paradoxes and extravagances.[18]

Many of those who filled the Savoy in those years recognized the justice of the satire against peer and against commoner, but others there were who, laughing at the fun, did not sense the fact that it was their

[18] Allardyce Nicoll, in his *British Drama,* 1925, aptly compares him to Shaw in this capacity to see the opposite side of the picture of conventional life. Gilbert, he says, dethroned an artificial imagination by a fanciful realism.

own smugness and stuffy rectitude that was being castigated. Therein lies the most delicious contribution of the operas to the humor of the world. The audience laughed at the play, the play laughed at the audience, but we of today have the last and the best laugh, as we view the situation with the perspective of the years.

> When they're offered to the world in merry guise,
> Unpleasant truths are swallowed with a will—
> For he who'd make his fellow-creatures wise
> Should always gild the philosophic pill.

So sings Jack Point in *Yeomen of the Guard* and so says and does W. S. Gilbert, who was often most serious when he was funniest. It was in the very nature of the man to impregnate his merry operas with maxim and precept concerning conduct and manners. In tabulated form let us note what some of these are.

Sorcerer. Satirizes " old-fashioned stilted manners " and " the pose of aristocratic benevolence." [19] In the opera a love potion is dispensed that will break down all barriers of rank, wealth, and age. Love is to rule without a peer. Lords and ladies are enamored of those of low degree. The parlous situation that would result is averted by the intervention of the sorcerer.

Patience. Satirizes an amusing but harmless esthetic craze of the early seventies, which had already aroused the satiric ire of Du Maurier in *Punch* and of Burnand in his play, *The Colonel.*

Pinafore. Satirizes jingoism and a blatant and affected patriotism. And again, love levels all ranks, but the social proprieties must be observed. One must stop somewhere in the leveling process. After all there are limits. Love is love and rank is rank.

Pirates of Penzance. Takes some stout raps at respectability,

[19] H. M. Walbrook, *The Gilbert and Sullivan Opera,* p. 43.

at the "snobbery of the *nouveau riche*," and the "exhibition of over-mature feminine sentimentality." [20]

Iolanthe. Satirizes a social caste that puts manners above intelligence and the emoluments of leisure above culture. The House of Lords is the especial butt. Stuffy importance is not dignity.

Mikado. Full of temporal and local "gags" that may be altered as the circumstances of presentation suggest. Takes a fling at suffragists, philanthropists, socialists, diplomatists, and all manner of knaves and fools in the kingdom.

Utopia Limited. A multifold satire on the English nation in a variety of aspects. Red-tapery and prudery are humbug. Officialdom and so-called polite society appear ludicrous.

Gondoliers. In the republic of Barataria perfect equality has been established by law. King and menial are on one plane. Yet social chaos ensues. The cook at once takes to himself perquisites and titles commensurate with his new dignity of equality. As Gilbert says:

> When all are promoted to the top of the tree,
> Then everyone is somebodee,
> And no one's anybody!

Here is the basic social truth expounded later so differently in Barrie's *Admirable Crichton*. Whatever be the criterion by which the branches of the social tree shall be occupied, there is no significance in one's being at the top, if he does not know that the lower branches are peopled as well.

A glance through these tabulated comments will suggest what an auriferous vein of social comedy Gilbert could have opened up, had he chosen a different method of treatment. Through his experience as a captain in the militia, as barrister, and as government employee he had come in touch with the various classes of society, and while sanctioning the social order as such, he had

[20] Walbrook, *op. cit.*, p. 56.

the humor and the insight to sense the follies that attended it. Although he exalted true worth wherever it is found, he was far from recommending a new democratic order of things, which would simply shift human snobbishness and affectation to a different pair of shoulders. As Lord Lololler sings in *Iolanthe,*

> Hearts just as pure and fair
> May beat in Belgrave Square
> As in the lowly air
> Of Seven Dials!

If his operas delight in setting all the time-honored distinctions of society in a dizzy whirl, it is only to meet the exigencies of the moment. At the end everything settles back into the *status quo.* But meanwhile the little teapot tempest has been highly amusing—and salutary. It is corrective, but it conforms. In the *Sorcerer,* Alexis would put marriage on a basis of love, not rank; yet how different a complexion the theory wears when his prospective mother-in-law of noble lineage would marry one beneath her. In *Penzance* the pirates court General Stanley's daughters, but they succeed only when it has become known that they are lords in disguise. The quixotically democratic Captain Corcoran in *Pinafore* shies at the notion that his daughter should wed with a common sailor.

It remains only to acknowledge the indebtedness of English nineteenth-century comedy to the author of these operas. They undoubtedly did much to dissipate the banality and dullness of mid-century burlesque and farce, and give back to comedy somewhat of her ancient prestige.[21] They demonstrated what verve and spirit and keen perception could achieve without vulgarity.[22] A class of intelligent, circumspect persons who had been getting their theatrical fare at the tasteful, decorous little drawing-room entertainments of the German Reeds at the Gallery of Illustration and later at St. George's Hall now flocked to the Savoy and thus re-established a contact with the world of the theatre. In matters of stage management Gilbert deserves to rank with Planché, Boucicault, Fechter, and the Bancrofts in demanding a presentation that in accuracy, variety, and naturalness should deal justly with actual life. Gilbert's insistence on long and careful rehearsals, personally superintended, was an inheritance from Robertson. In fact, the later man was quick to acknowledge his discipleship to him who was first to make significant a quiet reading of life and to emphasize the delicate nuances and shadings of the dramatic art.

As the century passed into its ninth decade the student of the manners genre finds some slight encouragement. Not only were comedies of native composition becoming more numerous and gradually supplanting in favor the Anglicized French play,[23] but they displayed

21 As William Archer succinctly says in his *Real Conversations,* they helped to " restore literary self-respect to the English stage."

22 Gilbert's insistent emphasis upon the wholesomeness of his operas for everybody's mother and grandmother seems to us a trifle " Victorian," but we must recall the character of some of the burlesque and opera bouffe which had preceded. Said Gilbert: " Finally, we agreed that no lady of the company should be required to wear a dress that she could not wear with absolute propriety at a private fancy-ball."

23 Between 1879 and 1888 the Hare-Kendal management at the St. James's offered London a tasteful fare of good comedy. Of twenty plays

a marked tendency to come to grips with reality and to recognize society as a living entity, not merely as a convenient background for a story. Toward the close of the decade, especially, we are conscious of a new formula in the work of Grundy, Pinero, Jones, and Godfrey. Comedy in their hands was an earnest attempt to reflect the men and manners of their time. As the years go on we shall see this earnestness intensifying into seriousness and society coming to be looked upon as a problem and not simply as a multifarious world, seductive to the artist. If it is true that the comedy of manners is not born of genre painting or sociology, at the same time it has a better chance of flourishing where plays are substantial, written with conviction for audiences and not for actors, and breathing the fresh air of real life, not that of the footlights, as did their paler predecessors. In a playwright an ounce of observation is worth a pound of invention. In the days of Elizabeth and of Anne drama went straight to contemporary life for its inspiration. In the latter years of Victoria it was tending to do the same thing after long weary stretches of servile imitation lying darkly between, and in despite of the tyranny of the commercialized theatre with its inevitable policy of "long runs" and its acquiescence to a bourgeois standard of taste. The gap between drama and culture was appreciably narrowed through the collaboration, as writer, producer, and patron, of the intelligent few for

presented, eight were from the French, seven were new English plays and five were revivals. Yet this percentage of foreign work is probably above the average.

whom the word "drama" connoted more than "theatre."

Outside of comedy itself were signs of a change for the better. The old eccentric burlesque and farce (usually employed as a *lever de rideau*), with their French flavor of salacity or their English flavor of buffoonery, were making way for a three-act type of farce only a shade less responsible than comedy in its characters, dialogue, and motivation. If it was unquestionably farce, it was reflective of the farcical element which life itself contains, now and again. Such plays, for example, as Pinero's *The Magistrate* (1885) and *The Schoolmistress* (1886) were demonstrating the improbable things that may happen to probable people. Of course, all jingle and tomfoolery had not vanished; the interesting thing is the appearance of something better.[24]

The eighteen-eighties were great crop years for melodrama. At the hands of G. R. Sims, Robert Buchanan, Henry Pettitt, and others the public was surfeited with thrill and sensation. Railway accidents, burning buildings, brutal murders and the like became more lurid

[24] Walter Pollock in *National Review,* July, 1885, and Sydney Grundy in *Dramatic Review,* March 14, 1885, bewail the decline of the comedy of the Robertson school, and the ascendancy of farce. William Archer took exception to these gentlemen, by contrasting the insipidity of the former with the frank, robust treatment of the ridiculous in life in the latter. Out of the artistic honesty of Robertson and the Bancrofts, and the ingenuity and occasional smartness of the farce-writers, he looked for the evolvement of an improved type of comedy. The position of H. A. Jones on this subject is expressed in his introduction to Filon's *The English Stage:* "Just as surely as the circulation of bad money in a country drives out all the good, so surely does a base and counterfeit currency in art drive out all finer and higher things that contend with it."

than ever because of an increasingly realistic stagecraft.[25] Deplorable as such plays were in many ways, they had a vigor of presentation that other types were coming to emulate. Their intense realism was in time to burn itself out by its own fires; imitation was to be followed by interpretation. Meanwhile, in melodrama as in much of the comedy the play was a show, the playwright a showman.[26] In *The World* (1880) by Paul Meritt, Henry Pettitt, and Augustus Harris, we have staged before us a raft at sea, the embarkation of an ocean steamer, an explosion aboard ship, the interior of the Aquarium, a madhouse, and a fancy-dress ball. Scarcely less ambitious are *Lights o' London* (1881), *Dark Days* (1885), *Harbour Lights* (1885) (played 513 nights with Jessie Millward and William Terriss in the leading rôles), *London Day by Day* (1889), and *Alone in London* (1891), all of them lusty offspring of Pierce Egan's *Tom and Jerry; or Life in London* back in 1821 (revived in 1870), a kind of theatrical slumming-party for delighted audiences. While these plays may have contributed something to the achievement of verisimilitude, they were noxious in the falsity of their moral perspectives.[27] Their pandering to middle-class

[25] "The drawback to realism is the fate of the realist. If he goes into the slums, he becomes base, if he goes into society, he becomes soprano." Wilton Lackaye.

[26] Speaking of the mania for photographic realism in comedy, an American editor refers to it as the "Upholstery School of Comedy," with Tom Taylor as its founder. "The decorations and novel effects derivable from the appointments and accessories form the prominent features."

[27] Dryden: "A play is an imitation of nature—we know we are deceived, and we desire to be so, but no man was ever deceived, but with a probability of truth."

taste for bland, happy endings George Moore deplored when he said: "The conversion of bad men into good men is the besetting sin of modern art."[28] To him the outlook for sincere drama was gloomy enough, in the midst of so much moral cowardice and deadly mediocrity.

[28] *Fortnightly Review,* LII (1889), 624.

V

DRAMATIC PRODUCTION INCENTIVES AND DETERRENTS

IF it is true that during the eighties drama in general and comedy in particular were seeking a new level, it was in response to a more sympathetic and intelligent attitude toward the theatre by the people. The drama is, of course, potentially either true or false, beautiful or ugly, exactly to that degree which its patrons will permit. If the better element of the London public absented itself from the theatre in 1885, on the ground that the theatre catered only to those who wanted to laugh or to shiver with the least amount of effort, then the result was manifestly poor plays. The manager says to the man who thus deprecates existing conditions, "I don't put on good things because you don't go to the theatre," and the reply is, "I don't go to the theatre because you don't put on good things." And so each points the accusatory finger at the other and naturally to no avail. Henry Arthur Jones, an ardent crusader as well as a dramatist, blames the public when he says, "When the best and most serious classes of the nation detest and defame their theatre, it instantly justifies their abuse."[1]

At all events, there began to emerge in the late eighties a small but cultivated coterie of theatre-goers

[1] *Fortnightly Review*, LXXXVI (1906), 1091.

which increased steadily in numbers as the theatres responded to their tastes. Others came from the ranks of more or less sincere objectors to the depravity of the professional stage who had been finding no scruples against attendance at dramatic entertainments in some building not labeled with the invidious word "Theatre." For years the Howard Pauls at St. Martin's Hall and the German Reeds (Mrs. Reed herself had been a successful actress) at the Royal Gallery of Illustration and later at St. George's Hall had attracted crowds of conscientious folk, to whom the professional stage was anathema. Many of the recruits, however, were thoughtful men and women, ready to welcome in the theatre any drama that would hold the mirror fairly up to nature. People of position in the state, in the professions, and in letters began to take cognizance of a stage that was no longer dispensing only comfits and baubles. It became fashionable for the upper set to attend the theatre as well as the races and boxing-bouts. The latest play was everywhere the topic of conversation. Reputable magazines now took their theatre seriously and gave ample space to dramatic criticism and review, which had appeared before for the most part only in the cheap professional periodicals.

In 1870 Henry Morley's *Journal of a London Playgoer* certified to that appeal of the theatre for a man of distinguished mental attainments, to which George Henry Lewes's book, *On Actors and the Art of Acting*, attested in the same decade.[2] Matthew Arnold, like

[2] Be it remembered that Lewes had written dramatic criticism from 1850 to 1854, had been something of an actor as had been his grandfather and

Gladstone, was another of the intellectual élite who was a frequenter of the theatre, although he published but little criticism—only five *Letters of an Old Playgoer* to the *Pall Mall Gazette,* 1882–1884, and a paper on "The French Play in London" when the Comédie Française visited that city in 1879. In the earlier article he writes that "we in England have no modern drama at all," only Elizabethan drama and eighteenth-century comedy. "Then we have numberless imitations and adaptations from the French. All of these are at bottom fantastic." Yet at the same time he sees a wide interest demonstrated in things theatrical. "I see our community turning to the theatre with eagerness and finding the English theatre without organization or purpose or dignity—and no modern English drama at all except a fantastical one." In 1882 he speaks with more encouragement of the plays he has lately seen. He finds the theatre more generally and spiritedly attended and by an audience representative of the different classes of society. From the change in the tenor of his words in 1879 and in 1882 we sense something of the increased responsibility which English drama was appropriating to itself.

In nothing is the decline of prejudice against the stage-world better revealed than in the change in the social position of actors, which in the eighties began to approximate, at least, that accorded to other kinds of artists. No longer were they without the pale by edict of a puritanical *idée fixe.* John Coleman, the actor,

had made a number of successful adaptations from the French for the London stage under the pseudonym of Slingsby Lawrence, the most noteworthy being *The Game of Speculation* (1851).

tells us that Mrs. Bancroft, Mrs. Kendal, and Helen Faucit (Lady Martin) were all country actors' daughters, that Irving, Barrett, and Toole sprang from very humble antecedents; and yet all were honored by society. The actor found the doors of reputable clubs open to receive him, if he did not care to join in organizing one of his own. One calls to mind the Savage, Garrick, Hogarth, Fielding, the exclusive Beefsteak, and the distinguished Arundel. T. H. S. Escott, a foreign resident in London, wrote in 1886 an entertaining book called *Society in London,* which testifies to this new social status of stage folk and adds dryly that society was not unconscious of the tradition of the risqué that hovered about the stage, and accepted its denizens as a thrill or novelty, as if it were doing something a little daring. The prudish notion, born of ignorance, that the stage world was of necessity a place of unholy mysteries died hard, like most prudish notions.[3] With the breaking down of moral prejudice against all Thespians, numbers of young people of gentle breeding were drawn by the glamor of the footlights. As a result, the minor parts in social comedy were coming to be filled by those whose instincts conduced to a sympathetic rendering of those parts, and thus the whole standard of interpretation of society life tended to be raised.

While a saving tenth of the public were coming to the aid of the drama in the closing decades of the century, the other nine-tenths continued to be then, as it ever will with little change, moribund and parochial,

3 This is one of many reasons why Thackeray called the English public "the great big stupid."

impervious to new ideas, frivolous and crotchety. It abstains from what sincere representation of life the theatre affords, either because of puritanical bigotry or because of a philistine complacency with mediocrity.

The fact of Puritanism in nineteenth-century life is too well known to require amplification. From the time of her accession and throughout her long reign, Queen Victoria exerted a quietly sobering influence upon society, much of it beneficent, to be sure. In many quarters, however, the morality of life she encouraged was tainted with hypocrisy and ignorance. People gave tongue to their respectability by denouncing the theatre. The Church was too often arbitrary and superficial in its pronouncements. Although the public, as a whole, was considerably more enlightened than in Sidney Smith's day, yet his comment, "There is something in the word 'play-house' which seems so closely connected in their [the people's] minds with sin and Satan, that it stands in their vocabulary for every species of abomination," would not have been inapplicable had he uttered it in 1890.[4, 5]

John Hollingshead, during his years of management of the Gaiety, was continually in hot water with those who decried his noisy but prevailingly harmless variety shows. Being the belligerent foe of all breeds of prigs and prudes, he was made the butt of much unnecessary persecution. Because he allowed women to appear in

[4] On Gladstone's twenty-third birthday he recorded in his diary that the theatre was to him as sinful as the race-course.

[5] "We owe the imbecility and paralysis of our drama today to the insane rage of Puritanism that would see nothing in the theatre but a horrible, unholy thing to be crushed and stamped out of existence." H. A. Jones in a Harvard lecture, "The Corner Stones of Modern Drama," 1906.

tights upon his stage he was blackballed by the Reform Club. It later developed that the gentleman who discredited him was a wholesale manufacturer of those very garments. Hypocrisy is not without its amusing side.[6] With all the pronounced moral consciousness of the nineteenth century it has produced little drama which is an honest attempt to pass a stream of life through the temperament of an artist. The people who flocked to shoddy plays in which all characters in evening clothes were naturally villains and all those in rags or working clothes were perforce virtuous, voiced righteous approval when that villainy was laid low and that virtue exalted; but they compelled such plays as *Widowers' Houses* and *Ghosts* to be presented almost furtively as things of ill repute. Even playwrights like Jones and Pinero have too often compromised with truth and made their plays comfortable for the sake of the Mrs. Grundy whom they openly flaunt but to whom they secretly conform.

The Philistine is a more universal fellow than the Puritan and more injurious to drama; the one accepts nothing, the other, everything. To the latter plays are an amusement, and the playhouse a rendezvous, not a temple of art. He wants his plays served up piping hot, well seasoned, and easily digestible. Anything that makes him think turns his stomach. He deprecates refinement of manners on or off the stage as mere flunkey-

[6] In 1877 a French farce, adapted by James Albery, from which all the Gallic naughtiness had not been expunged, created a sensation. Said an editorial in *Contemporary Review,* XXX (1877), 1052, "The virtuous indignation of the British public at the idea of anything immoral being placed upon the British stage is filling the theatre to excess."

ism. Evidences of good breeding and the pride that should accompany it are to him mere "side."[7] He, more than aught else, has always been the chief impediment in the path of a truer and finer dramatic expression in the theatre. Evidences of his blighting touch are everywhere apparent to the reader of the dramatic history of Victorian days.

In 1876 the Imperial Theatre was built as an adjunct to the Westminster Aquarium, where one could not only satisfy his curiosity regarding fish but could be entertained by dancing, topical songs, and acrobatic feats, such as Zaza being fired from a cannon's mouth, and the like. Vainly the Imperial tried to maintain legitimate drama; in fact, it often borrowed acts from its thriving neighbor to replenish a waning patronage. From 1879 to 1882, while Marie Litton and Lily Langtry were acting there, the theatre flourished intermittently and then closed for good. In 1895 the Anglo-American Theatrical Syndicate put on at the Olympic a musical-comedy version of *Pilgrim's Progress,* exhibiting a voluptuous ballet and Christian as a kind of panto-

[7] Gilbert makes sport of the lack of any worthy standard of taste in a theatre audience in the dramatic sketch, "Actors, Authors and Audiences—A Trial by Jury," contributed to the December issue of *Holly Leaves,* 1880. At the conclusion of a play heartily execrated by the house, a trial of the author is held, the audience acting as jury and selecting a judge from their number. Different types and classes of people present testify to the merits of the piece with amusing disparity. A nobleman thinks the tradesman scenes abominable, a clerk claims that those between the Duke and Duchess were highly improbable. Gilbert was frank to admit in his own case that he had to give the public twaddle to meet its taste. "If you serve up tripe and onions for the gallery, it offends the stalls; if you dish up sweetbreads and truffles for the stalls, it disgusts the pit. Therefore, a plain leg of mutton and boiled potatoes is the most stable fare for all."

mime prince. To cite one other instance of the public taste, Emma Cons conducted the affairs of the Royal Victoria Hall ("Old Vic") with the idealistic purpose of elevating the standard of public entertainment. In the eighties she attempted a policy of variety show of the music-hall type, but minus rowdyism and vulgarity. Later she tried opera and Shakespeare. In 1912, her niece, Lilian Baylis, made ventures of a similar character. For years the house flirted with bankruptcy because of the standards of performance insisted upon by these two women. The average playgoer demanded claptrap, bunkum, and novelty, of one sort or another. He wanted to laugh much, cry a little, and think not at all. Hence among the greatest hits of all those years of the closing century one must name *The Lady of Lyons, The Corsican Brothers, The Two Orphans, Our Boys, Our American Cousin, Box and Cox* (all these were written earlier but were frequently revived), *Under the Red Robe, The Prisoner of Zenda, The Private Secretary, A Message from Mars,* and *Charley's Aunt,* a perennial farce, which at one time forty companies were engaged in playing in America, in Europe, and throughout the British Empire.

What should we expect to be the behavior of our Philistine as a spectator at a play? Rather more demonstrative than refined; responding to the performance according to the appeal of the actor rather than of the play itself. He was a hearty, impulsive sort of fellow, very quick to resent aspersion against his intelligence and sometimes forgetting his vaunted British love of fair play. He liked what he liked—because he liked it. If he occupied a seat in pit or gallery he was much more inclined to demonstrate his reactions to the play than if he viewed the proceedings from the stalls, where the proprieties were more exacting. As the century wore to a close, audiences improved materially in decorum, although outbreaks from the pit were still of common occurrence. We find evidence of more repression of the emotions, a curbing of enthusiasm, at times becoming a positive front of apathy.[8] Indeed, toward the end of the century, criticisms are not wanting that lament the excessive toleration of audiences for shoddy plays. The pit seemed to have become by comparison as mild as any sucking dove. Decorum does not necessarily imply refinement of taste or critical discrimination. The actress, Mrs. Kendal, speaks in 1889 of applause having largely gone out of custom except on first nights.[9] G. R. Sims, writing in 1917 and looking back over sixty years' acquaintance with the London theatre, says, "The luxury of woe that the playgoers of the sixties loved to indulge in ceased to be in demand long before the century closed. West-End playgoers were the first to control their emotions and check the briny tears that at one time had been permitted to flow freely. Even in the gallery there were protests against too much sobbing in sympathy with the heroine."[10]

The following words by an eminent dramatic critic

[8] An audience that declines to be swept by sentiment is in a receptive state for comedy of manners, but one that is blasé without patrician acumen certainly is not.

[9] "Dramatic Opinions," *Murray's Magazine*, VI (1889), 601.

[10] G. R. Sims, *My Life: Sixty Years' Recollection of Bohemian London*, p. 291.

and editor might have been written in 1930 instead of 1881. (They apply, one would think, to the stalls rather than to the pit, which begrudged to neither side of the footlights a display of its allegiances or disaffections.) "Our youths are worn out and dissipated before they have arrived at years of discretion. It is a tired, tedious, unmanly, broken-backed age. Enthusiasm is considered 'bad form.' No one dares to applaud at the theatres."[11, 12]

Evidences, however, of barbarian taste and behavior in the theatre, particularly on the part of the middle and lower classes, are not far to seek during these same years. Referring to Scott again, this time from his very readable and informative book, *The Drama of Yesterday and Today,* we are surprised at the uncharitable, utterly rude treatment accorded players or plays, once the crowd had become tired or nettled. In 1870 the opera bouffe, *Chilperic,* at the Lyceum was preceded by Frank Marshall's comedy, *Corrupt Practices.* Not liking the acting of Miss Inman, the audience howled in derision. Marshall's protest in her behalf only added fuel to the fire. In the same year Lord Newry's little piece, *Ecarté,* at the Globe was damned on its opening night by a Saturday-night audience that had become restless and fretful (not without cause) before the curtain rose. They kept up such a fusillade of ragging and chaffing during the performance that the actors

[11] Clement Scott, *Theatre* (London), III, ser. 2 (1881), 175.

[12] In his *From "The Bells" to "King Arthur,"* he comments on the fact that at Irving's excellent revival of Albery's *Two Roses* an audience which had accepted *bona fide* the embraces of Jack and Lottie in 1870 now in 1881 received them with guffaws.

became nonplussed and the play spluttered out with no great loss to dramatic history. However, these scenes illustrate the ruthlessness of Philistinism. Years later (1899), the gallery made themselves very obstreperous during and after a performance of the opera, *The Coquette,* apparently because they understood that there were hired applauders throughout the house. The manager of the theatre, foolishly enough, defied them and an undignified and by no means orderly altercation ensued. Be it said in their behalf, the pittites frequently had a grievance at the hands of inconsiderate managers, but if no especial issue presented itself they were quick to find one. At one time Irving decided to number the pit-seats at the Lyceum, making them a reserved section, but the habitués resented the move so audibly the first night that he had to assure them he would return to the time-honored custom. A similar case occurred at the Princess's in 1886 during a run of Jones's *The Lord Harry.* Some extra stalls had been erected to accommodate the increased attendance. The boos and hisses of the pit so disturbed the play that Wilson Barrett, the manager, had to intervene.

One of the most unsportsmanlike phases of all this turbulence was the humiliation it brought to sincere if sometimes ineffectual actors. Scott cites[13] an instance on Christmas Eve, 1887, when Miss Farren, a gifted, deserving lady, was fairly driven from the stage by a distempered crowd that did not like her play. Just the year before, the Haymarket had been the scene of shameful conduct, when the pit and gallery stormed

[13] *Theatre* (London), XI, n. s. (1888), 94.

with abuse a talented Austrian actress, Emily Rigl, because the play, *Nadjezda,* did not please them. In the same way, not approving of Wilkie Collins' *Rank and Riches* at the Adelphi in 1883, the house went into a frightful uproar of cat-calls and howls, compelling Miss Lingard to retire at the end of the first act.[14] One is led to remark that you cannot expect to find manners portrayed on the stage when none are to be found in the audience. One last example of philistine demonstrativeness. Tennyson's little rustic drama, *The Promise of May,* was given its première at the Globe in 1882. It was hooted from first to last. Although the play was inexcusably late in starting and was not in itself a satisfying production, nevertheless for an English audience to cast such indignity upon their poet laureate was in wretched taste.[15] It is needless to say that neither all audiences nor all the members of any one audience were guilty of such vulgarism. Nor were audiences slow in voicing their approval when they felt that approval was due. The point is that the drama of the latter nineteenth century was subject largely to the verdict of a jury of inferior taste and sense of the proprieties, either dramatic or social.

[14] Charles Hawtrey, *The Truth at Last,* p. 96.

[15] As late as 1895 Henry James's picturesque, delicate little costume play, *Guy Domville,* was greeted at the close of its initial performance at the St. James's by boos and roars "like those of a cage of beasts at some infernal 'Zoo,'" as James put it in a letter to his brother William. It was certainly a needless affront to a sensitive, sincere artist. "The thing fills me with horror for the abysmal vulgarity and brutality of the theatre and its regular public," wrote James, and Meredith felt the shame of it in a letter to Mrs. Walter Palmer: "The treatment of Henry James at the close of his play will prove to Americans that the Old Country retains a fund of the cowardly part of barbarism."

Having before us the fact that the patrons of the drama were in large measure creatures of prejudice and exemplars of inferior taste; that the dramatic profession was a precarious one in remuneration and in reputation; and that the drama is from its very nature peculiarly sensitive to its environment, a thing of crowds and public places, and so dependent on the fashion and temper of the moment; that it is the natural fate of most plays to perish, it is of little wonder that nineteenth-century genius for narrative and portraiture found expression in the novel and not upon the stage. In prose fiction was greater stability and greater security. It did not depend upon an immediacy of appeal to the popular favor. It offered the selective audience of the single reader, not the heterogeneous, collective audience of the crowd, only imperfectly in rapport.

It is in this medium, for example, that the Comic Spirit bade her noblest avatar, George Meredith, to write. What a recorder of manners (at least potentially) was here lost to the stage! It would be idle to engage in surmises concerning the fitness or unfitness of Meredith's genius for the constrictions of the drama. His only venture in the field was in a fragmentary comedy, *The Sentimentalists,* of which the later scenes, in blank verse, were written about 1870 and the earlier in prose, somewhat before that date, but rewritten about 1895. It was not published until after the author's death. At a performance afforded it on March 2, 1910, at the Duke of York's, its dramatic ineptitude became apparent. The play lacked movement; the dialogue was too penetrative for oral purposes. All the characters spoke in Meredithian phrases, crisp and cryptic. The little comedy has been well likened to a fragment of porcelain, exquisite, fragile. Yet in its contrived artifice one may discover the germinal ideas of his *Essay on Comedy* (1877), delivered first as a lecture and then published in the *New Quarterly Magazine*.

In an age more propitious for dramatic writing, a first experiment like *The Sentimentalists* might have flowered into full-blown pictures of character and manners for the theatre, the counterparts of *Evan Harrington* and *The Egoist* for the study.[16] Perhaps his was too patrician an art, too committed to its own high ends to be acceptable to the general public, but the disheartening outlook for dramatic effort in his day would alone account for his adherence (and that of other great novelists) to printed fiction.[17] Certainly no man of his time was more eligible in his mental aptitudes for the writing of manners comedies. These words from the prelude to *The Egoist* prove that: "Comedy is a game played

[16] From a letter of Meredith's to Mrs. Walter Palmer, January 29, 1898, we learn that young Alfred Sutro had recently come to Box Hill with a proposal to dramatize *The Egoist*. Forbes-Robertson, it seems, fancied taking on the rôle of Sir Willoughby Patterne. A draft was submitted to Meredith, who made extensive emendations and additions, but the play was never produced. In 1920, thirty copies of *The Egoist, Arranged for the Stage by George Meredith and Alfred Sutro* were privately printed. It professes to be merely a telescopic version of the novel, but it must be acknowledged that this recension of Sutro's is an adroit piece of work.

[17] One recalls, also, William Morris's privately played extravaganza, *The Tables Turned or Nupkins Awakened* (1887), based on socialistic premises and satirizing contemporary men and manners. Shaw has said that under more favorable auspices Morris would have included drama among his literary accomplishments, a statement to be taken for what it is worth. Apropos of his "masque-morality," *Love is Enough,* Morris once said that he refused to write for the stage because the actors were incapable of speaking blank verse.

to throw reflection upon social life and it deals with human nature in the drawing-room of civilized men and women, where we have no dust of the struggling outer world, no mire, no violent crashes, to make the correctness of the representation convincing." Further testimony, if needed, is afforded in the sagacity and sympathetic insight of his brochure on the Comic Spirit.

If the English public and its theatre failed to lift drama to the dignity of an art in the days of Meredith's apprenticeship, how much less in earlier years did they have to offer a Dickens and a Thackeray who, with Meredith, have recorded the English *Comédie Humaine* of the nineteenth century! To these two men, as to Collins and Reade, the world of the stage was one of the deepest interest. In the Elizabethan age they would have been playwrights of distinction; in the Victorian they can reach a representative public only as novelists, and the picturing of middle- and upper-class manners finds its way into *Dombey and Son* and *Bleak House,* into *Pendennis* and *The Newcomes.*

Dickens, we all know, was an habitual theatre-goer. The stage held him in its thrall. Its bustle and stir, its emphasis upon crises in human experience, fascinated him. Although he never became a professional actor, he played with great promise in amateur companies in his younger days, both in England and in Canada.[18] Had there been the affinity between the stage and the public that should exist, he might have cast in his lot with the theatre, perhaps first as actor and later as a

[18] For instance, in Lytton's *Not So Bad as We Seem,* dealing with high society in the time of James II.

writer of plays. As it was, he wrote or collaborated in the writing of several burlettas and farces. His early literary success, however, led his mind permanently into another channel of endeavor.

It is interesting to learn that Dickens at one time contemplated leasing the old Strand Theatre and becoming its manager, but was dissuaded from the enterprise because of legal involvements. He had always taken a great delight in superintending the amateur performances in which he participated. Shortly before his death he told his friend Charles Kent that one of his most cherished day-dreams was "to settle down now for the remainder of my life within easy distance of a great theatre, in the direction of which I should hold supreme authority." At least fifteen of the master's major novels found their way upon the stage and were received with acclaim, beginning with *The Peregrinations of Pickwick* by William Rede at the Adelphi in 1836, six months after the first instalment of the novel, and continuing through the century, particularly from 1840 on into the seventies. Despite grievous piracies committed upon them, the stories retained upon the boards their sentiment, humor, and animation, giving pleasure to thousands and influencing the productions of such play-writing contemporaries of Dickens as Tom Taylor and H. J. Byron.

Like Dickens, Thackeray was an inveterate habitué of the theatre, and fully sensed the virility of drama as an art-form. Every Thackeray lover will recall the number of kindly, if sometimes satirical, references to stage-land—in *Vanity Fair*, a Drury Lane performance back in the palmy days of Elliston; in *Pendennis,* Mr. Bingley's stock company, and the inimitable Miss Fotheringay; in *Henry Esmond,* the young hero's attendance at the theatre in Lincoln's Inn Fields. In Thackeray's novels people are always witnessing or writing plays. His letters, also, teem with allusions to plays he has seen. In it all is the fervency of a boy's enthusiasm for the world of the footlights. Besides a one-act burlesque, *King Glumpus,* the novelist essayed in 1854 a comedy, *The Wolves and the Lamb,* which, however, was rejected by both the Olympic and the Haymarket as deficient in dramatic incident. Whereupon he transmuted the comedy into his story, *Lovel the Widower.* The drama is indeed a jealous mistress, brooking no divided allegiance in her votaries.[19]

As we have seen, the popular tastes and prejudices respecting the theatre were a source of discouragement to any potential dramatist. Then, too, the economic factor entered with tremendous force. Publishers of books and magazines were in a position to offer monetary inducements to writers, which were beyond the reach of theatrical managers until very late in the century. One reason why playwrights were being so poorly paid was the lack of protection afforded by the copyright laws, which permitted, without remuneration to authors, the influx of foreign plays and foreign employment of native work. These conditions, of course, discouraged the publication of plays except for professional uses within the theatre. Although drama is in-

[19] His *Rose and the Ring, Esmond* and *Vanity Fair,* have been adapted for the stage. Only the latter lends itself readily to the exigencies of dramatization.

dissolubly associated with stage presentation, yet the opportunity for publication is for the aspiring playwright at once a challenge and a stimulation to a higher literary standard of expression. In 1852 Parliament enacted legislation protecting foreign authors against the piratical use of their plays in deliberate translation, but it was not until 1875 that the pernicious practice of adaptation of foreign, particularly French, plays was checked by more stringent laws. Thereafter a native playwright could compete on at least equal terms with the foreigner. As a result of the Treaty of Berne, the literary output of foreign authors was placed on exactly the same footing as that of the native Englishman. And when the United States Congress, in 1890, secured copyright protection in America for English authors, all barriers were removed against the printing of plays. In 1891 both Jones and Pinero began to publish.

One other factor which played a part in deterring candidates from the profession of play-writing was the dramatic censorship, an institution which has crystallized into a governmental tradition, despite fitful but fervent protests. This is not the occasion to examine the history or to weigh the merits and demerits of an office whose decisions may be arbitrary and are unappealable. Certainly it seems to exist in despite of the genius of British independence and justice. What should merely be a wholesome check on salacity becomes in stupid hands a suppression of the free current of ideas in the theatre. The censorship has played its part in holding nineteenth-century drama down to the level of mere ephemeral amusement, an entertainment for the eye and ear alone, isolated from the intellectual and imaginative life of the time. The censoring of plays by one man, irresponsible to Parliament and unimpeachable, would seem to be an anomaly in modern England. Yet the office persists, at times blundering, at times reasonable, according to the incumbent's sympathetic understanding and vision. Too often he has strained at a gnat and swallowed a camel; he has admitted farce of thinly veiled naughtiness and has banned plays of candor and power that cut deep and clean into the living tissue of human society.

We have seen in an earlier part of this paper how obtuse the acts of the censor often were in the fore part of the century. They may be matched in later years, although the general standard of intelligence in the office has risen materially. W. B. Donne, as Examiner of Stage Plays in the time of Robertson, was scarcely less pedantic and meticulous than the George Colman who had refused Miss Mitford's *Charles First.* In John Oxenford's *Daddy Hardacre* at the Olympic in 1857, "O God" was altered to "O Heaven" and "O Lord" was everywhere omitted. The next year he excised from *The Amazon's Oath* the phrase, "And am no more worthy to be called your son," because it was Biblical. For the same reason in 1875 the title of Albery's *The Good Samaritan* was altered to *The Spendthrift.* In Gilbert's dramatized version of *Great Expectations* (1871), it is said[20] the Licenser of Plays returned Magwitch's words "Here you are in chambers fit for a

[20] Sidney Dark and Rowland Grey, *W. S. Gilbert: His Life and Letters,* p. 53.

Lord" with "Lord" changed to "Heaven," a piece of obtuseness it is difficult to believe. The censorship displayed a reverence not only for the Deity above but for the lords of earth. Passages referring possibly to titled families or to government officials[21] were deleted. "Mr. Holloway's Ointment" could not be spoken of as "Mr. Highgates' Ointment," for the said Mr. Holloway was a reputable tradesman, employing many people.

Under the regime of Edward F. S. Pigott, 1875–1895, the office of the Examiner of Plays was conducted somewhat more intelligently. Yet protests continued and were oftentimes justified. Grundy and Mackay's *A Novel Reader* (1878), adapted from Meilhac and Halévy, which satirized deservedly a school of feminine fiction, was suppressed, and no reasons for the action were permitted the adapters. In the same way, Mr. Pigott refused to license Arthur Mattison's *A False Step* (translated from Augier's *Les Lionnes Pauvres*), a delicate theme but delicately handled, saying that it would give much offence, although it was "profoundly moral in its ultimate purpose." And yet the innuendo of Parisian farces was continuing with little expurgation. The theatrical pabulum of the London public was being dealt out erratically. When a French company attempted to produce *La Petite Marquise,* the examiner promptly rejected it, but when they changed the bill to *Divorçons,* of which the other play is but a less salacious redaction, he was forced to admit it to performance, since it had already been licensed three or four years before.

[21] "May Gladstone keep his temper" was expunged from a topical song.

Although seemingly an effete institution, the censorship of plays has continued, despite frequent reputable protests at various times against the autocratic rejection of Shelley's *Cenci,* of Maeterlinck, Ibsen, and Shaw. In 1907, for example, seventy-one men of letters united in deprecation of the censor's act in prohibiting Edward Garnett's *The Breaking Point* and Barker's *Waste.* Among the signatures were those of Barker, Barrie, Conrad, W. L. Courtney, Galsworthy, Gilbert, Hankin, Hardy, Frederic Harrison, Henry James, Jones, Masefield, Meredith, Gilbert Murray, Pinero, Ernest Rhys, Shaw, Swinburne, and Arthur Symons. As to the reliability of the contention that the public itself will automatically eliminate deleterious plays by refusing them patronage we need here have no concern. It is indeed a question of grave doubt. Conducted sanely, the censorship becomes a wholesome safeguard to the public, even though in theory it may always be a discrimination against the drama. It must be admitted that it relieves the theatrical world of endless litigation concerning the moral fitness of productions; it protects the worthy dramatist against the public as well as the public against the charlatan.

We have been considering various phases of the dramatic situation in England in the latter decades of the nineteenth century, presenting, as they do, an inhospitable, forbidding front to prospective or potential writers for the drama and for the comedy of manners in particular. We have seen the deterrent effect of social and moral prejudice, inferior public taste, inadequate remuneration and copyright protection, and of a censorship that could be autocratic and stupid. In every one of these respects we have witnessed an appreciable improvement as the eighteen-eighties swing into the last decade. We have encountered, from the days of Robertson's *Society,* and shall continue to encounter in increasing numbers, plays presenting the social life and manners of the day, plays in which the aristocracy appears generously in the *dramatis personae.* And yet, with few exceptions, the tone of such comedies is domestic and plebeian. The patrician self-sufficiency and self-approbation of the old comedy of manners has disappeared. The emphasis has shifted and for an explanation we must look to the spirit of the age.

VI

PATRICIAN EVIDENCES IN A MIDDLE-CLASS AGE

1880–1900

THAT the reign of Victoria was scientific and commercial, and that it was permeated by a new democratic conception in government and in society, are commonplaces that do not call for verification. We need only point out the effect of these new conditions on the particular comedy type with which we are engaged. Sheldon Cheney in his exhaustive history of the theatre[1] asserts that the birth and growth of democracy from the days of the French Revolution brought no awakening of dramatic art but rather a stultification. Its emphasis was practical and materialistic. Power and prosperity were its watchwords. Long before, William Hazlitt ascribed the decline in comedy in his time to the democratizing of life, which levels out so many of the picturesque inequalities in society.[2] Comedy, he thought, gradually wears itself out by what it feeds on; scenes and situations are gradually used up and no new ones arise to take their place. Perhaps this is an over-melancholy view of the case. The perversities of human nature bid fair to furnish material to the writers of comedy and satire until the end

[1] Sheldon Cheney, *The Theatre, Three Thousand Years of Drama, Acting, and Stagecraft*, p. 380.

[2] The single fact of uniformity in dress throughout society may be taken as a kind of symbol of this process of standardization.

of time. Nevertheless, Hazlitt makes a point, for the contrasts which are so picturesque and even vital a part of comic presentation on the stage were leveled away as the class distinctions disappeared which created them. Such outward, distinguishing marks of caste as apparel and general deportment were matters of charm in themselves, exciting envy and respect. Sedan chairs and linkmen are not essential to the comedy of manners, but without their equivalents as symbols of rank and station, the illusion it must create is materially reduced.

With Victoria sobriety, simplicity, and decorum were ushered into English life after the pomp and display of the Regency. Whereas the coronation of George IV cost the state £243,000, that of his successor cost but £70,000. We note a restoration of Sunday observance. In matters of court etiquette the young queen showed little inclination to be punctilious. Throughout her reign the great middle class was coming gradually into its own. The industrial revolution brought in material prosperity and the growth of city life; from step to step the franchise gave the commoner a new political and social consciousness, until at last the Reform Bill of 1887 put the reins of authority into his hands. The abolition of the stamp duties made available a cheap press to quicken and enlarge his interests. His composite photograph is the John Bull that we have so often seen—a solidly practical and prosperous fellow, whose goodly girth would hint rather at physical well-being than at a concern for the arts or the humanities.

From early in the reign of Victoria and the Consort

the hereditary power of the old nobility through its political and social prestige and its vast possession of property began to be broken. The lavish creation of new peerages changed the aristocratic complexion of society. Representatives of commercial wealth, the sciences, and the arts and letters were encouraged by court patronage. As Lord Beaconsfield said, the plebeian aristocracy was blended with the patrician oligarchy. Much of the late nineteenth-century peerage, especially, was of recent elevation, in recognition of party support, philanthropy, or other uses of wealth. In the face of this mushroom aristocracy and these *nouveaux riches*, the old Tory families sat stern or disconsolate. The parvenu aristocrat was often more snobbish than the old-fashioned one had ever cared to be. The upper rank in society was slowly changing from an aristocracy to a plutocracy and the wheel had come full circle.

The patrician instinct died hard, but it was becoming an anachronism. Mayfair and Belgravia continued to wear their badges of preferment but they wore them with a difference. The swell of the fifties and sixties with his immaculate if finical toilette played his picturesque part and disappeared. There were Alfred Montgomery, Count Alfred D'Orsay (the "Alfred" remained a dandies' club until well on in the century), Morgan John O'Connell, Lord Kilmarlcock, probable source of Thackeray's The O'Mulligan, and Mr. Arcedeckne, a prefiguring of the novelist's Harry Foker. All of them were the very stuff on which the comedy of manners should thrive but they rarely appeared in a play except to be deprecated. Inheriting directly from the eighteenth-century beau and the buck of the Regency, they gave way in turn to the masher or dandy of the eighties with his toothpick, his limp, and his eccentric apparel, who was caricatured endlessly, in music-hall burlesque, in the press and in *Punch*.[3]

Meanwhile, the great professional and mercantile classes were flourishing in a life of larger privilege and opportunity, little desiring to invade the social precincts of the upper circle. Snobs and social climbers were repudiated by all well-bred members of either class. And yet the striking fact to note is that the boundaries between the upper and middle classes were now no longer inviolate, for reverence for wealth was now breaking down the barriers which caste-prejudice for so long had maintained. If the nobility were loath to accept the newly rich socially, they readily imitated his business practices and were not reluctant to be associated with remunerative enterprises in the City. Then, too, intermarriages were constantly blending the old blue blood with that of traditionally redder hue. Thus the upper class, coming into ever closer association with the better middle class, found itself surprisingly assimilable, and the lower shopkeeping class was lifted by its greater affluence into the enjoyment of privileges formerly denied. " The toe of the peasant comes near the heel of the courtier." Herein lies one of the most significant social phenomena of the century—this process of fusion and leveling up and down, and this trend from insularity to cosmopolitanism. Through this instrumentality a fringe grew up around an aristocracy for-

[3] In a sense of the comic and in satiric power, Du Maurier's drawings may be called the pictorial counterpart of the comedy of manners.

merly intact—a borderland in which pursuits, pleasures, manners, and general appointments of life were indistinguishable from those of the time-honored inner circle itself. The members of this enterprising new "high society" may be deemed as intelligent as the old but wanting in its patrician air of grace and distinction. By the eighties we may say that the social standardization and uniformity which Hazlitt had vaguely sensed had been effected, and political power really passed into the keeping of a middle class, self possessed, assertive but of limited horizons.

It must be at once admitted that the traditional comedy of manners found such social conditions as we have been discussing foreign to its nature and uncongenial to its perpetuation. In the past it had been the reflection of a social group isolated and distinguished, and had been written largely by members of that coterie and patronized by them. In the nineteenth century, however, that class was deprived of its political emoluments, and its social behavior became a matter of little moment because its prestige was gone. It had lost its piquant identity. Neither did it continue to cherish the traditions which a former gentility and privilege had bequeathed to it. Society with a capital "S" could no longer furnish the author nor the audience for a comedy of manners, because it was no longer proudly conscious of itself nor had reason to be so. As society at large became impregnated with the leaven of democracy, the title "Lord" and "Lady" lost caste inevitably, and yet there is ever a prestige accruing to station and family, a certain glamor for those in the more crowded levels below. These emoluments may take unto themselves honor and dignity or they may be worn as badges of preferment merely. In a Victorian age old comedy with its *haut ton* had become quite impossible as a representative type, but yet an upper class that was vigorously conscious of its own integrity and that took an interest in ideas might have been more respectfully treated upon the stage. Instead of inspiring high comedy, where wit and courtliness reign, it had to be content with playing a secondary and often disparaging part in a prevailingly middle-class comedy and farce.[4]

Manifestly, the impotency of the nobility was not only the result of their own deterioration but of social forces and conditions which they were helpless to control. The nineteenth century was a century of social revaluations,[5] of mingled disillusionment and vision. The very founts and springs of life were muddied and had to resettle. The old aristocracy had waned, and no new group had as yet been evolved, which in terms of culture, education, and attendant leisure had acquired the good manners that are the index of taste and breeding. Middle-class supremacy implied the drab manners or lack of manners of the "respectable" philistine. In an age of vast readjustments in man's physical and mental life, the fine arts languish, among them living itself, which is the finest of the fine arts. We hear de-

[4] A "comedy of the manners of South Sea islanders under City veneer," Meredith called it. And he added, "It is unwholesome for men and women to see themselves as they are if they are no better than they should be."

[5] "We in England have no modern drama at all. Our vast society is not homogeneous enough for this, not sufficiently united, even any large part of it, in a common view of life, a common ideal, capable as serving as a basis for it." Matthew Arnold.

plored the desuetude of good talk, which is also one of the graces. What we call manners is the consequence of these very arts. They blossom in a quiet air which is not surcharged with polemic discussion and commercial enterprise; they are a flower that does not flourish at a time of transplanting, vigorous pruning, and experimental grafting.

The comedy of manners, therefore, in the historic sense, cannot be looked for in the nineteenth century as a representative type of comedy. It may and does occur sporadically either as a quaint revival, an antique like its costumes and furniture; or as the picture of a contemporary aristocracy which still exhibits, now and again, the spectacle of a *beau monde*. As the reflection of the life of a unified, homogeneous, and imperious class, in which manners are crystallized by precedent and sanctified by custom, it does not exist except as an occasional anomaly.

At some future day the middle class may acquire a code of manners worthy of the name, one that will reflect self-discipline and taste and a good ordering of society. But the emphases of civilization must shift ere that is possible. When good manners arrive, the theatre will depict them, but it cannot create them. Here and there, we hope, are intimations of a better standard of middle-class social behavior, which is neither blasé nor gauche, neither bohemian nor philistine, neither that of a decadent aristocracy nor of an upstart democracy. It has been the dubious pride of our democratic age to exalt the "man" over the "gentleman" and yet in the existence of the latter will rest the proof of the finer flowering of our so-called civilization. In Lord Chesterfield's words, "A gentleman has ease without familiarity, is respectful without meanness; genteel without affectation, insinuating without seeming art," we sense a kind of opportunism, wherein gentility exists as a useful commodity. On the other hand, Beaconsfield's "Propriety of manners and consideration for others are the two main characteristics of a gentleman," and Thackeray's "It is to be honest, to be gentle, to be generous, to be brave, to be wise, and possessing all these qualities, to exercise them in the most graceful and outward manner" posit both the possession of virtue and the comely expression of it in behavior. At the present time, we are too busy with the utilities to have perfected the amenities. The manners of the old aristocracy were punctilious because of tradition; those of the modern gentleman will be animated by a higher motive. The old régime had its *noblesse oblige;* so will the new. As the former had its comedy of manners, so may the new. Meanwhile, in the eighteenth- and nineteenth-century comedy of manners which we possess, we may find relish in those social arts and graces which are all too rare in the daily round of experience.

Comedy, by its very nature, reflects the changing life of society from decade to decade, adapting itself with protean ease to new modes and aspects. Unlike its sister, tragedy, it is concerned at first hand with the temporary and the local. It presents us with "the very age and body of the time." Under the impress of those social conditions in the latter half of the nineteenth century which have been already indicated, comedy therefore became prevailingly a reflector of middle-class people, manners, and morals.[6] It became domestic in scene and plebeian in taste. Humor superseded wit; nature, artifice. Tired of the inanities and irrelevancies of early Victorian comedy, people turned to Robertson and Taylor and later to Grundy and Jones to confirm their own experience of reality. They sought recognition in the theatre instead of escape. Lamb's imputation still applied in all the years that followed him: "We carry our fire-side concerns to the theatre with us." In a veritable comedy of manners the public would have found escape, rather than recognition, in a world of unnatural wit and sparkle. It would have been an intellectual excursion—a glass of champagne after so long an indulgence in tepid tea.

As a result of the cry that comedy should be only a faithful mirror reflecting life's mingled wisdom and folly, humor and pathos, gladness and sadness, dramatic lines between types tended to break down. A closer adherence to the normal introduced a variety of qualities and elements which life in the unselected aggregate

[6] Back in 1869 Tom Taylor had this to say about the changes a democratized age was effecting in audience and theatre: "So long as the patent theatres survived, there was a home in them for artificial comedy as for formal tragedy, and a body of actors trained to represent both with more or less finish and completeness. But the same influences, call them popular or democratic if you will, which were gradually modifying manners, political opinions and literature, were at work in the theatre, both to sap theatrical privilege and to new-mould theatrical amusements. The patents were broken down; all theatres were opened to all kinds of entertainments; actors became scattered; and whatever of artificial or stately in stage art had been maintained by the barriers of privilege, or the influences of tradition, began to melt away, and make room for ways of acting and forms of entertainment bearing a more popular impress." "Some Thoughts on the English Stage." *Every Saturday,* VII (1869), 194.

possesses. Villain or hero, utterly satanic or utterly a paragon, merged into the common man. The object of laughter in a play was also the object of sympathy. Farcical characters rubbed shoulders with seriously drawn characters in a story full of sentiment and romance. Comedies represented the manners of a social group only as one of their many glinting surfaces.

Before considering some of the social comedies of the eighties and nineties, it will be well to refer again to a fact, already hinted at, that interest in aristocratic life and manners did not ever entirely cease during the middle-class régime in the theatre. In fact, at the close of the century we shall witness a noticeable augmentation of such interest. Traditional genteel deportment, if no longer so pronounced, as formerly, as a class characteristic lived on in little corners of society. Sometimes it appeared, in comedy, as a pathetic relic of the past, a proud gesture, a warming of the hands before a dying fire. Or it might be the tasteful expression of the individual's own temperament and philosophy, an artful artlessness. (The manners of the nobility were not always so blatant as they are represented in the fiction and particularly in the drama of the period.) Then, again, gentility in comedies often manifested itself as mere "side," a conscious exaggeration in dress, in carriage and the like. One step more and we pass over into the counterfeit world of the *nouveaux riches* and the social climbers, where manners become the object of deserved satire.

A perusal of London play-bills from the days of Robertson's *Society* reveals the veneration of caste of the English public, even when the nature of the piece did not require upper-class personages. The aristocracy becomes a kind of fetish to give a play tone and distinction. Democratic England has not lost its veneration for the deities of Mayfair. In the theatre it still prays that

> God bless the Squire and his Relations,
> And keep us in our Proper Stations.

A kind of aura of glamor and mystery encircles the heads of those of station and wealth, and this fact authors and managers are of course quick to recognize. Men and women of title are given place in a large proportion of the comedies, sometimes making a legitimate contribution to the theme, at other times merely strutting and fretting upon the stage. They add luster to romance as in Anthony Hope's delicate, piquant cloak-and-sword romance, *The Adventure of Lady Ursula* (1898), with its smart, lively dialogue distinctly in the comedy of manners vein. Or again, they may appear in historical plays, in which the manners of a vanished day are resurrected and we are caught in the spell of their quaintness and charm. To this class belong Douglas Jerrold's *Beau Nash* (1834), Blanchard Jerrold's *Beau Brummell, or the King of Calais* (1859), Stevenson and Henley's *Beau Austin* (1890), and Grundy's *A Marriage of Convenience* (taken from Dumas' *Un Mariage sous Louis XV*), a romance laid in a setting of brilliant manners.

We are reminded, too, of Robert Buchanan's adaptations of the eighteenth-century novel: his *Sophia* (1886), which ran for 500 nights, and *Joseph's Sweet-*

heart (1888), based on Fielding, remind us somewhat in their characters and *mise en scène* of the comedies of Sheridan and Goldsmith.[7] They may be called a series of vignettes of eighteenth-century high life or *tableaux vivants* of the tinsel age rather than integrated plays. The very names of Lady Booby, a woman of fashion, her maid Mrs. Slipslop, and Lord Fellamar, a dissolute roué, take us back to the reign of early comedy in the balmy days of Drury Lane and Lincoln's Inn Fields.[8]

Such adaptations call to mind the late nineteenth-century revivals of the standard old comedies of manners, revivals which may be attributed to a number of causes. Sometimes they were mere stop-gaps; oftener they were a tribute to the literary and dramatic vitality

[7] In 1890 he put on at the Vaudeville *Miss Tomboy,* a sanitary version of Vanbrugh's *The Relapse,* with dialogue rewritten and characters carefully remodeled for Victorian consumption. Fanny Hoyden becomes a guileless romp instead of a vixen. The author said, "The vein of heartlessness so characteristic of an artificial period has been abandoned altogether." Even then, the comedy did not lose its irresponsible good spirits.

[8]
So, times are changed indeed since wits and lords
Swaggered in square-cut, powdered wigs and swords!
Picture the age!—A lord was then, I vow,
A lord indeed (how different from now!)
And trembling virtue hid herself in fear
Before the naughty ogling of a peer.
. . . .
And now our task is, in a merry play,
To summon up that time long past away;
To bring to life the manners long outworn,
The lords, the dames, the maidens all forlorn.

From Prologue to *Joseph's Sweetheart.*

Buchanan's successful flair for the eighteenth century is later manifest in his *Dick Sheridan* (1894), a series of scenes from the days of *The School for Scandal,* centering around the life of its author. He has sketched for us the gay whirl of the frivolous world of fashion at Bath—its fops and exquisites, its lords and lordlings, its belles and its *grandes dames.* We may compare Gladys Unger's *Mr. Sheridan* (1907).

which those plays possessed. The public enjoyed to the full their atmosphere of a bygone time and their aristocratic flourish. There is space here to refer to revivals of only a few of the more memorable out of a number, and only to those revivals in which the players enacted their parts in the grand style which these comedies require. Without *élan* and a slight touch of exaggeration in the presentation, they fail to become that "Utopia of gallantry" which Lamb called them.

Equally alluring to the actor and to the public, Sheridan enjoyed many brilliant revivals during the latter half of the century. For instance, in 1874 at the Prince of Wales's, and again in 1884 at the Haymarket, the Bancrofts staged *The School for Scandal* with their characteristic attention to exactness in furniture and costume.[9] With Mr. Bancroft as Joseph Surface, his wife as Lady Teazle and John Hare as Sir Peter the play was performed with an easy naturalness rather than with the touch of artifice which it demands. In 1882 the Vaudeville Theatre was the scene of a brilliant restoration of *The School for Scandal,* which ran to crowded houses for 400 nights. William Farren and Ada Cavendish were the Teazles. Late the same year *The Rivals* was put on by one of the greatest casts that has ever interpreted it. At the hands of William Farren (Sir Anthony), Mrs. Stirling (Mrs. Malaprop) and Winifred Emery (Lydia Languish) the comedy was the very spirit of wit and gaiety *redivivus.* Later memo-

[9] Later they presented *The Rivals* in the same way. Under the direction of Bancroft and young Pinero the British Museum was ransacked for details for the Bath scenes. Forbes-Robertson designed the costumes with archaeological accuracy.

rable revivals of *The School* need only be mentioned: that at Daly's, 1893, with William Farren and Ada Rehan as the Teazles; at the Lyceum in 1896; at the Criterion the same year, with Mrs. Campbell, Cyril Maude, George Alexander, and Charles Wyndham; and the very excellent one in 1900 at the Haymarket with Cyril Maude, Winifred Emery, and Constance Collier. Repeated successes of the Sheridan masterpiece in our own century continue to attest to its lustiness. At the St. James's and at His Majesty's in 1907 and 1909 respectively it was given exceptional interpretations.[10]

Reappearances of certain other old comedies need give us pause only as they were presented with unusual distinction. *Beaux' Stratagem,* Imperial, 1879, William Farren as Archer, Lionel Brough as Scrub, Marie Litton as Mrs. Sullen, Mrs. Stirling as Lady Bountiful. *Clandestine Marriage,* Gaiety, 1874; Strand, 1887; Haymarket, 1903. *Jealous Wife,* Strand, 1892. *Belle's Stratagem,* Strand, 1873, ran 250 nights, William Terriss as Doricourt; Lyceum, 1881, Ellen Terry and Henry Irving. We shall not recount the occasional revivals of the Robertson comedies. Even *London Assurance* and *Money* have not been allowed to die out entirely on the modern stage. Frank Archer, the actor, records nine presentations of the latter play between 1872 and 1911, the last being a notable command performance at Drury

[10] Perhaps the most brilliant performance of the play in the entire century was at a grand complimentary benefit to J. B. Buckstone at "Old Drury," June 8, 1876. The cast was superlative, consisting of Phelps (Sir Peter), Irving (Joseph), Mathews (Charles), Buckstone (Sir Benjamin), Coghlan (Careless), Bancroft (Trip), Miss Neilson (Lady Teazle), Mrs. Stirling (Mrs. Candour).

Lane in honor of the German Emperor and Empress, in which every part in the cast was taken by a star.

As we consider those comedies of the eighteen-eighties which, in some degree, exhibit the characteristics of the comedy of manners, we encounter again and for the last time the ubiquitous Byron, whose *The Upper Crust* (1880) presents an interesting situation for the student of manners, despite its shallow and at times farcical treatment. As we must always expect in Byron, the play is overlarded with verbal filigree and surfeited with all manner of quips and cranks and wanton wiles. Byron's wit is pyrotechnic—flashy, explosive, soon forgotten. The comedy has to do with the attempt of Doublechick, a thoroughly vulgar, self-made man, to break through the upper crust of county society, with money-bags as his credentials.[11] If the broad-comedy aspects of the vulgarian soap-boiler were less stressed the play would present a study worthy of high comedy. Yet the mingled arrogance and servility of the barbarian manufacturer and the equally barbarian snobbishness and toadyism of the "Upper Crust" are propounded with more than Byron's usual cogency. When Doublechick has had an overdose of snubbing from titled folk of the county, he recovers his equipoise by going out to the gardener and "letting 'im 'ave it 'ot." Therein lies the touch of human nature at the back of all caste-systems. One serious defect in the play is its arbitrary motivation. Byron is confronted with the situation of a young lady betrothed to a baronet at the solicitation of her bourgeois father, and in love with a penniless

[11] J. L. Toole, the prince of low-comedy actors, played the part with magnificent unction.

gentleman. What must the author do to arrive at his foreordained conclusion? Nothing simpler. First, make the young baronet (who is really quite honorable) fall suddenly in love with a designing woman and then endow the penniless gentleman with a title and an inheritance. Here, as so often, the dramatic libertinism of farce frustrates the aims of comedy.

Another " old-timer " wrote a play at about this time that deserves a moment's notice—Boucicault, whose long and prolific dramatic career leans to the side of melodrama rather than social comedy. *The Jilt* (1886), however, presents an interesting picture of a turf-loving, horse-fancying Yorkshire aristocracy, stroked in with the author's customary liveliness. The story, nevertheless, is an artificial concoction, dealing with the triumph of a breezy, rather horsy sort of hero over a blackmailing villain, in defense of a lady who, now safely married, has been a breaker of hearts in her time. The characters we have met again and again; the dialogue is amusing, cynically flavored, reminiscent of *London Assurance*.

An interesting little three-act comedy of Burnand's, *The Colonel* (1881), may be classed in the manners genre. It is a redaction of an older play, *The Serious Family*, by Bayle Bernard, and in them both are elements of Bayard's *Le Mari à la Compagne* and very possibly of Murphy's *The Way to Keep Him* back in the eighteenth century. In *The Serious Family* a young married couple are seen under the thumb of a rigidly puritanical mother-in-law. Their struggles to release themselves furnish material to a farcically inclined plot. The whole philosophy of puritanism is subjected to some pointed satire, and this satirical element *The Colonel* inherits in good measure. Burnand, however, has replaced religious fanaticism by the esthetic craze of the seventies and eighties, which we find ridiculed in *Patience* and in the illustrations of Du Maurier. The hilarious attack upon this silly affectation for art is the one important thing for us in the play. Its lively entanglements and disentanglements and its plentiful contributions of puns and quibbles are the element of burlesque which Burnand constantly employs. That the play was somewhat more than a nine-days' wonder is attested by the fact that it had completed its 550th performance at the Prince of Wales's on the night that theatre closed its doors.

In 1882 appeared *The Parvenu* of G. W. Godfrey (for many years a clerk at the Admiralty office), a member of the Robertsonian cup-and-saucer school, in the best sense of the phrase. Certainly *The Parvenu* deserves to rank among the pleasantest and truest pictures of genuinely English social life of the decade. The over-used situation of the rich upstart breaking into high society is given a fresh turn. The central figure is Mr. Ledger, M.P., a loud, swaggering sort of bounder, who has built himself a fortune, with which he knocks for admittance at the doors of the aristocracy. Philistine though he is, he is not incapable of a noble renunciation, and his life of energy and resourcefulness contrasts to his advantage with the impecunious idleness of the baronet, Sir Fulke Pettigrew. His wife is snobbism incarnate, which suffers a tremendous blow when a humble young painter is mistaken for the Lord Clydesdale for whom she had set her cap as a son-in-law. The play reflects its age in its endorsement of the middle-class point of view, and yet it was heartily accepted by audiences of smart folk. The dialogue is witty above the average. Ledger and Lady Pettigrew, who affects the grand manner but is herself of obscure origin, may be termed real characterizations. In reading *The Parvenu,* one is reminded of Galsworthy's *Skin Game,* a much later satirical study in contrasts.

The plot of *A Great Catch* (1883) by Hamilton Aïdé is similar to that of *The Parvenu.* The De Mottevilles, a titled family of meagre resources, seek a match for their daughter with a rich Australian. The girl's aunt discovers his fraudulent past (for which he has done all possible to atone) and hounds him to the verge of suicide. His generous conduct to the girl in withdrawing from her life awakens our admiration. As usual the aristocratic members of the story are snobbish or eccentric or both. The character-drawing is above the average, and what of polish of manners the play affords was heightened on the stage by the acting of Genevieve Ward and the young Beerbohm Tree, whose reading of the part of the asinine Lord Boodle was a neat bit of satire.

Except for Pinero, to whose early plays reference will be made later, the most considerable dramatist to essay society comedy in our decade was Sydney Grundy, a man with a fine sense for the theatre but falling just short of the insight and power to translate experience into a genuine dramatic reading of life. Much of his work was French adaptation, which he defended as a legitimate form of dramatic activity. The influence of France is also seen in the Scribe-like workmanship of the man. He carves and whittles his plays with the most meticulous care, until he has achieved a perfect co-ordination of every part to the whole. He was one of the first of our playwrights to realize the value of complete economy of word and of action in the fulfilment of his theme. Grundy's dialogue is admirable in its clear, crisp configuration. Altogether, one feels that he handled the tools of his craft with masterly skill but never had quite the vision or grasp of reality to strike off an impressive *chef d'oeuvre.*

Two of Grundy's plays of the eighteen-eighties deserve our attention, *The Glass of Fashion* (1883) and *The Silver Shield* (1885). The former is a comedy of manners trenchantly satirizing scandal-mongering society journals and the frivolous, hypocritical society that fosters them. John Macadam, a rich brewer and incurable bourgeois, has bought up "The Glass of Fashion," a society journal that traffics in scandal, that he may effect an entrance into fashionable circles. Instead he is soon engulfed in trouble, as the aggrieved victims of his slanderous columns find means to persecute him. In the end he is glad to creep out from under his undertaking. Col. Trevanion, a soldier and a gentleman; his wife, a giddy, spoiled child of fashion who compromises herself by meeting her card debts with money borrowed from Prince Borowski, a Polish adventurer; and Peg, her breezy young sister, who saves her from an embarrassing situation in the Prince's studio, in a scene reminiscent of the screen-scene in *The School for Scandal,* are all characters that we may visualize before us. And yet they fall short of complete fulfilment. Rather we sense them as creatures of a shallow, empty, pleasure-chasing world. The conversation is natural, compact, lively, but not brilliant. The piece impresses one as a piece of artifice, handily contrived, a thing of the theatre.

In *The Silver Shield* we are conscious again of a play struggling, not quite successfully, to be freed from mere ingenuity and artifice. Too much dependence is placed on absurd misunderstandings arising from the chance reading of letters (an old stage device). Such jerry-building as this William Archer calls "second-hand Sardou." Manners are less emphasized than situation. The characters hover between type and full-rounded identity—the cleric with his humbuggery, his prudish wife, the old baronet, the vain but charming young wife; and yet they are closer to *vraisemblance* than would have been possible even a decade before. The dialogue is Grundy's—terse and incisive. One epigram deserves quotation. "And what's a cynic? A poor devil, who's fool enough to put into words the harshness wise men put into their deeds, and fool enough to put into deeds the kindness wise men put into their words."

Other plays depicting the social scene deserve but a passing mention, for the emphasis is not primarily upon manners. As a group they are rather "small-beer." Mr. and Mrs. Herman Merivale's *The Butler* (1886) is a domestic comedy, leaning to farce. The dominant figure in a quasi-aristocratic home is the butler, given vitality by Toole's acting. A play called *Cousin Johnny* (1885) by J. F. Nisbett and C. M. Rae glimpses the manners, or rather the bad manners of society, but is prostituted into farce by gross improbabilities. A country bumpkin is pawned off on Sir George and Lady Desmond as their long-lost son. His loutish attempts to live up to his conception of a young gentleman, which is that of an idler and a braggart, are passingly amusing. Farquhar would have treated the situation with different result. Westland Marston's *Under Fire* (1885) falls short of what we might hope for from its author's literary attainments. Lady Fareham's obsession to become a figure in good society, even at the sacrifice of others' happiness, furnishes the motive. Although possessing lively, cynically flavored dialogue, the comedy may be passed by as inconsequential. In the *Half-Way House* (1881) of Sims, we have a three-act farcical comedy of middle-class country life pleasingly presented. The aversion of an old established family of landed gentry against marrying into a family of petty tradesmen affords an interesting side light on rural society. Squire Hesseltine is a type of the superannuated coxcomb, but in general the characterization is undistinguished. The play breaks no new ground.

In comedies of the later eighties is evident a tendency to treat titled characters with more sincerity. Such treatment is, of course, a *sine qua non* of the comedy of manners, but it yet remains incidental to story for itself alone. Thus in the *Fascination* (1887) of Harriet Jay and Robert Buchanan, a philandering young army officer, Lord Islay, becomes enmeshed in a siren's net. Like Viola, his fiancée assumes males attire and in that rôle almost wins the heart of Islay's inamorata, besides winning back her recreant lover. For a play of this kind the deportment and conversation of gentlefolk are adequately rendered, but they do not exist as ends in themselves. The same comment applies to J. W. Pigott's *The Bookmaker* (1889). Although most of the characters are lords and ladies, we feel that the demands of the plot could be equally subserved in a home of the middle class. In Derrick's *Plebeians* (1886) a young aristocrat, without distinguishing caste attributes, is beset by two vulgarians who seek to marry him to eligible daughters. Derrick is a coarser Byron.

To *Modern Wives* (1887) by Ernest Warren is due a word because of its connection with a type of society play coming increasingly into vogue—the satire on the "New Woman." This comedy seems from reports to have been a mirthful, lively little piece which laughs at the extravagant, coquettish, unmanageable wives of the day. Tuned in the same key is the merry comedietta, *The Duchess of Bayswater & Co.* (1888) by M. A. Heathcote, a satiric skit on the aristocrat gone into business. Sir Jeremy Jobs contemns his daughter's affection for a mere plebeian, whose father has made a fortune in tinned meats, but looks with favor on the Duke of Bayswater, until he discovers to his disgust that both the young man and his duchess mother are up to the ears in the food business themselves.

In his book, *The Eighteen-Nineties,* Holbrook Jackson has nicely estimated the closing decade of the century. He emphasizes the paradoxes it exhibits: lassitude and exhaustion after a century of confused endeavor, and yet already the impulse toward new experiments in the re-creation of man's physical and mental world; egoism side by side with altruism; dilettanteism and virtuosity in literature and at the same time a most relentless spirit of inquiry; a Decadence which is perverse and artificial but which is also ecstatic and full of vision; a romantic, adventurous spirit, a revolt against the *status quo* which may be degenerate and may be regenerate. It is a decade of criticism and of protest against the moral inhibitions of puritanism and the banalities of philistinism. But in the same ten years we find also an expression of life oblivious to all claims save that of art itself. The paradoxical nineties find place for the sturdy conventionality of Henry Arthur Jones and for the esthetic paganism of Oscar Wilde.

These characteristic features of the *fin de siècle* find their natural expression in the drama. For one thing, we meet in the theatre a type of play coming to the grapple with contemporary life with an earnestness and a singleness of purpose not manifest in the past. Plays examine into the relation of men and women in modern society and often drag the family skeleton from its closet to become a member of the cast. They inquire profoundly into the springs of human behavior and seek to identify the individual with the society of which he is a part. To explain man's knavery or folly, we must reach out beyond the confines of personality. Society becomes the villain of the play. The mighty shadow of Ibsen has fallen athwart the English stage. The so-called romantic revival from about 1895 may be called the reaction of the public to this "problem play," as Grundy called it. *The Prisoner of Zenda, Under the Red Robe, The Seats of the Mighty,* and a sweet, charming little play like Parker's *Rosemary* were the answer to *John-a-Dreams* and *The Second Mrs. Tanqueray.* The fact that they were almost all dramatizations of novels spells, of course, the invalidity of the whole movement.

When the theatre becomes a kind of forum or even a clinic for the presentation of ideas on such subjects as woman's place in society, marriage, moral reform, philanthropy and class prejudice, drama in general is in danger of becoming sociological instead of social, and comedy is threatened with suffocation. At a banquet of the Dramatic and Musical Benevolent Fund in 1891, Beerbohm Tree said, apropos of the intense social consciousness in the drama: "If things progress at the rate they are progressing, we may look in the near future for a stage which will be a platform for the discussion of the mysteries of psychology, the teachings of esoteric Buddhism and for the exposition of the doctrines of evolution and heredity." The saucy, ever mirthful face of Thalia is threatened with a frown. And yet her laughter, heard in mockery or in hilarity, redeemed many a serious play from sombreness or acted as a nepenthe altogether from the vexing problems which had crept into the theatre.

The awakening of a social consciousness put its impress upon all forms of drama, serious and comic alike. One finds it with a varying gravity of treatment in the work of Pinero, Grundy, Jones, of Haddon Chambers and R. C. Carton. Intent observation and criticism beget satire, which in itself may indicate the scrutinizing, detached mind that often writes powerful drama. But unless treated with great propriety, it is too caustic and ill natured for the uses of comedy, especially the comedy of manners. High society still continued a favorite *milieu* for playwriters, though often taken beyond the confines of pure comedy, as in *The County* (1892) by Estelle Burney and Arthur Benham, *An American Bride* (1892) by Sir William Young and Maurice Noel, and the *Marriage* (1892) of Brandon Thomas and Henry Keeling.

In a number of comedies of the early nineties in which intrigue rather than manners prevails, one catches now and then in a scene or in a character an impressive glimpse of high life *à la mode,* as in John Hare's ever memorable personation in 1891 of the haughty, irascible Lord Kilclare in Coghlan's *A Quiet Rubber.* Percy Gauntlett, the young ne'er-do-well in Pierre Leclerq's *This Woman and That* (1890), as interpreted by Otis Skinner, was a type out of the true comedy of manners, and the same may be said for Harry Grahame, the unscrupulous fascinator of women in Vernon's *Sowing and Reaping* (1890) and the Earl of Bromber, the old roué in Leclerq's *Illusion* (1890). The former was played by that urbane and polished gentleman, Charles Wyndham, and the latter by Lawrence D'Orsay, who was for so many years to take off the vacuous nobleman to the life. One pauses to wonder to what extent the success of these portraitures was due to the sympathetic interpretation of these talented actors. Not only in the major but in the minor parts of comedies throughout these years one meets personages familiar to the manners type—the superannuated dandy, the harum-scarum tomboy and the elderly woman of real or affected gentility.

But the decade had also something more significant to show—a reflection of high society in and for itself, in which moral and critical values were obscured or completely disclaimed. The *beau monde* took on again something of its former glitter and charm as a world worthy to stand alone and not to function merely as a foil to the classes below. In this group of comedies, beginning with Oscar Wilde and continuing on through the decade (and into the next) in plays of Jones, Pinero, and Carton, the requisites of the comedy of manners are met to a large degree,—an amoral approach, witty, clever dialogue, sympathetic characterization, and a certain atmosphere of ease and elegance.[12] It can be said that here we have

> Some fairer trace
> Of wit than puns, of humour than grimace.

Beneath this veneer of polished manners and sparkling talk is an aristocracy that is not Sheridan's in dignity or in patrician exclusiveness but is like his in its counterfeit respectability. While middle-class vulgarities were

[12] The tendency in the literature of the nineties to glorify the artificial over the natural and to cultivate a style of calculated rather than spontaneous effects, delighting in verbal preciosity and ingenuity, was a tendency favorable to comedy of manners. A greater sophistication in audiences at the theatre seems to be another *fin de siècle* mood. They had become a little too blasé to be swept into ecstasy by the old-fashioned melodrama.

being objurgated in thoughtful plays, upper-class vulgarities were made the occasion for laughter, with or without the satiric note.

Before examining the social comedy of the leading dramatists of the day, let us clear the ground of the work of less conspicuous writers. In a time of such a considerable output of plays dealing with society, it is difficult to determine with accuracy those which conform at least partially to the manners type, especially as only a comparative few found their way into print.

Who is there to whom reference was made in the previous decade that now demands our attention? Concerning Sydney Grundy little need be added. *Sowing the Wind* (1893) the author was right in classing with Pinero's *Sweet Lavender.* Like it, it is a comedy of sentiment and old-fashioned charm, although with more of a moral issue involved to give it substance. Although the time is 1830, there is little in manners or dialogue that is of the period. Grundy's usual alertness of speech gives place to a leisurely prolixity. Mr. Brabazon, wealthy and well born, refuses to allow his adopted son to marry the daughter of a notorious woman, until it devolves that she is his own daughter. "Sowing the Wind" as a title is in reality a misnomer, for the play has to do with retribution rather than with transgression. Brabazon's espousal of the conventions and prejudices of society above the worth of character bespeaks the tyranny of caste. Two of the characters are eligible for the full-fledged comedy of manners of the days of Bath and Tunbridge Wells—Sir Richard Cursitor, a young sport of the town, and Lord Petworth, a withered debauchee. *The New Woman* (1894) appears never to have been published. From all accounts it would seem to strike deeper than a comedy of manners is wont to do. The situation was that of a well-born young man, leaving Oxford with his mind teeming with ideas for social amelioration. After marrying a good woman of lowly station he takes up with a Mrs. Sylvester of advanced ideas on woman's freedom. In the end he comes to realize his folly. Grundy would appear to have shown that the so-called "New Woman" is really as old as Eve under her theories. Three of the minor characters, as faddists of the "New Woman" movement, he scarified with ridicule. The critics were unanimous in regarding the dialogue as the most brilliantly witty and satirical that the author had written. In the following year appeared the light and very amusing *The Late Mr. Castello* (1895), in which a charming young widow restrains the ardor of her suitors by the uncomfortable fact that her explorer husband may never have perished. How Captain Trefusis makes use of this fact to bring the obstreperous young lady into submission furnishes the material for three acts of good fun. It is a kind of modern *Taming of the Shrew,* confessedly a farce, but in its rollicking gayety a little reminiscent of the madcap comedies of the eighteenth century.

G. W. Godfrey, whose *Parvenu* ranked high among the comedies of the eighties, wrote another social comedy in 1895, *Vanity Fair,* which he called "A Caricature." The satire here is far more astringent and less effective. As the title suggests, the affectations and sham respectabilities of the social world are held up to view. Shaw, writing in the *Saturday Review,* explained Godfrey's exaggerations on the ground that he did not know high life at first hand. The scene at Mrs. Brabazon Tegg's Grosvenor Square reception calls to mind the second act of Jones' *Masqueraders,* but is more extravagant and with no decisiveness of characterization. Mrs. John Wood's travesty of a *nouvelle riche* was meritorious.

Like *Vanity Fair,* most of the comedies present a most unflattering picture of high life. That it was the nursery of scandal and the playground for puppets is unquestioned, but we must deplore for the sake of comedy the trenchant and even splenetic tone of many of these plays. For instance, *A Society Butterfly* (1894) by Buchanan and Henry Murray is called a comedy of modern life, but it is too warped in vision to be a representative cross section of the social world. Mrs. Langtry took ample opportunity of the part of Mrs. Dudley, who, in revenge for her husband's infidelities, emerges from her chrysalis into a full-winged butterfly of fashion, warming herself in the sunlight of every man's favor. The play started inauspiciously; the first night it was roundly hissed by the gallery gods. Reports fail to state the effect of the play on "the opulent and somnolent stupidity of the stalls."

In the same general category may be placed Lady Violet Greville's *An Aristocratic Alliance* (1894), a redaction of Augier's *Le Gendre de M. Poirier.* The play was rendered emasculate by its inevitable failure to reproduce the language and social *milieu* of the French play. Lady Greville affords us a contrast between an indolent young spendthrift with a title and his simple-hearted wife, daughter of a bourgeois pickle manufacturer. The denizens of the patrician and the plebeian worlds are equally repellent. The one is parasitic, the other arrogant and pushing. The part of Gerald, Earl of Forres, the aristocratic cad, was redeemed by the suave, elegant manner of Charles Wyndham. One other French borrowing may be mentioned here as having proved a striking but disagreeable play, *The Fringe of Society* (1892), a clever adaptation of Dumas' *Le Demi-Monde.* It is a sinister rather than a gay scene on which the light of comedy here searches and probes—society jealously guarding its portals against the outsider who matches chicanery with chicanery in his efforts to break through. Wyndham played Sir Charles Hartley, a blasé man of the world who wears with an easy distinction the badges of good breeding, a part which Wyndham took superbly in his later years. Cyril Maude was a senile roué and Mrs. Langtry the scheming adventuress who tried in vain to batter down the walls of society. To these artists the play was largely indebted for its atmosphere of high comedy.

J. P. Hurst's *Woman's World* (1896) missed an admirable opportunity for comedy of manners by its cynicism. It is another of the satires on woman in business and politics. The world of clubs for business women is set forth with a mordant wit. The comedy abounds in glimpses of the manners of contemporary society and industrial life, but the author approaches his task heavy handed.

The *Today* (1893) of Charles Brookfield illustrates one of the many uses to which Sardou's *Divorçons* was put. Lacking his architectonic skill, Brookfield has outdone him in his vehement exposé of a frothy society. Bertie Twyford, one of those epicene dandies that only an affected and emasculate social world could engender, is a kind of nineteenth-century Sir Fopling Flutter or Sir Novelty Fashion who sauntered so mincingly through the pages of Restoration comedy.

Somewhat nearer to our purpose is *The Plowdens* (1892) by Otto Benzan and Edward Rose, in which affectation of manners as well as of morals in the upper middle class is presented with considerable spirit. Like Jones, the authors call attention, with some tinge of bitterness, to the hollow shams of society and its prostration before Mrs. Grundy. The Plowden family discover that a hired companion to one of the daughters is in love with a son. They cast her out when they learn that her past is not stainless, but pharisaically continue to encourage a baronet's suit for the daughter's hand, even when they discover that he was responsible for the other girl's downfall. Produced at Grein's Independent Theatre, it was acknowledged to be a comedy of well-drawn society types and smartly contrived dialogue.

H. A. Kennedy's *The New Wing* (1890) is full of amusing side lights on class prejudices. Hester Singleside, daughter of a gentleman of the old school, has become enamored of the new socialism and the cause of the workingman. Her admirer, Sir Edward Strangeways, is a young architect who takes advantage of some building operations at the Singleside mansion to disguise himself as a workman and test the validity of her views. Amusing complications ensue, and by the final curtain-fall Hester has been disillusioned regarding social equality.

Other comedies that similarly contain a bit of social criticism and a glimpse of manners through the medium of farcical situations may be dismissed briefly. In R. R. Lumley's *The Volcano* (1891) the Duke of Donoway (played admirably by Arthur Cecil) is secretly the owner of a society journal and comes to regret his venture. The modern "go-getter," who dominates abroad and domineers at home, and whose religion is the worship of rank and riches, is the central figure of a lively, smartly written comedy, *The Gudgeons* (1893), the joint work of Thornton Clark and Louis N. Parker. Miss Costello's *The Plebeian* (1891), in its marriage of an impoverished young lady of gentle birth to a rich parvenu, is reminiscent of plays we have met. Though the play begins promisingly as comedy, it deteriorates into melodrama. A clever little *jeu d'esprit,* a mere duologue, but reflective of manners, is *An Underground Journey* (1893) by Mrs. Hugh Bell and Charles Brookfield. A duke and his prospective cook are thrown together in a railway journey, and each mistakes the other's identity. Comedy is inevitable when the solemnities of caste catch people napping.

A very brisk little farce is *Husband and Wife* (1891), written by F. C. Philips and Percy Fendall and presenting with just a brush of satire the ever merry theme of hen-pecked husbands and militant wives who dream of emancipation from the thraldom of petty man through the august medium of the "Association for the Amelioration of the Morals of Married Men." The piece is a pleasant contribution to the "New Woman" group of plays. Jerome and Phillpotts's *The Prude's Progress* (1895), an entertaining little satire on pseudo-reform and pseudo-philanthropy, scarcely invades the field of manners. One of the most sportive of the lighter comedies of this group confronts us at the very close of the decade. It is *The Canary* (1899) and is by Miss Constance Fletcher ("George Fleming"). Back of its engaging study of Mrs. Temple-Martin are the tyrannizing traditions of society. She is a lady who longs for the romance she finds in books as an escape from her prosaic existence. Since she is as incurably a conformist as she is a sentimentalist, she shrinks back in horror when opportunity comes to her door. A flickering heat-lightning of satire pervades the comedy.

Two plays of somewhat different texture are *The Gay Lothario* (1891), a comedietta by Alfred Calmour, and *Niobe* (1892), an anonymous fantasy. The former is a neatly turned, gay little trifle in eighteenth-century costume, showing how a man and a woman matched wits in the game of love to the eventual satisfaction of both. The love-making has something of the sauciness and self-assurance found in the old comedies of Mrs. Centlivre or Samuel Foote. The latter play effects a fantastic blending of the antique and modern worlds by means of a statue which comes to life in the manner of *Pygmalion and Galatea*. The suggestion has been made that it may have been inspired rather by Anstey's little book, *A Tinted Venus*. The situation of a lady of ancient Greece suddenly transported into a nineteenth-century English society naturally afforded ample opportunities for ironic flings at modern modes and usages. It had a successful run at the Strand of over 300 nights. *The Mummy* (1896) of Day and Reed is a weak attempt to mine the same vein.

A Pantomime Rehearsal (1891) by Cecil Clay and Mrs. Henry de la Pasture's *The Modern Craze* (1899), given at St. George's Hall, are two farcical contributions of the decade to the contemporary vogue of society theatricals. They sport entertainingly with the frequent crassness of titled amateur actors and may be dignified here as lowly descendants of *The Rehearsal* and *The Critic*.

VII

RETURN OF THE COMEDY OF MANNERS

1890–1915

IT now becomes our duty to consider a number of plays which are very distinctly comedies of manners and which possess, in many cases, a literary merit apart from their validity as pieces for the theatre. The question as to the relation of literature to drama or what constitutes literature in a play need not lure us into argument. It will be admitted that when a play reflects or interprets for us some segment of life through the medium of distinctive characterization expressing itself in action and in speech, and so employs the imagination as to make the beholder conscious of the truth and beauty of the presentation, that play is a part of literature. Literature in a play certainly does not mean fine writing *per se,* as some writers have believed to their cost. Rather is it a glimpse of the universal through the particular that in some way becomes memorable to the individual. Pinero's opinion is interesting: "The literature of a play I understand to be contained in the development of character and the suggestion of the unwritten portions—those which, by stimulating the imagination, suggest all that the novelist would describe. Really literary dialogue, if you must use the word, is that in which the right word always appears in its right place, and conveys its exact meaning with reference to the evolution of the dramatic idea."

Since Sheridan, literature and the drama had seemed permanently divorced, but in some of the plays of Pinero and of Wilde there are indications of a reconcilement. The nineteenth century, which had known many plays that were actable but not readable and a few plays that were readable but not actable, was, at its close, to discover plays that were satisfying in both capacities. As we have already noted, playwrights were beginning in the nineties to take their plays into print after giving them to the theatre, as a kind of verification of their success upon the boards. In the quiet perusal of a play at home, a reader may be made aware of a literary quality which the stage spectacle itself did not suggest. It was a healthy sign when plays took their places on library shelves.

As William Archer has observed, there are three stages in the modern English drama. The first two are identified with Robertson and Pinero and are of and in the theatre. Both these men were actors as well as playwriters. The third stage, which he calls that of Shaw, found its impulse from without the theatre and its expression largely at the hands of men of letters. The names of Wilde, Stevenson, Barrie, Moore, Galsworthy, Maugham, Bennett, Ervine, and Phillpotts are cases in point. It is worthy of note that with the advent of better plays we find also a more independent and intelligent dramatic criticism appearing in the press and in periodicals. The influence of such men as Clement Scott, A. B. Walkeley, Archer, Shaw, Beerbohm, and W. L. Courtney in stimulating a more just appraisal of plays in the theatre is not to be gainsaid.

At the very outset of the nineties appeared a very pleasant little comedy picturing the aristocratic manners of a bygone time. *Beau Austin* (1890) by Henley and Stevenson, like *Beau Nash* and *Beau Brummell,* introduces us to one of those courtly dandies of impeccable manners but censurable morals who lent grace and charm to the society life of the eighteenth and early nineteenth centuries.[1] Beau Austin, however, in his repentance, gives a Victorian stamp to the play, which we have already observed in Buchanan's *Miss Tomboy.* Some critics have considered it a dramatic incongruity that the old rake, having perfected all the heartless graces of society, should suddenly emerge from sinner into saint and marry his former mistress at the mere solicitation of her sweetheart. It must be said, however, that the authors have consistently emphasized the chivalry of the beau rather than his profligacy and have handled tastefully the emergence of penitence and passion through his studied elegance of demeanor. From the viewpoint of form and organization the play is shown to be the work of amateurs. The speeches are often long and not "in character," but they are couched in the graceful and delicate language of the literary artist. Individual scenes are to be commended for their dramatic contrasts: Dorothy's young brother, the fine young blade in his new uniform, and the aging roué,

[1] Clyde Fitch's *The Last of the Dandies,* played at Her Majesty's Theatre in 1901 and harking back to the early Victorian days of the Count D'Orsay, and Constance D'Arcy Mackay's one-act miniature in verse, *The Beau of Bath,* are further contributions to the type.

equally proud in his attire, but in such a different way; and the scene between Fenwick and the beau, the one all nature without art and the other art almost without nature. Perhaps the play is too remote from reality to be ever a stage success, but it makes very pleasant reading. The following lines from the Prologue by Henley show the kinship of the play with the fashionable comedy of the preceding century:

> To all and singular, as Dryden says,
> We bring a fancy of those Georgian days,
> Whose style still breathed a faint and fine perfume
> Of old-world courtliness and old-world bloom;
>
> . . . .
>
> When manners reigned, when breeding had the wall
> And women—yes!—were ladies first of all.

With the comedies of Oscar Wilde, *Lady Windermere's Fan* (1892),[2] *A Woman of No Importance* (1893), *An Ideal Husband* (1895), and *The Importance of Being Earnest* (1895), the English comedy of manners achieved the prestige of literary style for the first time since *The School for Scandal.* Inheriting something of the temper of Congreve and Sheridan, and Sardou's facile effectiveness, they are at heart a saturated solution of their creator. In them are curiously mingled cynicism and sentiment; their plots, though often faultily and arbitrarily motivated, reach strictly orthodox moral conclusions, but the dialogue is audaciously pagan.

Wilde was a part of the aesthetic protest against the

[2] Charles Brookfield's *The Poet and the Puppets,* of the same year, is a genuinely clever travesty on characters and episodes in the play that rises above the usual silly parody.

drab moral consciousness of the time. He was a gentleman in that he was a wit, a *raconteur,* a diner-out, an inheritor of fine instincts and gentle breeding; and he was also the mere dandy in his faddish display of mannerisms. His very life was theatrical; he himself embodied much of a comedy of manners as he moved and talked. He and his comedies were brilliant *tours de force,* arresting by their very compulsion of talent; but they were a passing phase. They were as serenely oblivious of the streams of contemporary social life as Boccaccio's lords and ladies sheltered from the plague-stricken city below. Wilde was inherently a virtuoso in art, an adroit craftsman, a seeker after effects, not truths. He startled, he titillated the mind, but he was at the last unsubstantial, lacking the sincerity and conviction of a spokesman for the people. All his comedies, except *The Importance of Being Earnest,* are mere transcriptions of conventional characters and situations out of farce and melodrama, touched upon by an inimitable capacity for clever talk. Conversation becomes a fine art in the abstract, but of an essence far too rare for human nature's daily food. With all of his theatricalism charged against him, he must be forever credited with bestowing upon social comedy the rare gift of witty, graceful dialogue. If he was an insolent *poseur,* his was the attitude of one to the manner born. He could give to the theatre a vivid picturing of society's Upper Tenth because he himself was a part of it. We feel that he speaks as one having authority.

It will not be necessary to rehearse the plots of these *comédies de Salon* or to discuss them in detail. In fact, it is rather by viewing them as a group that one senses best the polished and sophisticated society whose manners and philosophy they so excellently present. It is a society over-civilized and under-civilized at the same time, one that thrives only in the sunless, scented air of London drawing-rooms. Hester Worsley in *A Woman of No Importance* says of it, a little self-righteously: "You shut out of your society the gentle and the good. You laugh at the simple and the pure. . . . You have lost life's secret. Oh, your English society seems to me shallow, selfish, foolish. It has blinded its eyes, and stopped its ears. It lies like a leper in purple. It sits like a dead thing smeared with gold." Her American democracy revolts at reverence for caste. Lord Illingworth voices an old tradition when he says, "A well-tied tie is the first serious step in life," and "If a man is a gentleman, he knows quite enough, and if he is not a gentleman, whatever he knows is bad for him."

In Wilde's first three comedies we find little variation in treatment. His was a brilliant but a narrow mind. All three plays present a problem in the manner of melodrama and against a background of high society. In the first two, manners and dialogue exist for themselves, almost to the subversion of the story; *An Ideal Husband* is dramatically the most impressive—a twisted skein of political intrigue and manners with silken threads of nuance and epigram. Everywhere the machinery of melodrama is apparent—dry bones which he has ingeniously concealed beneath the artistry of his style. The adventuress; the sacrificing, guiltless friend; the dove-like wife; eavesdropping; blackmail;

the compromising glove or fan; such antiquities as soliloquies and asides—all these are the furniture of a hundred decently buried theatre-pieces.

Wilde's characters tend to repeat themselves—the types of people with whom he was personally conversant. Algernon Moncrieff and Viscount Goring are dandies, toying exquisitely with life; Lady Windermere and Lady Chiltern are much the same sort of tame, sentimental wife, a bit overconscious of her rectitude. The dowager and the *grande dame* are played upon with variations in Lady Pontrefact, Lady Bracknell and the Duchess of Berwick. Wilde is distinctly at his best with his women with a past like Mrs. Erlynne and Mrs. Cheveley. The former is a characterization not without subtlety. As a mother she is capable of a beautiful sacrifice for her daughter; as a woman she senses her nature too well to accept domestic respectability. The conclusion of *Lady Windermere's Fan* is thus redeemed from the cheapness of maudlin sentimentality. Lady Cheveley, on the other hand, is proudly unregenerate. When Wilde says she is "a work of art but showing the influence of too many schools," he has said all. Lord Illingworth in *A Woman of No Importance* is certainly one of his finest creations—the cynically clever, accomplished denizen of the *beau monde*. Gerald and Hester in the same play barely escape priggishness, if they do escape. Wilde's forte is in the vices, not the virtues. Of his characters in general it may be safely said that he has envisioned their surface characteristics with verve and skill, but that is all. In questions of motive, for instance, he is indifferently successful.

If Jones and Pinero effected the comedy of manners through plot and situation, Wilde achieved it conspicuously through dialogue. Much has been said, and deservedly, in detraction of the unnatural brilliance of his wit. Epigram, paradox, and verbal fence at times completely stifle the action; they find their way to lips that could not have uttered them; they are, many of them, mere audacities and perversities of a gentleman-mountebank. And yet they are always provocative and scintillating, and their artificiality is a part of that legitimate heightening of effect which the comedy of manners appropriates. Wilde whetted the appetite of the intellectual playgoer for distinguished conversation. Shaw shrewdly estimates the worth of this dialogue in saying, "The six worst epigrams are mere alms handed with a kind smile to the average suburban playgoer; the three best remain secrets between Mr. Wilde and a few choice spirits." And in another place (in *Dramatic Opinions and Essays*) he catches so well the humor of the impact of a Wilde witticism upon a typically stolid British mind that the passage is worthy of quotation:

"There is nothing in the world quite so exquisitely comic as an Englishman's seriousness. It becomes tragic, perhaps, when the Englishman acts on it, but that occurs too seldom to be taken into account, a fact which intensifies the humor of the situation, the total result being the Englishman utterly unconscious of his real self, Mr. Wilde keenly observant of it and playing on the self-unconsciousness with irresistible humor, and finally, of course, the Englishman annoyed with himself for being amused at his own expense, and for being unable to convict Mr. Wilde of what seems an obvious misunderstanding of human nature. He is shocked too at the danger to the foundations of society when seriousness is publicly laughed at."

The Importance of Being Earnest marks an advance in the author's dramatic proficiency. In it he was breaking away from the machine-made perfection of Scribe and approaching an easier manner with less brocade of dialogue, which stiffens while it furbishes. It is a trifle, of course, but a delicious one, insouciant and irresponsible, the very apotheosis of clever funning and dainty persiflage. If it is a farce, it is true to its nature as a farce. "Its title was a pun, its story a conundrum, its characters lunatics, its dialogue a *galimatias,* its termination a 'sell,'" some one has said. And yet in this lightest of his plays, Wilde was the most sincere.

It is idle to surmise what further successes Oscar Wilde might have achieved in the comedy of manners had his dramatic career been prolonged. While admitting that he lacked the higher capacity of the artist to see life steadily and see it whole, he was a brilliant painter of a social scene. If he was a dilettante, he possessed the dilettante's nicety of perception at its best.

Unlike Wilde, Arthur Wing Pinero is to be thought of as a playwright of wide horizons and varied interests. His dramatic activities have run the gamut from light farce to unrelieved tragedy, and it is in the serious drama rather than in comedy that he will be longest remembered. He differs markedly from Jones in that his best work, with few exceptions, has been concerned less with society than with the individual. He has remained studiously aloof from the crowd and has never allowed his art to become turbulent with social reform. Jones is perhaps more intellectual or at least more concerned with ideas; Pinero is more broadly intelligent, more intuitive, and hence his plays are not prone to be topical or didactic. He comes a little nearer the universal. And yet he, too, has been a popularizer of the sentiments and opinions of his day rather than an originator with a consistent, continuous criticism of life.[3] It is with the outer, not the inner realities of existence, that he is content to deal. He is noteworthy as the first to bring the stage back within measurable distance of contemporary life and thought, but he has only at inspired moments identified the two. In other words, he has succeeded again and again with the drama of observation, but only imperfectly realized a profoundly arresting drama of criticism.

Much more consistently and with much greater success, Pinero's social comedies have reflected the life and manners of the upper classes. He never strays for long from the neighborhood of Hyde Park or the fashionable country-seats of adjoining shires. In a conversation with William Archer,[4] Pinero justified his predilection for the aristocracy in the following terms: "I think you would find, if you tried to write drama, not only that wealth and leisure are more productive of dramatic

[3] The fact that he acceded to the public taste and wrote happy endings for *The Profligate* and *The Big Drum* has often been cited as indicative of his attitude toward his art.

[4] William Archer, *Real Conversations,* p. 21.

complications than poverty and hard work, but that if you want to get a certain order of ideas expressed or questions discussed, you must go pretty well up in the social scale." In so speaking he aligns himself with a past rather than a present tradition in dramatic writing.

The Pinero comedies of manners fall naturally into two divisions: an earlier group of so-called farces ranging from *The Hobby Horse* (1886) to *The Amazons* (1893), and a later and smaller group consisting of *The Princess and the Butterfly* (1897), *Trelawny of the Wells* (1898), and *The Gay Lord Quex* (1899). *The Thunderbolt* (1908), one of the most powerful plays he ever wrote, is distinctively a middle-class study.

In the Introduction to *The Cabinet Minister* (1890) the author remarks that "farce must gradually become the modern equivalent of comedy, since, the present being an age of sentiment rather than of manners, the comic playwright must of necessity seek this humor in the exaggeration of sentiment." Pinero is apparently using the term "farce" with some latitude, for plays like *The Cabinet Minister* and *The Times* (1891), while containing indubitably farcical elements, have not the caricature in characterization and the want of proportion between the persons of the play and their motives which "farce" ordinarily implies. The term can be applied more closely to earlier productions like *The Magistrate* and *Dandy Dick*. In *The Hobby Horse* a slight element of manners first seems to take its place in a plot that is only partially farcical. This combination of comedy of character and farce of situation developed in Pinero's hands to the gradual elimination of the latter. Mere possibility became probability and sometimes something more.

Lords and Commons (1883), which has never been printed, need concern us only long enough to observe that it was apparently an early study in contrasts between upper and middle-class life. Mrs. Devenish, a rich American "widow," takes possession of Caryl Court, the titled owners of which are no longer able to support it. It eventuates that the lady is really the wife of the Earl of Caryl, who had deserted her years before because of her inferior social position. The play makes clear how ill-bred a family of so-called "breeding" can be. The play concerns the student of manners only indirectly. Of equal inconsequence for us is *Mayfair* (1885), a denatured version of Sardou's *Maison Neuve,* adapted with indifferent success to London life and lifting the social level of the French originals to the comfortable middle class. Once again we are afforded a contrast between the old régime, conservative in business and in social morality, and the new, with its showy affectation. The road to Mayfair is beset with pitfalls for those who are blinded by the glamor of wealth and social position.

The Hobby Horse may be quickly disposed of, for it is an immature though pleasant little comedy of turfmen and jockeys and the London slums, with scarcely any consciousness of social background. Spencer Jermyn (one of John Hare's best parts), with his plans for a home for decayed jockeys, his wife with her quixotic love for the downtrodden, and Noel Brice, the Eastside social worker, combatted in his efforts by the self-righteous people of the church, all are types of futile, ill-directed philanthropy. Mrs. Pigott-Blundell, who contributes copies of the *Illustrated London News* to the cause of uplift among the poor, represents the stupid, pharisaical charity of the rich. The play is merely a foretaste of Pinero's handling of a social group. The phenomenally popular *Sweet Lavender* and *The Weaker Sex,* which followed in 1888, do not concern us here. The former, especially, is an inheritor of Robertson's sentiment and easy naturalness. The latter looks ahead to Pinero's later excellent studies in womanhood and its capacity for sacrifice. It satirizes playfully "gentlemanly ladies and zoölogical gentlemen" and the whole tribe of faddists and agitators that swarm about society. Lady Vivash and Mrs. Boyle-Chewton furnish two other examples for the stage of the "New Woman," who just beneath the surface is eternal woman, the mate of a man and the mother of children. Lord Gillingham is one of Pinero's delightful minor characters—the cheery old aristocrat, too sleepy of an evening to be more than vaguely conscious of his social obligations as a host.

The farce formula of "possible people doing improbable things" still obtains in *The Cabinet Minister.* Sir Julian and Lady Twombley, who find wealth and rank a none too enviable experience, are quite well drawn, and so are their daughter and her young man, Valentine, a couple whose fresh naturalness of manner contrasts with the blasé artificiality of Brooke Twombley and Lady Euphemia. Mrs. Gaylustre and her brother, a bland, unctuous money-lender, are the types of social climbers we so frequently meet in social comedy. In the latter character and in Sir Colin Macphail, the sly, tongue-tied young lord, we are in the realm of caricature and low comedy. In all these characters we are dimly conscious of a social world and a social code, but they are overshadowed by farcical situation.

Pinero, the craftsman, writes with a surer touch, and Pinero, the dramatist, looks upon his social scene with a more discriminating and a soberer eye in his next play, *The Times,* a slender but entertaining comedy of the manners of aristocrats and would-be aristocrats. "Can the depths be sounded of ignorance, of vulgarity of mind, of vanity, and of self-seeking?" Pinero asks, and we ponder for an answer. Percy Egerton-Bompas is a rich, assertive shopkeeper who seeks for himself and his wife social recognition. They are both hopelessly bourgeois. Their life is a round of calls, half blatantly, half furtively made. And yet in all their servile efforts to placate the Brahmins of society, they have a redeeming sense of their own ridiculousness. It is in this that the play rises superior to its predecessors. Their attempts to foist off an ill-bred daughter-in-law and her mother as ladies of good birth prove futile, not because society recognizes the imposture, but through the disclosures of a piqued woman-journalist. The society jackal and go-between, the hireling of the social climber, is neatly portrayed in the Hon. Montague Trimble.

The Amazons Pinero justly termed a farcical romance. Its absurdity of incident is that of a Gilbert extravaganza, but in characterization it approaches comedy. The situation of three girls brought up to assume a masculine rôle in life is, of course, improbable, if highly entertaining, but Miriam, Marchioness of Castlejordan, and her three blooming daughters are more than merely fantastic. When nature brings out the eternal feminine beneath their masquerade, and the hilarious antics of the play near an end, a certain innate girlhood in the daughters and motherhood in Lady Miriam assert themselves. The Earl of Tweenwayes, constantly mindful of his noble lineage and quoting heroic verse inopportunely, is patently an amusing caricature. The play is, of course, a charming little satire on the "modern" woman of the nineties, clamoring for equality of opportunity with man. Nature alone disqualified her from demanding that she become the father of his children.

Two quite different strands go into the texture of *The Princess and the Butterfly* (1897), the one romantic, the other realistic and satirical. The Princess Pannonia and Sir George Lamorant are old friends in robust, early middle life, who have talked so much in a self-pitying kind of way about their lost youth and the encroachments of age that they are actually becoming old in spirit. They agree very calmly to seal their platonic friendship in marriage that they may slip into old age together. Meantime, an ever-busy Cupid causes each to fall in love with a person much younger, and life renews itself in a new devotion. "Those who love deep never grow old." The *Academy* for April 3, 1897, shrewdly suggests the cynical possibilities, which Pinero did not choose to employ, of presenting the decline of love in the couple from passion to mere acceptance, culminating in a marriage of convenience as a "haven of content." It is undoubtedly true that Pinero would have met the demands of high comedy more successfully had he shown the couple as visioning the incongruity of their proposed acts and accepting each other with the humor and the irony that the situation invited.

This fantastically handled theme is superimposed on a picture of a jaded, philandering society, which affords Pinero one of his finest excursions into the province of manners. Three out of the five curtains go up on a stage well populated with the tastefully dressed, smartly behaved denizens of exclusive society. Fops and dandies, "foolish virgins and malicious matrons," are alike seeking to forget the boredom of youth or the blight of age in a forced gayety. It was from the folly of all that that the Princess and her Butterfly turned, hoping to find solace in each other. One remembers certain ironical touches—the supposedly virtuous Mrs. St. Roche condemning the frankly vicious Mrs. Ware, and the young man who was invited to parties solely because he was the means of making another young man give his funny laugh.

In *Trelawny of the Wells* (1898), Pinero reverts to sentiment rather than manners. The scenes he depicts of the actor's life back in the days of Sadler's Wells have the flavor of Dickens and the Crummles company in *Nicholas Nickleby*.[5] He has not varnished his pic-

[5] Pinero has told Clayton Hamilton that practically every one of the stage-characters was taken from life. The play is at many points reminiscent of Sir Arthur's own early experiences in the theatre.

ture with romance; it is a squalid, shabby, precarious life the actor leads, and yet it has an unmistakable glamor, and back of its bohemianism are the basic virtues. Over against this very emotional life is to be placed the solemnity of Sir William Gower's establishment (it could hardly be called a home) in the West End. The contrast between the manners of these two diverse worlds the dramatist has managed with his usual skill. It is little wonder that Rose preferred the vulgar *camaraderie* of her own world to the smug decorum of the Gower's.

Pinero rose once to the full possibilities of the comedy of manners, and that was in his *The Gay Lord Quex* (1899). The vivacious dialogue has the audacious savor of the eighteenth century. Like Congreve and Sheridan he is content to present a picture with a deft, ironic touch and without social or moral commentary. The Marquess of Quex with his debonair grace and faultless attire is a worthy successor to the roués of old comedy. He is the *bon viveur* to his finger tips. Pinero has skilfully blended in him the man of honor and the gentleman of the world in whom profligacy is the perquisite of rank. Marriage he professes to be "a dull depravity permitted to the respectable classes." His is the world of pleasure and fashion, of bored idleness, of posing and flirting, of ultra-smartness. With possibly one exception, there is not a character in the play that is wholesome. Muriel Eden professes to be true to her fiancé, the Marquess, while playing a dangerous game of flirtation with the unscrupulous Captain Bastling. The Duchess of Strood, Quex's aforetime mistress, is a frail and shallow *poseuse*. Pinero has limned them all in with a master touch.

Set over against these pets and toys of life is Sophy Fullgarney, the manicurist, an essentially common person, and "innocently vulgar," as Pinero calls her. Had the fates permitted, she would have graced the drawing-room with her designing charm and her shallow wit. Although the author recognizes the nobility of her motive in wishing to save her foster-sister, Muriel, from a marriage with Lord Quex, he shrewdly contrasts the vulgarity of her methods with the imperturbable good breeding of the nobleman. Blood will tell in the critical decisions of life. The workings of the aristocratic and the middle-class mind were excellently contrasted in the acting of John Hare and Irene Vanbrugh in the original cast.

It has been said of Pinero that he is primarily a craftsman, who has achieved remarkable economy and precision in technique, and that this very skill has sometimes lured him into the making of plays where incidents evolve at the dictate of Pinero and not of the characters themselves. Such a stricture is not applicable, at least, in the case of *The Thunderbolt*, a powerfully sardonic study of provincialism, which can be construed as a true play of manners only by the greatest liberality in definition. It is deserving of reference at this place, however, as showing the unrelieved intensity with which the artist can set forth a social group, with each member completely individualized. The sordid, shabbily genteel Mortimore family represent the very essence of philistinism with all the offense that the term may connote. Their vulgarity and snobbery may be placed against that of the social set in *The Gay Lord Quex*. Pinero has painted both groups with a well-nigh faultless stroke.

A late comedy of Pinero's, *The Big Drum* (1915), is an able satire on self-advertisement and notoriety-hunting in society that has added nothing, however, to the luster of the author's name. A young novelist, Mackworth, has become engaged to Ottoline, the attractive daughter of the Filsons, a noisy, pushing, parvenu family of title. He stakes his claim to their acceptance of his suit on the success of his latest book, only to find later that his intended has secretly bought up large numbers of copies to insure its success. He allows his chagrin at this discovery to outweigh his love and breaks the engagement. Ottoline herself comes to realize that the parvenu, "drum-beating" strain in her would always offend his over-nice sensibilities. The reader finds his allegiance divided. Like Pinero he decries the vulgarity of "drum-beating," but he also sympathizes with the loyal gesture of the lady. He is repelled at the blatancy of the Filsons, but he feels that they, like the Egerton-Bompases in *The Times,* are simply decent folks out of their element. The fact that both groups or classes in the play share our interest was a recent development in comedy. In the decades before, the characters were clearly marked for our approval or disapproval.

Any examination of the comedies of Henry Arthur Jones for a depiction of manners will be embarrassed by the very pronounced social consciousness and moral conscientiousness of the man. In his early comedies, especially, he set his hand so zealously to the task of castigating the stupidities and hypocrisies of society that he almost lost sight of the larger issues of his art. The *saeva indignatio* of the reformer cannot beget a comedy of manners. *The Crusaders* (1891) is, for example, a bitterly ironic, almost fantastic arraignment of the empty, fruitless, quixotic efforts of the classes to uplift the masses. All social idealism that is not based on love and understanding becomes Dead Sea fruit in the mouth. None of the members on Cynthia Greenslade's Reform Committee was qualified for his adventure in human destinies. Cynthia herself and her friend Mrs. Campion-Blake approach social service as the latest fad, as an escape from ennui. Ingarfield and Una Dell are enthusiasts and dreamers. Lord Burnham and his son represent the politely interested, sceptical man of the world. Jones laughs all such reformers to scorn. The world wags along as it is, little the worse for their efforts—that is the tragedy and the comedy of it all. At the end of the play the very essence of irony is reached in the fact that of all the crusaders none are free from the taint of meanness and hypocrisy save Ingarfield and Miss Dell, the hopeless Don Quixotes of the play.

Again in 1895 in *The Triumph of the Philistines* he lets fly a satiric shaft—this time against the middle-class philistinism which he knew out of his own experience, and detested. He calls it a preachment on the text, "Be not righteous overmuch." A drab, hypocritical morality and a fanatic suspicion of the beautiful deserve Jones's hardest blows, but drama is not the gainer thereby. In none of his thesis plays is Jones the revolutionary. He presents no panacea for the ills he inveighs against, nor does he depart from the well-trodden paths of social conformity. He handles unconventional themes conventionally.

Our first picture of society and its manners is to be found in *The Masqueraders* (1894), in which it is cast, however, in the minor key of intellectualized melodrama and romance, not in the sparkling major of comedy. The second act, in which we are present at a reception by Lady Skene, is one of the playwright's most brilliant sketches of a social group. Were the entire comedy cast in that mould, it would be excellent comedy of manners, except for the insistence of the satire. The social set in which this lady moves is the loud, vacuous kind, where the men are horsy and the women catty. It is all very insincere and very futile, and lest that thought ever occur to them, they dance madly and feverishly through life in a kind of *bal masque*. Nobody believes in thinking for himself. It isn't done. One says, "I came because everybody else comes. Why did you?" to which is replied, "Because everybody else comes. Do we ever have any other reason for going anywhere, admiring anything, saying anything, or doing anything?" *The Masqueraders* contains much that is typical of its author: his flair for satire, his splendid gift for story-telling (two of his situations reveal the hand that had written *The Silver King*), his brisk, incisive dialogue and his telling portraitures that seem to fall just short of full-bodied reality. His types of people tend to reproduce themselves at will throughout his work—parvenus and prigs and discontented wives, idealists and reformers, women hiding a past and women hoping for a future. We may say that he never quite shakes off the artisan and becomes the artist, because of a limited range of experience and power of imagination. There is the impression that the material of his plays has been cleverly devised and assembled, but has not been evolved from a profound acquaintanceship with life. He has written a body of effective stage-pieces that attain their ends by a broad, forceful stroke, not by subtlety and discrimination. He has said no new thing but has mirrored expertly the modes of his day.

In *The Case of Rebellious Susan* (1894) and especially in *The Liars* (1897) and a later comedy, *Mary Goes First* (1913), Jones came very near to achieving the pure comedy of manners. In them is much of that flourish and that air of amused tolerance with life and unconcern for the moral consequences of action which has ever characterized this type. The dramatic resolution of these comedies is determined by no other purpose than to bring to a natural conclusion the amusing incidents presented. The aim in writing is purely to afford amusement at the gay, irresponsible picture which genteel society affords. Jones's gentlemen and ladies, however, are not completely convincing, for he cannot create them out of his experience. He could not draw a gentleman with perfect certitude, because he was not a gentleman himself. He sprang from sturdy yeoman stock of Buckinghamshire, and in instinct and experience, as well as origin, was essentially bourgeois. His urbane, polished gentlemen of the world like Sir Christopher Deering in *The Liars* and Sir Richard Kato in *Rebellious Susan* were given authenticity by the sympathetic acting of Charles Wyndham, a gentleman to the manner born.[6]

While Pinero's talent came into full ripeness in somber studies like *The Profligate* and *The Second Mrs. Tanqueray,* Jones's mellowed and warmed into comedy. As the years went by, he set aside somewhat the rôle of Physician Extraordinary to society and contented himself with painting the social scene as he saw it, realizing that the very ailments of the social body furnish the most picturesque material for the artist. His conformity to the social and moral code stands him in good stead as a recorder of manners, for while violating the sanctities of convention, society never repudiates them.

Jones's essays at the comedy of manners were ushered in under most favorable auspices in *The Case of Rebellious Susan.* Author, actor, and audience were happily met and of one accord: a capable playwriter recreating himself, Wyndham and his sympathetic company of players, the smart audience of the Criterion.

The play revolves about the situation of a very attractive, high-strung young wife, Lady Susan Harabin, and her revolt against the complacent infidelities of her very average husband. She is weary of the policy of

[6] John Drew in the Wyndham parts achieved the outer man of society in the perfect appointments of apparel and in deportment, but there was lacking the *savoir faire* which only instinctive breeding can afford. Dr. Weygandt aptly calls Drew " the glorified floor-walker."

forgetting or at least of forgiving; she wants to pay him back in kind. This we are led to believe she does during a trip to Egypt, or at least some degree and kind of retaliation by the impulsive Susan is implied. She feels that society having placed woman at a disadvantage in marriage, she has a right to take what measures she may in her own behalf. That is her defense for the lies she tells. Knowing she has lied about her acquaintance with Lucian Edensor, we are naturally uncertain as to what part, if any, of her declaration of innocence is true. At all events, she learns that young Lucian, whose protestations of devotion she had encouraged, has remained faithful to her just three weeks, and at the end of the play we see her accepting her husband's earnest proffers of affection and returning to uneventful domesticity with untarnished reputation—but with the stipulation that no questions shall be asked or answered about the past. It is as who should say, "Life is perplexing but amusing withal. So let's go in to dinner," and with that gesture the comedy closes—without desiderata, without wholesome application of truth to anybody, and with a challenge to Mrs. Grundy to find a moral if she can. Sir Richard asseverates, to be sure, that women should be the wives and mothers that Heaven intended, but that bit of wisdom is directed rather at Elaine Shrimpton, a raw, brusque young woman, whose hunger for self-expression and whose callow youthfulness have combined to make her absurd.

Such a plot might have been handled with the seriousness of *His House in Order*, but Jones's vivacity and quizzical spirit of levity have kept it on the plane of high comedy. Although we do not meet society at first hand, we can sense in the background the set of which Susan and her urbane, imperturbable, faultlessly correct guardian, Sir Richard Kato, are a part—where smartness is at a greater premium than intelligence, and the responsibilities of life are worn with a careless grace. Jones's dialogue rises to meet the requirements of the comedy of manners. It is fresh, sparkling, at times brilliant. It is not a mere brocade as in Wilde, but relates itself fittingly to the characters.

One of the greatest charms of the comedy is the aura of mystery which envelops it. The play is an unanswerable interrogation. Did the pert, mutinous Susan transgress with Lucian? Would she have gone back to her unpalatable James if her young man had remained true? Our curiosity is titillated by the author's skill in veiling, and rightly veiling, these facts from us. Of course, if we knew that the lady had overstepped the proprieties, we should feel that her complete exoneration was a breach of dramatic justice. As it is, the spirit of the comedy of manners has been admirably maintained.

In *The Liars* (1897) the Comic Spirit dominates the scene with the same triumphant smile. In many ways the play resembles its predecessor. A lady, piqued at her husband's neglect, seeks solace in a flirtation with an attractive but rather priggish young man. Her little game is interrupted by the spying of her brother-in-law. When disclosure threatens, Lady Jessica and her allies resort to a veritable campaign of falsehood, which promises success until at last the wrong lie is told and the truth comes out. The matter at issue—who was the lady's partner at a private dinner—concerns the comedy but little; to present the spectacle of a group of smart, dissembling society people enmeshed in the lies of their own weaving is the sole end. As in *Rebellious Susan,* the play has its *raisonneur,* a kind of focal, philosophic center in the person of that gentleman of the world, Sir Christopher Deering, who persuades Lady Jessica from an elopement.

Like the previous comedy, *The Liars* is morally inconclusive. There is no deep solicitude on the dramatist's part to explain his characters ethically and to provide berths for them at the end according to their deserts. We hear no fulminations against lying. It is amusing, it is also dangerous; prudence and *savoir faire* say to walk gingerly, that is all. And women are such lovely morsels of waywardness! They lie so prettily, one is tempted to encourage them. After all, isn't Gilbert, Jessica's morose and self-important husband, really to blame? Such is the casuistry to which the spirit of comedy invites us. Jones has come close to the gay insouciance, the banter and moral holiday of Restoration comedy or of a delightful French comedy like *Le Monde où l'on s'Ennuie.*

We are again teased by a query. If George had not caught Lady Jessica in deception, her husband would not have known. To what lengths would she have gone if circumstances had not forced her hand? And who knows, pray, when she will not repeat the little game? "I hope she does," whispers the Comic Spirit. Lady Jessica, like Lady Susan, is such an irrepressible

Machiavellian, it seems very likely. Certainly, at the curtain-fall, they offer no guarantees of domestic felicity to their none too attractive spouses.

The Manœuvres of Jane (1898) marks a decline from the high pinnacle of *The Liars.* In it we are conscious of individuals rather than a social group. When we first meet the fastidious, vacuous Lord Bapchild and his *entourage* at Chaney Court, we recognize the promising beginning of a comedy of manners, but the boisterous, assertive efforts of the girls to get mates to their liking quickly runs into farce. The husband-hunting and the hoodwinking of parents become a little tiresome. The two girls themselves are scarcely as likable as comedy would desire. Jane is petulant and unruly to a degree; Constantia is just as self-willed, but in the sly, demure fashion of a Becky Sharp. Jane, especially, is the descendant of many a headstrong minx in eighteenth-century comedy. Lord Bapchild, too (played admirably by Cyril Maude), is the dramatic scion of a long and noble lineage of aristocratic noodles and nincompoops. Although the play is perplexed by no moral issue, there is more conscious regard for the proprieties than in *The Liars.*

Dolly Reforming Herself, although coming as late as 1908, may be disposed of here; like *The Manœuvres of Jane* it is on a personal rather than a social theme. It is a breezy but rather thin comedy on the futility of, or rather the hypocrisy in, resolutions for self-reform. Dolly Telfer is a staccato little person, not altogether pleasant in her "cattiness" and zeal for reforming others. The quarrel scene with her husband, in which she alternately storms and wheedles as her temper dictates, is in Jones's liveliest vein.

Whitewashing Julia (1903) and *Joseph Entangled* (1904) mark a continuance of the saucy, nonchalant manner of the earlier comedies, but they place less emphasis, the latter especially, upon the manners of a group in society, and more upon the complications of a plot that at times imposes upon credulity. The first two acts of *Joseph Entangled,* however, are an excellent example of artificial comedy; in the third the deadly presence of a moral issue and the emotions which accompany it make themselves felt. In *Whitewashing Julia* Jones resorts to his favorite social setting—a country aristocracy, complacent in its own rectitude and solicitous about the moral welfare of those outside its sacred pale. Julia is a widow who has had an affair with a married duke somewhere on the Continent. Rumors have reached the smug, parochial little community where she had formerly lived. She is snubbed by all the best families, until it develops that she is to marry into one of them and that one of the most sacrosanct of their young married men has himself a not irreproachable past. At once Julia is beamingly accepted, without further concern for her own unexplained adventure.

Sir Joseph Lacy in *Joseph Entangled* is a kind of warm-hearted Lord Quex, who finds himself suddenly plunged into a scandal through an innocent indiscretion with a married lady. Lady Verona can claim kinship with the Lady Susan and Lady Jessica of previous comedies, as the fashionable young wife in a frivolous set.

The difference is that here the lady is entirely innocent of wrong. She is not the bored wife seeking dalliance; she is the victim of circumstances. Whereas the heroine of *The Liars* tells lies that no one believes, Lady Verona tells truths that receive a similar reception. The play treats of an imbroglio rather than manners, but the settlement of the issues at the dictates of good form rather than of moral necessity suggests what those manners would be.

With *Mary Goes First* (1913) Jones, then over sixty, returned to pure comedy, in a vivacious depiction of the provincial manners of an English town. The skirmishes for social supremacy and the petty rivalries and jealousies incidental to suburban life are set forth in all their amusing absurdity. Mary Whichello, a clever young matron of piquant personality, has been the acknowledged leader of the little town's social set. When a generous sovereign bestows knighthood on the Bodsworths, her prestige collapses. In the petty warfare that ensues, Lady Bodsworth is no match for her indomitable rival, who harries and badgers her into mortified surrender, and with the strategy of an old campaigner wins for her own torpid husband a baronetcy. Jones has not failed to make evident the bourgeois strain in it all—the instinct to push and scramble. Not the least source of irony which the comedy so generously affords is the fact that the whole tempest in a teapot grows out of the mere matter of who shall take precedence at a dinner. The play is a gem of dextrous, skilfully articulated plot construction. The part of Mary found its perfect interpreter in the inimitable Marie Tempest.

During those years of the nineties when the critics were acclaiming Pinero and Jones as the spokesmen of a new and better day in the drama, they were also finding cause to recognize, though often with a note of misgiving, the work of three playwrights of uneven workmanship, who were very seldom failing to entertain their audiences but were being content with the surfaces of the life they depicted. C. Haddon Chambers, Henry V. Esmond (H. V. Jack) and Richard C. Carton (R. C. Critchett) are of interest to us because each of them has, at least once, invaded the precincts of the comedy of manners and at other times has skirted its boundaries. As we read the available plays (mostly comedies or farces) of these men, we are conscious of a calculated stagecraft that has achieved its ends but that brings with it no reading of life, no depth of experience. This prevailing staginess each has happily violated, as we shall see; when we encounter the grip of a comic idea or the sharp perception of character, we find these men capable of comedy worthy of attention. As is too generally the case everywhere, they wrote for a public, rather than about something; and too often in their pot-boilers the pot is small and the blaze a meager one. Esmond and Carton, as professional actors, furnish but two further examples of men who, like Shakespeare and Molière and Ibsen, approached playwriting through an interest stimulated by professional contact with the theatre. Esmond went on the stage at sixteen, Carton at twenty-two.

Chambers' *The Tyranny of Tears* (1899), although bordering dangerously on farce, is the nearest he ever came to achieving the comedy of character and idea. Although essentially the study of a temperament, Mrs. Parbury, the vapid, shallow wife, who despotically rules her amiable husband through her childish petulance, is the type of many a tactless, lachrymose spouse and so lends the play the complexion of a comedy of middle-class manners. The characters are sketched in with a light, deft touch and with a good nature that contrasts agreeably with the sardonic studies of marital maladjustments which were so common a spectacle in the theatre. And yet, while the play skims along at such a merry gait, we cannot but think that the author, in his unprejudiced, sharp-eyed appraisal of human frailties, has touched momentarily on something basic and universal. Charles Wyndham and Eva Moore illustrated how large a part is played by talented acting in a stage success.

Sir Anthony (1908) is the title of a play in which the name-character never appears. In this spirited little farce-comedy Chambers acquaints us with the most disgusting of all snobbery—that of the middle class. And yet he has handled suburban vulgarity so banteringly that we experience no real resentment. A young Cockney ledger-clerk, Clarence Chope, has chanced to pass words with a Sir Anthony Mellish and plays up that event to his employer and his friends as the mark of an intimate friendship. When the former investigates, Clarence is of course made an ass and repents of his folly. Chambers' methods are not drastic; what might have become tart with satire is kept sweet with humor.

Nowhere else has Chambers remained long within the realm of manners. His *The Idler* (1891), remade into *The Great Pursuit* (1916), never rises above the old-fashioned comedy-melodrama of which any high-school dramatic club would be capable. *The Impossible Woman* (1913), from Mrs. de Sélincourt's *Tante,* is an admirable sketch of a popular pianist of sham artistic temperament, imposing her selfishness on a condoning world, but the credit is due largely to the novelist. *The Awakening* (1901) starts auspiciously in a drawing-room amidst well-groomed, smooth-spoken people of leisure, whom Max Beerbohm calls " the well-bred but ill-behaved," but by Act II the limelight has centered upon Mr. James St. John Trower, the handsome veteran of many an affair of the heart, and we are forced to watch him mellow into contrition under the sweet influence of an unspoiled country girl. Chambers, like many another, takes love much too seriously for the uses of artificial social comedy. In the same way, a later and much finer play, *Passers-By* (1911), foregoes, for the sake of sentiment, a most promising opportunity for a study in manners. Peter Waverton, a young bachelor aristocrat, bored with the tedious round of fashionable life, calls in chance passers-by to get their " slant " on life. The first two are delightful studies of social misfits. The condescension of Waverton's butler toward these derelicts is a shrewd comment on the iron and the irony of caste.

For purposes of our investigation Esmond is almost hopelessly saturated in emotion of a superficial but sugary variety. He seems to be forever exalting the inherent goodness tucked away in even the most unpromising of us. He likes to stress the bravery and true-heartedness of people. As we should surmise, he has a weakness for happy endings. We feel the lack of a strong hand at the helm of his plays. There is nothing in Esmond more than meets the eye—no glimpses of character, no unexpected nuances, no surprising twists to the story. He is always very pleasant when not tiring. *One Summer's Day* (1897), a delicate, idyllic play like *Sweet Lavender,* and *When We Were Twenty-One* (1901), with all their indisputable charm, do not emerge from the debatable land of " Perhaps " and " Pretty Well." Pathos and tenderness are there in quantities to stifle the laughter of pure comedy. The glow of a warm geniality prevails over the glitter and sparkle of wit. In *A Young Man's Fancy* (1912) we move among titled folk but only for the sake of the easy gentility which they can contribute. The play lacks a comic idea to galvanize it into action. Slightly nearer to our purpose is *The Dangerous Age* (1914), in which a widow of forty, still longing for the romance of youth, has a farewell tryst with a young man under compromising circumstances before settling down to an arranged marriage.

Two of Esmond's comedies, however, dip into the comedy of manners unmistakably. The first, *My Lady Virtue* (1902), is quickened into life by the realization of personality. Lady Ernestone is that rare individual who always tells the truth for its own sake without regard to the needless injury it can inflict. Like Mrs. Parbury she is well-meaning but muddle-headed, almost incredibly lacking in tact and common sense. What is mere priggishness she mistakes for devotion to principle. Her husband and a neighbor, Mrs. Burville, had had a love affair before either of them had married. Mr. Burville attempts to use a letter of Lord Ernestone's for blackmail and all but succeeds through the naïve stupidity of "My Lady Virtue." Esmond rises here to grasp a situation and to realize a social scene through a characterization that is as provocative of comic responses as Mary Whichello or Davies' Mrs. Baxter. *The Wilderness* (1901) is deserving of our regard largely because of its first act, laid in a fashionable Bond Street tea room, where we meet the *beau monde* in all its glory. There are the match-making mamas and the parasitic daughters and the faded, jaded duennas, whom their younger sisters will become some day. The men and women are all either predatory or victimized or both. It is out of this "wilderness" that Sir Harry Milanor and Mabel Weston escape to give their souls the room to breathe. Of course, in doing so they shunt a potential comedy of manners on to another track. Esmond's first act in this play marks his nearest approach to artificial comedy.

Carton, like Esmond, was hampered in character-drawing by fashioning so many of his heroines to meet the acting requirements of his wife. Katherine Compton and Eva Moore (Mrs. Esmond) were exceedingly competent actresses, but their continual participation in their husbands' plays was by no means an unmixed good. Carton's, like Esmond's, is a slender art, born of the theatre and conforming to its traditions. We are sometimes at a loss to know just what he is "getting at." He brings to his plays no fund of experience out of which some bit of the comedy of life may be compounded. The people of his plays smell too often of the lamp and are not quite focused into complete reality. They are creatures rather of artifice than of nature. This very fact, it must be admitted, qualifies him as an exponent of the comedy of manners, as a very humble but a very authentic descendant of Sheridan. In *Lord and Lady Algy* (1898) and *Wheels Within Wheels* (1899) especially, we find all the proper ingredients—an artificial world artificially presented, intrigue, definable characters, a dash of wit and the absence of all edification. Other comedies, as we shall note, are only less successful in attaining purity of mode.

Sunlight and Shadow (1890), an idyllic little piece strongly suggestive of Robertson, and *Liberty Hall* (1892), steeped in Dickensian sentiment, may be summarily dismissed. They mark an early manner that is like Esmond's in its heart-warming, gentle humor and pathos. Being a farce, *Lady Huntworth's Experiment* (1900) must not be scrutinized too curiously as to its probability. Lady Huntworth has allowed her dipsomaniac husband to divorce her and, wishing to disappear for a time, becomes a cook, and a very able one, in a vicarage kitchen. From the numerous proposals she receives from adoring males, she manages to select one that promises her a happy future. Some pleasant characterization relieves the play from unmitigated farce, but the depravity of the lady's drunken husband is rather out of harmony with the picture. In two plays of 1904, *Mr. Hopkinson* and *The Rich Mrs. Repton,* a potential comedy of manners is vitiated, in the one case by farce, in the other by melodrama. In the former, a withering sarcasm is directed against the aristocrats of Cavalier morals but not of Cavalier breeding among whom Lady Egglesby lives her life. The situation of the proud but impecunious lady planning to stoop to the hand of rich Mr. Hopkinson, a preposterous cad, and then to elope with the man of her choice, suggests the possibilities for manners comedy which Carton failed to utilize. In the latter of the two plays just mentioned, the rich Mrs. Repton in question sets aside a part of her mansion as a club room for a group of indigent aristocratic wastrels. Had not the sinister hand of melodrama interfered, we might have had the polished, irresponsible Carton at his best.

Mr. Preedy and the Countess (1909) and *The Eccentric Lord Comberdene* (1910) are too given over to mere high spirits and inconsequence to concern us here.[7] They are a little dash of paprika without the solid food which it should season. Their plots bewilder rather than allure by their labyrinthine windings. Set in a less extravagant tempo they might be modeled into social comedy. The *Saturday Review* thinks the latter a "melodrama that tries to satirize itself *en passant*."[8]

It is regrettable that *Lord and Lady Algy* and *Wheels Within Wheels* are not available in printed form, for in them Carton achieved that grace and polish of the fash-

[7] *The Bear-Leaders* (1912) was never successful, but it, too, touches the world of fashion, "bear-leaders" being people of good social connections who make a business of "coaching" the scions of titled families in the responsibilities of their position.

[8] *Saturday Review,* CX (1910), 674.

ionable world so brilliantly delineated in Congreve and Sheridan, but found in modern English drama up to Carton's day only in Oscar Wilde and imperfectly glimpsed in Jones and Pinero. From reviews we are able to learn that *Lord and Lady Algy* reveals the closely felt presence of *The School for Scandal* in characters, in dialogue, and in situation. The famous screen scene has its less ingenious counterpart in the later play. Lord and Lady Algernon Chetland have separated through general boredom with life and each other. The Marquis of Quarmby, his brother, an arrant hypocrite and a valetudinarian, arranges an assignation with Mrs. Tudway, wife of a wealthy bone-boiler, in Algy's rooms. The plans of this meeting Lady Algy overhears at a fancy-dress ball. At Tudway's behest, Lord Algy has come to this ball to dissuade Mrs. Tudway from a suspected elopement. In his befuddled state of drink he becomes the cause of many amusing complications. To add to the merriment, Algy's father, the Duke, comes seeking his son and is recognized by Mrs. Tudway's mother, a female of uncertain age, as her erstwhile lover. She tries simperingly to revive his interest. Tudway, the Duke, and Lady Algy all suspect Lord Algy of being the lady's partner at the clandestine meeting. When Tudway arrives and interrupts the little tête-à-tête, his wife is forced to hide in an ante-room. Lord Algy admits the presence of a woman there but will not name her. Lady Algy, arriving, states she has an appointment with Mrs. Tudway, thus resolving the situation with the reconciliation of both couples. Carton seems to have caught perfectly the sophistication and cynical playing with emotion that we find in eighteenth-century comedy. His epigrams and smart dialogue owe a debt to Wilde. Such comedies as these, while never being representative, yet reflect a verifiable side-current in modern civilization, and are an adornment to the dramatic art when expertly constructed. Charles Hawtrey and Katherine Compton in the name-parts were all that could be desired. In America in 1899 the same characters were impersonated by William Faversham and Jessie Millward.

Wheels Within Wheels runs in the same extravagant vein as its predecessor but combines intrigue with the presentation of manners. It is as unabashedly unmoral or immoral (as you will) as Etherege or Vanbrugh at their gayest. To briefly adumbrate the plot, Lady Veronica Curtoys is about to elope with her lover, Mr. Vartrey. Her sister-in-law, Mrs. Onslow Bulmer, a lady as sensible as she is unconventional, saves her by stealing a compromising letter from Vartrey's rooms and leaving a note that suggests herself as Vartrey's companion in the runaway. The expected outcome is the discomfiture of the blackguardly Vartrey, the reinstatement of Lady Curtoys, and Mrs. Bulmer's emergence unsmirched from her perilous enterprise. She is also relieved from the attentions of an atrociously vulgar bounder, Blagden, whom she had promised to wed. Miss Compton, who was always most at home as a self-possessed, slangily smart, lazily good-natured woman of the world, found the part of Mrs. Bulmer to her heart's liking. The author must be commended for the skill with which he has caught the smartness and wit of artificial comedy, as well as its gayety and impudence.

In pronounced contrast to the work of the three professional writers for the stage just discussed are the plays of Henry James and " John Oliver Hobbes " (Mrs. Pearl Craigie), both of whom came confidently to the drama as a vehicle for their literary talents, but (in the case of James especially) without the endowment of practical experience in the public theatre.

Henry James, the novelist, is the psychological analyst of personalities, subtle as personalities ultimately are, but with their subtleties magnified as they pass through his highly specializing, super-refined mind. And yet in his frequent studies of the social encounter of American and European civilization, as in *Roderick Hudson* and *The Ambassadors,* he has projected upon his pages many engaging pictures of the manners of a sophisticated, tradition-ridden upper-class society. Too somber some of his canvases are for comedy, but the James habitué will recall scenes in which an elegant, leisured, and iniquitous aristocracy is displayed with a quietly deprecating, intellectual laughter. James's failure to make the life and manners of high society a reality in the theatre may be ascribed to his inability to simplify, intensify, and animate his stories to meet the requirements of oral and visual presentation. They lack the lifeblood of a quickening emotion. The conversation loses itself in subtleties and refinements. In fact, James lays too heavy a responsibility upon his dialogue; it must not only fulfill its normal function but must explain and help carry the plot as well. A subjective novelist, whose clientele was always the select few, could scarcely expect to meet the promiscuous audience of a theatre in a successful play. James was too impatient of public moods and tastes to be a dramatist.

It may be well to rehearse briefly those stage ventures of his in which the manners of a cultivated and fashionable world are to be distinguished. In 1891 appeared a dramatized version of *The American,* affording ample opportunity for social contrasts between a New and an Old World civilization, exemplified specifically in Christopher Newman and the Marquise de Bellegarde. The *Athenaeum*[9] judiciously commented at the time on one probable reason for the failure of the play, pointing out that James had accentuated the melodrama in the story and that such "lachrymose" and "painful" elements were out of harmony with the neat exercise in social comedy which the novel invited. *Guy Domville* (1895), to which casual reference has already been made, was acknowledged by sagacious critics to be a charming eighteenth-century costume play of literary merit, presenting characters sketched in with rare perspicuity, but to be of too delicate a texture for the theatre.

The High Bid, from an earlier tale, was presented in Edinburgh in 1908 with Forbes-Robertson leading the cast, and the next year in London at a series of matinees at His Majesty's, but with no greater success. The play lacks incident to keep it moving; it does not project its ideas into the world of substance where things are done as well as said. It is little more than a succession of adroit but verbally incontinent duologues. Even the

[9] *Athenaeum,* Oct. 3, 1891.

slightest review of the plot will suggest the possibilities it contains for a comedy of manners. Prodmore, a typical representative of the vulgar man in business, holds mortgages over the estate of the impoverished Clement Yule. The price of his relinquishment is that Yule shall marry his daughter Cora. He is about to yield when Mrs. Gracedew, an attractive and indomitable American widow, intervenes. Cora is properly mated elsewhere, the mortgage is lifted, and the widow again assumes the rôle of wife. The author's leisurely, fastidious method ill conforms to the compression of drama. The characters lose the human reasonableness that his commentary as a novelist had accorded them.

The Outcry (1911), like *The High Bid,* was later converted into fiction. It concerns the wholesale deportation to America of English art treasures and reflects something of the modes of thought of an old conservative family of title. James came as close to the comedy of manners as was possible for him in a little play, *Disengaged,* one of a group of four comedies he wrote designedly for the theatre.[10] It had its first appearance at the Hudson Theatre, New York, in 1909. It is a dry, sharp satire on promiscuous philandering in "good" society. The atmosphere is typically that of a sophisticated, over-civilized world; the dialogue is correspondingly adroit and subtle, but an instrument too formidable for actor or for audience. One does not feel that the characters ever fully materialize, as they float through the mazes of an intricate plot.

[10] They appear in his *Theatricals,* vols. 1 and 2, 1894, 1895.

Like James, Mrs. Craigie was an expatriated American, although her identification with English life dated from very young girlhood. She displayed early an intense love for play going and play writing. While still a child she wrote the plays which she staged on her own toy theatre. Later on, she took part with zest in the amateur theatricals of London's West End, with which women of title and fashion combated the boredom of leisure. Lady Freake's private theatre at Cromwell House, for instance, was a popular rendezvous for these dilettantes of the drama.

Mrs. Craigie is of interest to us not so much on account of her two authentic comedies of manners as because of the fact that she writes of a refined and privileged world which she herself graced for many years. The advantage of wealth enabled her to gratify a taste for music, travel, and reading. Being a person of magnetism and charm she found the doors of a cultivated, selective society open to receive her. As a result she writes with the natural ease of one to the manner born and not with the possible overcoloring of an opinionated outsider. The delightful little trifle, *Journeys End in Lovers Meeting* (1895), in which the situations were suggested to her by George Moore from the French of Caraquel, may be passed over for more significant work to follow. In the hands of Ellen Terry, Forbes-Robertson, and William Terriss it proved an attractive curtain-raiser at the Lyceum. Captain Maramour comes at night to Lady Soupire's rooms to urge his suit, knowing the unhappiness of her married life. He is forced to hide at the approach of her husband. So sincerely does Sir Philip demonstrate the warmth of his affection, pleading, by way of proof, that he knows every inch of her boudoir, that the lady's heart is touched, and when she blindfolds him to search for a certain book, the Captain slips out of the room and out of her life. The play is not without its satiric implications. Beneath the smiling mask of society is often the anguish of the human face.

The Ambassador (1898) is a none too probable play of intrigue along conventional lines, which is lifted into comedy of manners by the wit and grace of its lines. Its *mots d'esprit* and its crackling repartee are perhaps too bountifully and promiscuously bestowed, but the fact remains that here we have a play of real literary distinction, written with the gesture of the well-born. The characters not only bear titles, but know how to wear them.[11] We see at once its kinship to the comedies of Wilde. There is the same polished, cosmopolitan society—diplomats, adventuresses, idlers, ingénues, and full-breasted dowagers. Lord St. Orbyn and Lady Basler have their close counterparts in *A Woman of No Importance*. And again, the epigrams take us back to Wilde, although they are less perverse and brittle and more freshly light-hearted in their conception. The exotic, slightly decadent atmosphere of the earlier comedies, however, is entirely absent. Lewis Hind,[12] testifying to the author's true patrician qualities, says that her talk sparkled even more than that of her char-

[11] Of H. B. Irving's Sir William Beauvedere, T. P. O'Connor said, "I have never read *The Egoist,* but it struck me that this is just what Mr. Meredith meant."

[12] Lewis Hind, *Authors and I,* p. 151.

acters. He aptly describes her work as "brilliant, metallic, artificially elegant and smart."

Two years later Mrs. Craigie's *The Wisdom of the Wise* corroborated but did not augment the reputation she had made as a gifted writer of social comedy. In the neatness and delicacy of the treatment we sense a feminine hand—a hand that might have learned to stiffen comedy with dramatic crisis, had death not so soon interposed. In all of the lady's work we feel she falls just short of complete objectification, of a focusing of her art in terms of life. Mrs. Craigie called her play an experiment after the manner of the light comedy of Molière, but while it succeeds as a piece of artifice, it lacks the shrewd comic perception of the great Frenchman. The play concerns mischief-makers and the injury they may cause. The Duke of St. Asaph has recently married a lovely girl, who worships him with all the strength of her ingenuous nature. Her virginal mind contrasts sharply with the artificial world into which she is cast. The Duke's two cousins belong to the class of "brainless, heartless, overfed and undereducated" women who are only happy when meddling in others' affairs. They attempt to instruct Georgine how unfashionable it is for a young duchess to remain the confiding, sentimental creature she was during betrothal days. Despite the scantiness of plot and characterization, the play impresses us as an intimately true picture of high society by one of its members. The author's manner of easy authority lends credence to her dialogue with its tasteful blending of sentiment and cynicism. At the initial performance, a part of the audience exercised its time-honored prerogative by rudely voicing its disapproval.

VIII

TWENTIETH-CENTURY TENDENCY AND ACHIEVEMENT

WHILE the lords and ladies of Carton and Mrs. Craigie were putting back into the comedy of manners somewhat of its lost glamor and *haut ton,* we must remind ourselves of the continued advance of the much more significant, representative movement to make the drama a vehicle for ideas, and by so doing, to appeal to a thoughtful, educated element in the public that had heretofore remained aloof from the theatre. The movement was a disquieted, very earnest effort to reach down to the vital issues of life. It proclaimed the right of testing all things. In its humanitarian concern for man as man, it became broadly cosmopolitan and sought through the publication of plays to reach an international audience. Such a profound interest in the problems of society was in danger of losing sight of the artistic ends to which the drama is dedicated. Social analysis might easily intrude upon observation, and the drawing of a picture give place to the propounding of a philosophy.

The answer to the demand of an intelligent minority for a cultural dramatic expression that should interpret and criticize modern life in terms of truth and not merely of stage-effect was naturally a theatre that should be independent of the commercialized interests that controlled the dramatic output in accordance with the popular taste. J. T. Grein's Independent Theatre, 1891–1897, through which such epochal plays as *Ghosts* and *Widowers' Houses* were made available to the London public, was the first step. Then followed the important pioneering, experimental work of the Incorporated Stage Society, founded in 1899 to promote "the production of plays of obvious power and merit which lacked, under the conditions then prevalent on the stage, any opportunity for their presentation."[1] Among such

[1] This same year, 1899, W. S. Gilbert composed the following fusion of sense and nonsense for the Lydia Thompson benefit at the Lyceum. The lines are inserted here with seeming irrelevancy, only to show what were the characteristic comments of a veteran dramatist and producer looking into a past in which a Stage Society could have had no place:

> What changes here I see since that dim age
> When little Goldenhair tripped on the stage!
> The Drama, struggling then in lodgings shady,
> Has made her fortune, and is quite the lady
> With endless hosts of highly cultured friends.
> Think how she dresses now, and what she spends
> On vast dramatic shrines—in sumptuous salaries,
> In real Venetian-leathered pits and galleries—
> In plays that run a year to houses packed,
> And cost, to stage, a thousand pounds an Act!
> . . . .
> Stock companies, completely out of date,
> Burlesque quite dead (it never had that fate
> When Talfourd, Planché, Brough and Byron made it,
> And Rogers, Clarke, and Marie Wilton played it);
> Then, strangest thing, of playhouses vast crops!
> Playhouses plentiful as grocers' shops!
> Ten in twelve months! Well, I don't want to prate,
> But if new theatres crop up at this rate
> Where will you find your pieces, if you please,
> And where your actors and your actresses?
>
> Ten months will build a playhouse per contractor—
> It takes at least ten years to build an actor,
> And, as our best authorities insist,
> Ten times ten years to build a dramatist!

plays was the early work of Shaw, Barker, Hankin, and Maugham. In the first ten years of its history, the Society produced thirty-seven English and twenty-five foreign plays.

A third expression of the attempt to liberate the drama from the shackles of commercialism and bring it face to face with life was the Vedrenne-Barker management at the Court Theatre, 1904–1907, and at the Savoy, 1907–1908. By a series of definitely stipulated short runs of only a few weeks each, these men introduced to the public a number of significant plays, tastefully interpreted and adequately staged. The individual actor was submerged; totality of effect was made pre-eminent. If Shaw's plays received the lion's share, Barker's, Hankin's, and Galsworthy's were not neglected. In all of these plays, as representative of the new drama, we have to note the spirit of social inquiry and of technical experimentation. All the old dramatic fences are cheerfully overleaped in the effort to come to the grapple with reality. To set forth an idea and develop it through the medium of character takes precedence over the elaboration of plot. The social and moral significance of separate situations is of greatest consequence. In the case of Shaw and Barker drama becomes, at times, practically static, with a minimum of action and a maximum of talk. The concrete, visualized stage presentation becomes an illustration, a case in point, of the author's opinions, and the different characters, from their varying points of view, ring the changes on the theme of the play. In the hybrid of treatise, homily, story, dialogue, and description that sometimes results, a drama devoted to the ends of art is no longer discernible.

One of the most significant characteristics of the new drama, as represented variously in the work of Shaw, Barker, Hankin, and Galsworthy, of Houghton, Ervine, Masefield, and many others, is its complete dedication to the life of the middle and lower classes. The common, ordinary man in his social and moral relationships, the man without the prerogatives of inherited wealth and station, holds the center of the stage. Nor, as we shall note later, is he confined to London and its suburbs. Through the promulgation of the repertory theatre in Dublin and in the provincial cities of England he can reflect the life of the country and the town.

Lady Windermere and Lady Algy seem scarcely of the same category of beings as Candida or the Huxtable sisters, not to speak of Masefield's Nan or Houghton's Fanny Hawthorn. Nor indeed are they nor should be, for they inhabit that artificial world against which the tides of social controversy and amelioration beat in vain. In a régime of social comedy in which cerebration shares so large a place with observation, the pure comedy of manners was in danger of becoming vitiated with social criticism or of being relegated altogether. And yet a strain persisted, true to its artistic destiny—to be the pastime of the educated gentleman and his lady. At the hands of Sutro and Maugham and a little later of Besier and Frederick Lonsdale the manners comedy received recognition down to and past the limits of this paper. To the intelligent of every class its wit and Corinthian refinement will ever be a diversion. Then, too, the denizen of the *beau monde* likes to see himself upon the stage. Outside of melodrama and musical comedy, he inclines chiefly to plays of smart society. Coming to the theatre after a late heavy meal and glowing with "post-prandial satisfaction," he does not want to think, and yet he may be tired of the frothy confections of the music halls. The comedy of manners affords him just that tasty, easily digestible fare for which he is seeking—intelligent but not intellectual, gay and witty without a lapse into nonsense. It is generally admitted that the London theatre-going public is more aristocratic and insular in its interests than that of New York, for instance. The theatres cater to the tastes of the West End rather than to those of the middle class.

Since much of the comedy of the new movement in the drama was social in its nature, it was of course intimately concerned with manners. That it did not evolve a genuine comedy of middle-class manners was the result of its didactic, doctrinal intent. In the comedies of Hankin and Houghton a social consciousness did not becloud the artistic impulse; in the comedies of Barker and Shaw it was allowed to do so. The creator of the Huxtable family, as we meet them in Act I of *The Madras House,* could have penned a superlative comedy of the manners of Suburbia, but instead the play veers off into talk, turning over various problems of sex, marriage, and woman's economic position in the modern world. The Barrie-like descriptive comments in Barker's stage directions are full of that luminous insight which a comedy of manners turns to such good account. *The Madras House* discusses conditions; a comedy of manners would accept them.[2]

In Shaw much the same is true—and to a greater degree. It is not necessary to say that Shaw uses the stage as a forum for polemic discussion, a kind of glorified cart-tail from which to promote his views. In his comedies he launches implacable war on the outworn morals and manners of today. Society is beridden, he believes; around its neck the Old Man of the Sea of convention and ignorance. "My reputation has been gained," he declares, "by my persistent struggle to force the public to reconsider its morals. . . . I write plays with the deliberate object of converting the nation to my opinion in these matters." And again, "I fight the theatre, not with pamphlets and sermons and treatises but with plays." Such a credo is of course at the opposite pole from the purpose of comedy as a form of art, and yet it is worth noting that he possesses abundantly the perspicuity and the sense for the comic which play so large a part in the manners genre.

Getting Married, as it stands, is merely a symposium, and a very prolix one, on matrimony as a modern institution. The characters are merely convenient forms on which to drape a point of view. Consistency and credibility are cheerfully sacrificed for the enforcement of an opinion.[3] Shaw refuses to let his characters be

[2] Barker's profoundly suggestive play, *The Secret Life* (1923), displays yet further a mastery of dialogue that is in itself dramatic and that preempts the function of plot. Its theme, the restless seeking of the spirit of man for the unattainable in a world of disenchantment, takes us into a philosophic appraisal of an epoch, not a concrete picturing of its manners.

[3] G. S. Street, in *Blackwood's*, CLXVII (1900), 832–836, contrasts Shaw, Congreve, and Sheridan. "Sheridan's weakness is his lack of ideas; Mr.

and do for themselves. He must be forever coaching them and interposing himself between them and their dramatic function. While Jones is employing one *raisonneur* in a play, Shaw is using a round half dozen. Hence the illusion of reality is always frustrated. The point we wish to make here is that *Getting Married* is replete with ideas which are capable of being expanded and concretely expressed in a comedy of manners.

The lambent spirit of mirth and mockery in *You Never Can Tell* bespeaks Shaw's capacity for social comedy without indoctrination—were he someone else than Shaw.[4] The play is full of banter at human affectations. The air is charged with satiric chuckles. The characters blurt out the truth with such aplomb that we might think them under the magical compulsion of some Palace of Truth. It is all very delightful farce, but it is also criticism. Gloria, presenting the conflict between the "New Woman" and the woman that nature urges her to be, and William, with his quaint philosophy of marriage, are richly endowed for the uses of social comedy.

How He Lied to Her Husband and *Pygmalion* might be educed as further demonstration of Shaw's potential aptitude for the comedy of manners. The former is a

Shaw's weakness is his superabundance of them. Congreve's ideas come naturally from the play of his characters and out of the fullness of his experience. Mr. Shaw's ideas have to come in at all cost, and character and experience may go hang."

[4] *You Never Can Tell* and Barrie's *The Admirable Crichton* touch each other in spirit, but at arm's length. The latter play is luminous with profound truths concerning the structure of Society, and *Quality Street* hints delightfully at the old-fashioned ways of a village like Cranford; but the genius of caprice and sometimes of ecstasy that infuses Barrie's plays is antipodal to that of the comedy of manners.

romping extravaganza, letting fly at illusions and delusions, with more than the usual Shavian agility. The latter play is also full of rollicking good fun. With a shifting of the emphasis it would become excellent manners comedy, for in it we have the emptiness of social pretensions and of class distinctions that we have encountered throughout our study. The duchess and the daughter of a dust-man are distinguishable only by the external touchstones of speech, dress, and etiquette. Between the fraudulent poor and the indolent rich there is little to choose. In both, the Comic Spirit finds food for laughter. In Shaw, the writer of comedy, we endorse the absence of the sentimentalist, but we deplore the presence of the doctrinaire.

While the intelligent minority were finding a new stimulus at the Court and the fashionable few were being regaled by "creased trousers and frock coats at the St. James's and talk and tea-cups at the Criterion," the unregenerate majority still continued faithful to the old gods of light entertainment. The cry of the populace was still for *panem et circenses.* With the accession of Edward VII a more liberal pursuit of pleasure and theatre-going was countenanced by the best society. Much of the old farce and melodrama was incorporated into the music halls[5] and variety shows, which began

[5] It would be interesting to trace the ancestry of the modern Palace of Varieties back through the old Canterbury Music Hall in Westminster Bridge Road, which Shaw Desmond in his *London Nights in the Gay Nineties* calls their immediate predecessor, to such popular supper- and music-rooms in the forties and fifties as Evans's Singing Room in Covent Garden, The Cyder Cellar and The Coal Hole, all of them the haunts of boisterous conviviality and good talk, where the singing of glees and ballads and other forms of entertainment were provided. It will be re-

in the late nineties to become a pretentious form of entertainment for the fashionable as well as for the crowd. In the more rapid, nervous existence of the new century they became more and more popular as places of mental diversion and relaxation. Well-to-do West Enders dropped in late of an evening to see the ballet and get a laugh or two. The atmosphere was informal. Men did not need to be punctilious in their attire. A writer of the day says that to dress befittingly they should appear in bibs and pinafores, carry a rattle and suck a lollipop. It was admittedly nothing but the tinkling of cymbals and the crackling of thorns under a pot, but it met the popular favor and that was enough. Perhaps it was the same cynic who observed, "When the public seemed to think any burlesque or extravaganza too long, the manager put things right by shortening the dresses." As the years went on, the tumbling and strong-man acts came to be supplemented by short skits and sketches, which were often telling little satires in light vein of the follies of the town and as such present us in a new setting with the material and method of the comedy of manners.[6]

It is well to note that with the advent of the music hall that part of the public which desired sensation and ribaldry now had its own demarked places of amusement, whereas in former years it took its demands generally to all the playhouses of the city. This segrega-

membered that Evans's was one of Thackeray's favorite resorts and that he had it in mind in creating his Cave of Harmony.

[6] In 1912 the London music halls were placed on a par with other theatres in being allowed to produce plays under license of the Lord Chamberlain. This enactment was a great stimulation to the writing of one-act plays.

tion of types of plays to certain theatres was beneficial to the drama. The St. James's, Haymarket, and Garrick, especially, came to be associated with high comedy of varying degrees of gravity; the Adelphi and Drury Lane, with melodrama, and the Empire, Tivoli, and Alhambra, with a pastiche of song, dance, and burlesque.

We have perused the work of Pinero and Jones, of Chambers, Carton, and Esmond, all of which extended well into the new century, although it is identifiable rather with the old. The first decade of that new century marked the beginning of the dramatic career of four new playwrights, all of whom find a place in any history of the comedy of manners. *Cousin Kate* (1903) by Hubert Henry Davies, *The Two Mr. Wetherbys* (1903) by St. John Hankin, *The Walls of Jericho* (1904) by Alfred Sutro, and the *Lady Frederick* (1907) of W. Somerset Maugham were the four plays in which they made their initial venture in social comedy. It is significant that these men brought to the writing of plays not the experience of the actor but that of the journalist and the novelist (in the case of Maugham). Before we consider their contribution to our subject or notice at all the work being produced outside of London, let us dispose of the minor comedies as succinctly as we may.

In looking over the miscellany of dramatic offerings to the stage for 1900–1914, we are embarrassed by the quantity of creditable performance. It will be well, therefore, to select the representative best according to two tentative classifications—those which are impregnated with social idea and purpose and those which exhibit a social scene merely for entertainment. As we should expect, the complexion of both groups is more often middle or upper middle class than aristocratic. Since in most cases these plays are unobtainable in print, it will be possible only to hint at their contents.

Of comedies verging on social criticism (the demarcation between our two groups is necessarily indeterminate) we are not primarily concerned, except where the picturing of manners is unmistakable. *Her Grace the Reformer* (1906) by Mrs. Henry de la Pasture (Lady Clifford) proved to be on the stage a pleasing but unimportant one-act satirical play, brushing lightly Jones's old theme of the hypocrisy of reformers. It centers around a duchess who advocates social equality abroad but presides over an unlimited monarchy at home. Charles McEvoy as an authentic member of the Manchester "school" contributed with Houghton and Brighouse to its first successes. After the ironic realism of *David Ballard,* he produced in 1911 *All That Matters,*[7] which he terms a comedy of English life. It is a *mélange* of melodrama, farce, and idyl with interspersions of drawing-room comedy of the tea-cup and small-talk variety.

A much more capable comedy is the very pleasant *Just to Get Married* (1910) by Cicely Hamilton, journalist, feminist, and ex-actress, who had already written two years before a romantic comedy of social significance, *Diana of Dobson's,* presenting the life of the shop-girl and the dreams that her rich customers

[7] This play well illustrates the conflict in the man between a natural gypsy strain of romance and professional experimentation in realism.

awaken within her. *Just to Get Married* is a reflection on woman's place in the new social order and particularly on marriage as her appointed destiny. Emmeline Vicary is an undowered girl who is forced into matrimony by her aunt. When she has ensnared a rich, noble-hearted young fellow and is about to marry him, she revolts from the sordidness of it all. Later she meets him under conditions that are honest, and finding that she has grown to love him, she herself proposes. Far from being strident or doctrinal, the comedy is genial both as a picture and as a criticism.

Two plays of Robert Vansittart's, both of 1913, deserve mention. His extended career in the diplomatic service should have given him first-hand acquaintance with the ways of the ruling class. In *The Cap and Bells* he has contrasted an English peer, Lord Chislehurst, an amiable, level-headed gentleman, with his daughter, who indulges a flair for politics and social service. A duke and a socialist are both dancing attendance upon her. Mr. Vansittart seems to have availed himself of the opportunities for humor and irony which his situation proffered and yet the play is almost over-weighted with views on capital and labor, with inevitable side lights on the aimlessness of upper-class society. *People Like Ourselves* comes more gaily to the task of true comedy. Sir Joseph Juttle and his wife are types of the newly rich. Their son brings into the house a popular actress with whom he is in love, and with her come a troupe of associates, representing the various kinds of society people who haunt the Green Room of the theatre. The possibilities here for the reflection of manners are infinite. Miss Magdalen Ponsonby's *Idle Women* (1914), put on by The Pioneer Players, seems to have been a veritable comedy of manners, sketching in with a mordant pen the familiar picture of the rich, scatter-brained woman in society. Lady Ditcham has an "urge" to found a new religion among her fashionable coterie of friends, who would doubtless be benefited by any religion at all but are quite inefficacious to assist in her enterprise.

Among the comedies which we shall include in our second group, the palm should be awarded to *The Man from Blankley's* (1901), a frolicsome little comedy of manners elaborated by F. A. Anstey (F. A. Guthrie) from some sketches he had written for *Punch*.[8] Lord Strathsporran becomes inadvertently a guest at a dinner party given by the Montague Tidmarshes, a hopelessly snobbish and vulgarian middle-class family, stuffy and unctuously respectable. The lord is mistaken for the man they have sent for from the caterers to "fill in" as a paid guest at table. The obvious farcicality of the play is lifted into something higher by the effortless *vraisemblance* with which the manners and the speech of the bourgeoisie are reproduced. We feel it to be an altogether genuine picture that Anstey has given us, without disguise and without coloring. It has an authenticity that comedies about the upper classes often lack. Skittles and beer are to be preferred to stale champagne. The dining-room scene of the second act is a gem of comedy in its amus-

[8] Anstey's *Voces Populi* were delightfully pungent, satiric sketches of social life. They have been called "Du Maurier dramatized."

ing conversation, appropriate to a group in which a veneer of gentility vainly conceals their inherent vulgarity. The play enjoyed a deserved success in America as well as in England, and in 1906 was honored by a command performance at Sandringham.[9] Anstey's *Lyre and Lancet* (1902), in which he introduces upper-class country-house society, is less starkly true, less contentedly a comedy of manners and nothing more.

George Hawtrey's *Lord of His House* at the Comedy Theatre in 1902 gives fresh glimpses of country society, but the story of the phlegmatic husband, the pushing lawyer, who would gain social and political prestige and who philanders with the gentleman's wife, and the neglected wife herself, whose dormant respect for her husband is awakened when he refuses to accept the evidence of her misbehavior, offer nothing new to the reader of drama. *A Sense of Humor* (1909) by Mr. and Mrs. Cosmo Hamilton (Beryl Faber, the actress) attracts us mainly because of its gayety and the neat artifice with which a story of intrigue is handled in characteristic eighteenth-century fashion. A slighted wife and her rival's husband seek to pay back their spouses in kind. Their tactics succeed in awakening dismay in the enemy's camp. But it so happens that the other lady is also acting only in pretense. After a brisk exchange of retaliations, the proper dénouement is of course effected.

A short but indisputable comedy of manners is Max Beerbohm's *A Social Success* (1913), as an epitome of

[9] Charles Hawtrey, the embodiment of urbanity and imperturbability with a dash of audacity, was Lord Strathsporran to the life.

the plot will suggest. Tommy Dixon is a young gentleman of means who has been received with suspicious warmth to the bosom of the smart set. He finds its giddy, empty round is jeopardizing his self-respect, and so he purposely cheats at cards to win his dismissal. For a time it would seem that his little coup has succeeded, as his friends leave him in disgrace, but soon they repent and take him back in forgiveness to the aristocratic bosom. That silken cords have proved strong as cables is Beerbohm's satiric admission in his play.

A satiric comedy of political and social life in high places is Anthony Hope Hawkins' *Pilkerton's Peerage* (1902). The title is suggestive of the ridiculous struggle of a parvenu to gain a title, but Pilkerton proves to be too dour a person for laughter, and after three acts of tepid dialogue the play at last drives home its ironic comment that the government distributes honors in trade for party support and not for service to the nation, but that it is distinctly bad form to give utterance to that fact. The play illustrates how a too fiercely satiric intent may curdle the pleasantry of comedy. In 1910 Hawkins collaborated with Cosmo Hamilton in *Helena's Path*, a dainty bit of artificiality concerning the dispute between a peer and a neighboring marchese over a right of way through their properties. It is an elegant piece of trifling in the manner of eighteenth-century comedy.

Still other comedies[10] afford glimpses, at least, of

[10] *An Angel Unawares* (1905) and *A Question of Age* (1906) by Robert V. Harcourt were coolly received by critics and public because of their want of organization. They need be no more than mentioned here.

the manners of society. G. S. Street's *Great Friends* (1905) possesses that dry wit, unimpassioned treatment, and detached point of view so much to be sought after in the manners type of play. It concerns a sensible woman's method of winning back a rather spineless fiancé from a more alluring woman. In Street's crisp, epigrammatic style his readers find a confirmation of that which has made his books popular. In John Valentine's *The Stronger Sex* (1906) we are in the atmosphere of the drawing-room. When a husband coolly informs his demure little wife that he had married her only for money, she ceases suddenly to be demure. By the end of the play she has effected a real union between them and has proved which is the stronger sex. Ernest Denny's *Vanity* (1913) is a nebulous piece of work but pictures for us the moving, populous world of the stage and its environs. *Peggy and Her Husband* (1914) is a smart, lively comedy by Joseph Keating, presenting the fashionable world with its vanities and its aimless chatter.

Three plays of the early twentieth century may be taken together in that they summon up the manners of a bygone day. *The Eighteenth Century* (1907) from the comedy of E. J. Malyon and C. James is fantasy, farce, costume play, and satire rolled into one. A nobleman who had long paid homage to the ideals and manners of the eighteenth century is conducted thereto by a potion and finds to his disgust that distance had lent enchantment. The play affords interesting social contrasts in two epochs. Those readers who have seen Louis Parker's *Pomander Walk* (1911) will testify what a dainty little Dresden china of a play it proved to be, as delicate as a bit of old lace—and as inviting. The episodes are trivial; the play's great merit is in its atmosphere of idyllic charm and unreality. The author takes us "out Chiswick way, half way to Fairyland," into a little nook, where the roar of the busy world is but a murmur. The characters of the play are all out of an old album of life—the admiral; the red-cheeked sailor boy; his father, Lord Otford, who finds an old sweetheart in the still lovely mother of his son's intended bride,—all of them, including the profane parrot. *Mary Edwards* (1912), put on by Miss Horniman's Manchester company, may be dismissed by saying that it is a slender play of one domestic situation and that manners appear as a by-product of the story.

In the ever-present farce, also, we may catch folly as it flies. To mention but a few will suffice for our purpose. Robert Marshall, a retired army captain, now deceased, and the author of these stage favorites, *His Excellency the Governor* and *The Second in Command,* possessed more than the usual ability to entertain in the theatre. In his dialogue he is a not unworthy follower of Wilde. *A Noble Lord* (1900) is too insouciant to take even itself seriously, but *The Duke of Killiecrankie* (1903), though a romantic farce, reveals the wit and satire of manners comedy. When the acid-sweet Lady Henrietta reproaches the Duke for his apathy as a lover, he abducts her to his castle in Scotland in true Petruchio fashion. One of the party, a Mrs. Mulholland, has made her money in glue, an odious as well as odorous source of income, and it is in the verbal encounters between the two ladies during their enforced intimacy that the comedy takes on a social complexion.

In passing, a word should be said of a vivacious farce-comedy, *An American Citizen* (1899), which dips too often into pathos to be more than remotely of the manners genre. The play was written for Nat Goodwin by Madeleine Lucette Ryley, an actress like Cicely Hamilton, and the author of over twenty plays. Although born in England, she is really to be identified with America, where she has long resided.[11] Percy Fendall's *Mrs. Dering's Divorce* (1903) treats farcically the theme of the divorced couple who discover their best qualities only after they have parted, a dramatic idea similar to that in *Divorçons* and in Cosmo Gordon-Lennox's *The Freedom of Suzanne* (1904), a comedy of manners carried up the dramatic scale to a more irresponsible key. Self-willed Susan, having divorced her husband, finds that the way back is the harder road. The part proved an excellent vehicle for Marie Tempest, the wife of the author, who was himself but another one of many to arrive at playwriting through the stage door. The comedy is of the stage-play type, as are his pleasant farce-comedy, *The Marriage of Kitty* (1902), and *The Indecision of Mr. Kingsbury* (1905), a combination of manners and intrigue, deriving from *L'Irresolu* of Georges Berr. Jerome K. Jerome in *The New Lady Bantock* (1909) hits upon a theme rich in possibility.

[11] The same may be said for Stanislaus Stange, a native Englishman whose name is associated with America as actor and successful librettist of comic operas. His *The School for Husbands* (New York, 1905, London, 1906) is a costume comedy of manners, leaning to farce, but echoing in title and in treatment the boisterous comedy of the eighteenth century.

A young nobleman marries a music-hall girl but, wishing to be accepted only on his merits, conceals his rank. To her surprise she finds herself mistress of a manorial estate. The servants prove to be relatives of hers, who make it their duty to instruct her in ladyship. The play drifts into shallows and miseries, whereas it might have ridden triumphantly into high comedy. There is just a glimpse of manners in Douglas Murray's *The New Duke* (1913), in which a very plebeian bachelor unexpectedly inherits a dukedom and finds his new world so hectic that he flees from a prospective duchess into the arms of a buxom girl of his own choosing. Social contrasts between two classes in society are laid down with the bold strokes of unapologizing farce.

In St. John Hankin is much of the intellectual curiosity and honesty of Shaw in approaching contemporary social life, but while the latter is shaking his fist, the former is merely shrugging his shoulders. In his detestation of bourgeois cheapness of mind and soul, Hankin never forgets that he is writing plays and not theses, and therefore does not exploit his characters by subjecting them to his dictation, but allows a social truth to evolve from what they do and say. "It is the dramatist's business to represent life, not to argue about it," he said. He elicits our admiration as a spokesman for sincerity. His plays evidence that sturdy, forthright honesty of the artist which is the prime requisite of all worthy endeavor. "They display the conflict between things as they are and things as people like to think they are." It is characteristic of him that he should champion the under dog, the social misfit, who protests against the conventionality of the comfortably adjusted and the "unrespectability" of the respectable. He likes audacious people who disturb the sanctified peace of society. And yet, uncompromising as he is, he has not quite the philosophy to let his sense of the comic rise above his irritation. He is a little prejudiced in his very gesture of eschewing prejudice.[12] Hankin never broke through into a full, clear utterance. His ironic death interrupted the complete dramatic fulfillment of irony in his work. But he was a substantial workman, who, unafraid and clear sighted, brought healthy ideas into comedy. His *milieu* is not primarily that of the aristocracy, but in his observation, in his moral inconclusiveness, and in his amused cynicism he is eminently qualified as exponent of the comedy of manners.

Wilde polished the surface of comedy and its glitter found a paler reflection in many of the men who came after. It is clearly present in the smart verbal exchanges of Shaw's earlier plays. And it is apparent in Hankin's dexterity and wit, but with a sounder conception of his craft he tempers them to the requirements of the middle-class country people with whom he deals. His dialogue is incisive, economic, pungent—the successful adaptation of a means to an end.

Hankin's characters are recognizable and intimately associated with his action, but their range is narrow.

[12] He has an exaggerated sanity, which in a robust nature is the comic spirit at its highest power, but in one of low vitality like Hankin, sanity becomes intolerable as it views the madness of the world. He was too sane to believe in a world of reason in madness; not robust enough to make of it a comic matter. John Palmer, *The Future of the Theatre,* p. 144. (Paraphrased, not quoted.)

Certain types tend to reproduce themselves. The easy-going, misunderstood fellow, who like Hankin himself is not tricked by the show of things and who is constantly disregarding the signposts and fences along life's road because of the lure of the open fields, is before us variously in Dick Wetherby, Hugh Verreker, and Eustace Jackson. So, too, the brutally frank, class-proud lady of station who appears as Lady Faringford in *The Return of the Prodigal* (1905) becomes Mrs. Eversleigh in *The Charity that Began at Home* (1906) and Lady Remenham in *The Cassilis Engagement* (1907).

Each of the major Hankin comedies is built on a comic idea admirably suited to the comedy of manners. *The Two Mr. Wetherbys* proclaims that a marriage can be ruined as easily by excess of ideals as by their absence, and that a good reputation may often become more embarrassing than a bad, because it necessitates hypocrisy. The "good" James is unfortunate enough to be saddled with a wife and an aunt who are meddlesome pietists and moral martinets. The "bad" Dick, married to a wife whose triumphant rectitude refuses to understand his good-humored enjoyment of life, remains honestly himself and accepts with alacrity the separation which his solemn spouse demands. The unerring logic of the play seems to break down in his final capitulation to her insistence for a reunion. Is this the conventional "happy ending" which Hankin repudiated as a sop thrown to a public too sentimental[13] to accept in the theatre the severe logic of life, or is Hankin's tongue in his cheek as he closes?

[13] "They dodder like romantic old women in an almshouse." Hankin.

In *The Return of the Prodigal* a very dumpy, conventionally correct parvenu family, the Jacksons, suddenly find their political and social aspirations jeopardized by the return of a ne'er-do-well son, whose sangfroid and embarrassingly clear appraisals of the family furnish excellent comedy.[14] In Hankin's next play, *The Charity that Began at Home,* he makes sport (as Jones's *Crusaders* did in so different a way) of the quixotic though well-intentioned people of good society, whose experiments in good works result distressingly for all concerned. It is like Hankin to put the only true wisdom and sympathy in the play in the mouth of the cynical egoist, Hugh Verreker. He, like Eustace Jackson, is capable of real sacrifice, not because he is sentimental but because he is not.

The Cassilis Engagement is the most typically comedy of manners of the group. It concerns a mother's love for her son, but there is no tug at the heart-strings. It is as luminous and as cold as a crystal. Mrs. Cassilis has brain as well as heart, and when Geoffrey becomes infatuated with Ethel Borridge, who is as commonplace as her name suggests, she does not defeat her own ends by opposing the match but sagaciously invites Ethel and her mother for a visit. Her son's illusions are soon dispelled. Of course, Hankin's popularly called unhappy ending is in reality not only the most rational but the happiest. For Geoffrey and Ethel it would have been wedding knells, not wedding bells.

[14] The title of the play affords an ironic contrast between the Prodigal Son of Scripture, a sincere penitent, and Hankin's prodigal with an impudence born of philosophic insight.

In sharp distinction to Hankin's trenchant social criticism is the geniality and charm of Hubert Henry Davies' social picturing, with just a fillip of satire here and there—a blending of elements that bespeaks the Robertson tradition. Davies is a master of gay and graceful comedy of middle-class manners, finding its setting in a natural world, not in an effulgent, artificial one. If his range of experience is limited, his dramatic performance is sound. He has the genuine enthusiasm of the recorder of manners for the kaleidoscopic social scene. He maintains consistently an amused, detached attitude that is rarely tinged with scorn. Like Hankin he is an observer of men but in him a lambent humor replaces wit. His comedies have caught the contagion of his own affability, but it is a geniality that does not degenerate into the sentimental. They are luminous with a warm glow of sunshine, not with the icy glitter of Maugham, let us say. It is this sympathy of his that enkindles his characters and endears them to us in a way that was impossible for Sutro or Hankin.

Davies' most memorable contribution to our modern drama is primarily a character study, but Mrs. Baxter in *The Mollusc* (1907) is so sentient a creation that she becomes the symbol of a class of women in society who coax and wheedle their way through the world. She is a potential comedy of manners in herself. Placid, unvexed, she makes flunkeys of her family and her friends but exacts the service with an indolent amiability that is disarming. She embraces routine and serenity and evades responsibility with the ardor with which some people welcome adventure. Her brother Tom brings into the serenity of the Baxter household a quickening presence that awakens the Mollusc to at least a momentary sense of her womanly duty. The author has been shrewd enough to bring his play to an indeterminate conclusion and has thereby enhanced its comic potency. Can the mollusc ever slough its shell?

Mrs. Baxter. . . . Tom shall never have another chance to call me a mollusc.

. . . .

Miss Roberts (*to Tom*). You've worked a miracle.

Tom (*quickly to Miss Roberts*). Were those miracles permanent cures? (*Shakes his head.*) We're never told! We're never told!

The comedy attracts our attention also by the neat adequacy of its technique. With a cast of only four characters, the situations are never forced. It is the comedy of manners in its most intimate form, as contrasted with the *Ideal Husband* or *Our Betters*.

Lady Epping's Lawsuit (1908) showed that Davies was not at home in a play of avowedly satiric intent. The personages in his flippant world of exclusive society are but lay figures. The countess herself is realizable but extravagantly done. She is a vain, selfish woman of fashion, pertinacious in doing anything that is not worth doing. She " takes up " a dramatist as her latest fad and bothers him with her own amateur effusions, which he sees to be incurably absurd. The play is episodic. The countess and the gentleman flirt; his wife returns the compliment. He writes a play that bears only the most casual resemblance to one of her own; she sues him for plagiary. It is all very inconsequential. The court-room scene descends into unalloyed farce. Lady Epping's evasive, noncommittal answers in the witness box are the best kind of theatre. She is at once too stupid and too clever to be cross-examined. Davies' dialogue in the play is characteristically crisp and sparkling.

Two other plays remain for consideration, *A Single Man* (1910) and *Doormats* (1912). The former is a theatrical piece put to a good use by Cyril Maude. The machinery of the play makes itself audible at times. It is a pleasant, mild little play in which an element of manners is barely perceptible. A middle-aged novelist suddenly realizes he should have a wife. Despite the kind offices of his sister-in-law and his own mistakes, he at last finds his chosen one in his own secretary. The second play is more self-revealing, more assuredly of comic stuff. Noel Gale, an artist, has petted and pampered his wife until she has her own way in everything. She diverts herself with a flirtation which reaches the verge of serious consequences, when she discovers that the gentleman is not of the condescending type. Noel has tried to do what so many uxorious husbands in our comedies succeeded in doing—revive his wife's affection by a simulated indifference. But at the first sign of her distress, poor Noel always weakens and thus loses his strategic position. Some people are born to be door mats and some to be the boots; some are givers and some are takers. The play ends with Leila in tears of contrition, but Davies is too candid to palliate us with a conclusive ending. Leila, like Mrs. Baxter, is incorrigible, and Noel will go on wearing his silken chains to the end of the reckoning. Therein lies the derisory laughter of the play. Had Leila undergone a permanent change of heart, we might smile but we could not laugh.

With the exception of the war years Alfred Sutro has been writing for the theatre almost continuously since 1904. His work represents the kind of comedy the best commercial theatres of London had to offer their patrons in the opening years of the new century—comedy that broached social topics because it was the mode of the day, that sought above all else to avoid dullness and generally succeeded, and that entertained the public through novelty of situation and adroitness of craftsmanship. In 1914 it had contributed nothing which the drama of 1900 did not already possess. Sutro's plays lack substance. We do not feel that they are constructed from the tissues of life. They stand strongly in need of the glamor of the stage for their effectiveness. Presenting the stereotyped forms of the nineties in character-drawing and dialogue, they yet are redeemed from flaccidity by the author's skill in handling his material. He is dramaturgist rather than dramatist. He has been compared, not inaptly, to Sardou, a Sardou of less range and power.

The Walls of Jericho, Sutro's first important play, exhibits him in more than his usual grasp of an idea and of character. It is a stark satire on an effete aristocracy. It is a Babylon of wealth and pleasure he presents, peopled by loungers and flirts. We have met this world many times before. Sutro paints it vividly again. We are in the chosen *milieu* of the comedy of manners, but the moral indignation and revolt which suffuse the play supersede the gesture of acceptance (cynical if you will) which our type characteristically displays. It is such animated puppets of fashion as the Marquis of Steventon and Lady Parchester who are the natural denizens of manners comedy, and not Jack Frobisher, whose manhood seeks for himself and his wife, Lady Alethea, the free air of the world's frontiers. One wonders if some day her sister, Lady Lucy, and the rich young man she has beguiled will be faced by the same problem and how they will solve it. The comedy and the tragedy of life go on endlessly. If Sutro has justly been imputed to be an imitator of Pinero, *The Walls of Jericho* will furnish the best evidence.

The next three plays offer little that is to our purpose. *Mollentrave on Women* (1905) is not robust but ingenious. Mollentrave is a man of sixty who suavely poses to his friends as an authority on woman and her behavior in love. When he advises and directs their love affairs, his specious theories go awry, and the ultimate happy mating of the couples results in spite of and not because of his efforts in their behalf. The irony of it all is that he is so fatuous as to think that his strategy has succeeded. He had attempted to study Woman, when in reality it is only women who exist. *The Correct Thing* (1905) offers ironic comments on society but is negligible as a play. The next in order, *The Fascinating Mr. Vanderveldt* (1906), would furnish a brisk, pleasant evening's entertainment for any talented group of amateurs. It is without any conspicuous mark of merit, but is neatly contrived. Lady

Hendingby, a Junoesque dowager, starched and domineering, and her elder daughter, with a misplaced zeal for social reform, are realizable but true to type. The latter's sister, the virtuous but indiscreet Lady Clarice, is tricked into a compromising situation by the gentleman after whom the play is named, in order to force her consent to a marriage. She outguesses him smartly and chooses a husband elsewhere. The sprightly encounter of wits between the two is reminiscent of the eighteenth-century comedy of manners, as is the absence of any moral consideration in the light-hearted telling of the tale.

We may pass over *The Making of a Gentleman* (1909) as being not a study of manners directly but of a middle-class family. A self-made man in blind love tries to give his children the "polish" he had been denied. When they turn out to be cads he learns that breeding cannot be bought in the open market. It is another example in comedy of the folly of putting the toga on plebeian shoulders. In *The Perplexed Husband* (1911) we are on surer ground. It is a satire on suffragism and the new freedom for woman, treated in a spirit of banter and with that touch of exaggeration so common in comedies of manners. Mr. Pelling, a practical business man, arrives home from a trip to find his wife under the influence of two "new thought" fanatics. He pretends that he too has caught the vision and brings an attractive typist into the house to convert to the higher life. His wife's jealousy of course dispels her delusions. Kalleia, the typist, is a very warm-blooded, human creature who seems distinctly out of key in this little piece of artifice. *The Clever Ones* (1914) ridicules different types of "intellectuals" in a middle-class home. The contrast between the affected mother and daughter and the common-sense father could have been employed for high comedy by other hands; in Sutro's it descended into farce.

By 1914 in *The Two Virtues* Sutro's slender art had become informed with a comic idea. We are once again within hail of our type of comedy. The play is pure funning, but shot through with glints of social criticism. The characters converse in that easy, bland, charming way that sophisticated comedy demands. Sutro has caught here the natural cadences of human speech. Jeffrey Panton is a dryly humorous, sentimental chap with a flair for historical research. He has long nursed the sorrow of a disappointment in love. The lady in question, now married, dotes upon his sentimental devotion. At her request he seeks to save her husband from an imagined intimacy with a Mrs. Guildford, who turns out to be a cultured lady with an unhappy past. An immediate friendship between Panton and the lady ensues, which ripens into love under the strenuous opposition of his sister, Lady Milligan, one of society's chosen daughters. Sutro has drawn the sister to the life—the podgy, strutting kind of dowager, of a mountainous self-importance. The pronouncement of the play that charity is a greater virtue than chastity is too lightly made to disturb its inherent mirth.

Sutro's post-war plays take us beyond the limits of our investigation. Suffice it to say they are farce or light social comedy each after its own kind, adding little to the playwright's reputation. The tenuity of so much of his work suggests the one-act play, in which he has written successfully, as his most happy medium for expression. *The Laughing Lady* (1922) and *Desperate Lovers* (1927) are comedies of a gay and heartless Mayfair. *Far Above Rubies* (1924) and *The Man with a Heart* (1925) are typical Sutro plays, well made, tartly satiric, skimming the surfaces of men and manners.

With the name of W. Somerset Maugham the twentieth-century English comedy of manners is most closely linked. The somber realism of his *A Man of Honour* (1903) hinted at a capacity for serious work which his long list of successful stage pieces has never verified. Having failed to please the public in that first endeavor, he turned deliberately to the light entertainment for which it was willing to pay. He has chosen to become a dramatic huckster taking his wares to market. He writes not so much about people as for people. As we think of his plays in the aggregate, we are impressed with the man's knack for being entertaining, but there is the feeling that he has never deemed it worth while to expend himself to any high end. Rather he has dextrously reassorted the stuff of the old dramatic lumber-rooms. The diagnostic habit of mind, to which his medical training might invite him, is seldom apparent as he sets forth the spiritual maladies of his "patients." He is a kind of stage journalist in his deftness of stroke and immediacy of appeal.

And yet, to the student of the manners comedy, the very absence of a warm humanity in Maugham's plays is a commendation. In many ways one senses in them the presence of Oscar Wilde. In him is that same hard, sharp depiction of the manners of a sophisticated society which the London playgoer is just clever enough to appreciate but not clever enough to participate in, if he could. Maugham's characters appear and reappear in his comedies in modified variations, never quite achieving three-dimensional reality. They talk with the insolent frankness of the smart set. They delight in epigram and repartee that are sometimes a trifle labored. Their persiflage is the froth of wit, not the rare distillment itself.

The chosen setting for the Maugham comedies is "polite" society. In his earlier performance he tends to treat it farcically or melodramatically; in his later work he emerges into unequivocal comedy of manners. His nearest approach to the type in his pre-war comedy is to be found in *Lady Frederick* (1907) and *Smith* (1909). In the former the author introduces us to that pleasure-seeking, migrant, cosmopolitan society whose habitat ranges from the Riviera to the Scottish Highlands. To that class belongs Lady Frederick Berolles, done for us in Maugham's best manner. She is a delicious Irish paradox—jubilant, defiant, caressing, dominant. Her past is not impeccable. She is, of course, swamped with debts, and yet she refuses to advantage herself of a scandalous secret in the Mereston family to marry the heir to their wealth. She sees, too, what a tragedy the disparity in their ages will some day become and shatters his illusions by making him witness to her morning rites at the dressing-table. The verbal fence and paradox in the dialogue is distinctly à la Wilde. It is a salt that sometimes loses its savor.

Smith is a more thoughtful play. In fact, the author's flagellation of the "tame cats" and childless women of society threatens to extinguish laughter. The young Rhodesian farmer can find in his sister's London set no woman whom he would choose as his mate. He finds at last in Smith, the housemaid, the womanhood he is seeking. As we have noted, the comedy is more than a picture of manners; it is, like *The Walls of Jericho,* an indictment. Smith's views on the social status of the servant are interesting to be compared to those of Barrie's Crichton. *Landed Gentry* (*Grace*), which appeared in 1910, is too distorted and cynically perverse a picture of county aristocracy to be within our field. The tyranny of caste and the double standard of morality for rich and for poor has been treated more temperately by Galsworthy.

The three farces written before *Smith* concern us little, not because of undue hilarity but because (except the first) they do not reflect manners. In *Jack Straw* (1908) we meet the Parker-Jenkinses, a parvenu family, whose exaggerated snobbery and vulgarity verge close on caricature. To satisfy a grudge, two of their "friends" palm off on them a waiter as a foreign peer. Even when they learn the deception, they are forced to continue the masquerade to save their face. Maugham has one last surprise for us in his bag. The waiter proves to be the archduke he was simulating. Charles Hawtrey excelled as the languid, unruffled Mr. Straw. In the same way the roguishness and April temperament of Marie Tempest made *Mrs. Dot* (1908) and *Penelope* (1909) the best of entertainment. The latter, like *What Every Wowan Knows,* tells how a wife cured her husband of a flirtation, not by opposition, but by complaisant acceptance. Maugham rings no new changes on an old theme. He is consistently the clever journeyman.

When Maugham wrote *Our Betters* (1917) and *The Circle* (1921) he achieved the full-fledged comedy of manners. The former lashes with contempt the American expatriate who buys his or her way into a London society which reprobates while it accepts. It is a sordid and ugly picture, limned in with hard, brittle strokes. Explicitly a comedy, the play is implicitly a terrifying tragedy. It wears a grin that is cadaverous on a second glance. The young American visitor, who revolts at the empty round of dissipation, is a stereotyped figure, whose function is to voice the protest of the play. Through him the author sits in judgment on his characters, and it is this moral consciousness that flaws the authenticity of the comedy as a specimen of the manners type.

With *The Circle,* as in *Home and Beauty* (1919) (*Too Many Husbands* in the United States), Maugham becomes more saturnine in spirit, as he sharpens his characterization and economizes his dialogue. *The Circle* abounds in the laughter of the comedy of manners, but the echo is sardonic. Elizabeth Champion-Cheney, a young wife with romantic notions about freedom from the conventions, is married, neither more nor less happily than thousands, to a priggish but good-hearted husband. When Teddie, a callow youth who exudes self-confidence, asks her to run away with him, she yields, because he offers her suffering, anxiety, and brute conquest. One might conjecture that the play is rising here to the note of idealism and spiritual emancipation of *A Doll's House,* but the play ends rather to the accompaniment of a shrug and a wry smile. "You never can tell. Youth must be served. Life is an endless circle. The 'Stop, Look, and Listen' signs in life are read only after the accident has happened." After a rereading of Maugham one queries what there is of the wit or wisdom of high comedy. As a comedian of manners has he done more than give back to his audiences their own traditional conceptions of high life? Does he carve out of the living granite or has he deftly pieced together quarry-chips?

Before leaving the comedy of manners as we have met it on the professional London stage, recognition must be paid briefly to the productions of Rudolf Besier and Cyril Harcourt (died 1924). *Don* (1909) by the former writer is a play of considerable literary merit and of a fresh originality. It tells of a quixotic, Shelley-like young visionary who befriends a lower-class married woman who is in great distress. He takes appalling liberties with the conventions but with the purest motives. When he brings her into his father's home (he is a Canon) for protection, the effect upon his family may be imagined. It is an incisive study in contrasts between idealism and a solemn respectability that loses sight of the larger charity in its veneration for half-truths. At the close the play deepens into something more than a presentation of manners. Besier's *Lady Patricia* (1911) has more of the dash and sparkle of light social comedy. In the garb of fantasy it satirizes dabblers in sentiment who have reached mature years. Lady Patricia is a Burne-Jones sort of woman—languorous, mellifluous, willowy, a living affectation. While she is playing at love with an amiable but very prosaic youth, her middle-aged husband is committing an equal folly with a very modern young woman of the neighborhood. Of course everything is adjusted according to the code of light comedy. The play is purely an artifice of the theatre, but it is adroitly done.[15]

In 1907 Harcourt's first play, *The Reformer,* given at a Vedrenne-Barker matinee at the Court, gave an adequate foretaste of the piquant, vivacious type of light drawing-room comedy which its author was to write. The entire group is reminiscent of *The Importance of Being Earnest* in frothiness of wit and satire and delightful inconsequence. They must be counted as something more than mere farce. In *The Reformer* a lady demands that on her marriage with a nobleman she shall remould his habits closer to her heart's desire. As her methods are foolish, she loses him. *A Pair of Silk Stockings* (1914) at the Criterion proved to be a good box-office attraction, having to do with a slangy smart set at a house party. In the first act amateur

[15] In the courtly environment of *Kings and Queens* (1915) Besier presents again his favorite contrast between the inhibited life and the life of realization. *The Prude's Fall* (1920), written with May Edgington, sets French tolerance over against English dogmatism in a sharply ironic comedy of manners that rivals in situation the Restoration comedy at its best.

theatricals appear again as a fertile source of comedy. The farcical theme in *A Lady's Name* (1916) of a woman novelist advertising for a husband for purposes of "copy" is informed with witty observations on class distinctions and social absurdities. No less smartly written is *A Place in the Sun* (1919), in which differences of caste between the county aristocracy and the tenant-farmer class are lightly ridiculed. Harcourt's skill in composition was due, in part at least, to his experience as an actor.

The experimental attempts to release the London stage from the constraints of commercialism (already referred to) had their counterparts in other sections of the Kingdom. In 1899 the Irish Literary Theatre was established in Dublin under the auspices of the National Literary Society (founded by William Butler Yeats) and chiefly by the united effort of Yeats, Edward Martyn, George Moore, and Lady Gregory. Through the initiative of Miss A. E. F. Horniman the movement found a theatrical home in 1903, and the Abbey Theatre became the first repertory playhouse in the English-speaking world.

With the encouragement which that theatre has given to the Irish folk-drama we are, of course, not concerned; we have only to recognize a distant connection of Martyn and Moore with our chosen topic. The comedy of manners has been practically non-extant in Ireland, for the life of the people is rural rather than urban. An assertive middle class, such as we have seen reflected in our English comedies, is lacking. Then, too, we must reckon with the turbulent social and political conditions that have so long prevailed. When Irish writers have not become absorbed into English life and thought, they have turned in earnest devotion to their own national and racial issues; there has not been in Ireland the leisurely and contented mind that can approach society with the careless gayety that the comedy of manners implies. It is therefore a question of circumstances and not of native aptitude; the Irish gift for a keen appraisal of personality for pungent satire, for wit and repartee, needs no exposition when we recall such names as Farquhar, Goldsmith, Sheridan, Wilde, and Shaw.

Edward Martyn was a man of wealth and education, who brought to the theatre sincerity of purpose, but lacked a sense of stage technique. Although a member of the landlord class, he did not share its views. His only approach to the comedy of manners was in his rather abortive comedy, *The Tale of a Town,* which first saw the footlights in Dublin in 1905. Its manner is naturalistic; its theme the snobbery and political corruption in an Irish town. One feels, as he reads it, the presence of the author of *An Enemy of the People.* It is a play which has felt the compulsion of reality but which could not dress reality in the habiliments of art. The characters fail to reach our hearts; their speech is stiff and unyielding. The author knows the landlord and politician classes of which he writes but is unable to evidence that knowledge in his dialogue. He girds too vehemently at social and political abuses to have realized the finer spirit of comedy. It is ironic that his Irish public should have hailed the play primarily for its propagandist value.

When Martyn's associates in the Literary Theatre deemed his comedy to be unsuited to their needs, he generously put the play into Moore's hands for revision. The result was *The Bending of the Bough* (1900). Both men were confessedly amateurs in the theatre, but if Moore did not bear so authentically the Irish stamp upon him, he possessed a literary gift which would not entirely forsake him even in an unfamiliar medium. The first act Moore kept virtually unchanged, but the latter four acts he has rewritten with clearer, sharper strokes, putting into the mouths of the characters lines that have a literary if they have not a dramatic virtue. The symbolism of the play in his hands becomes articulate. Northhaven, a poor and decadent town (Dublin), has bartered away its commercial advantages to its rich neighbor, Southhaven (London), in return for financial assistance and social patronage. The leader of the true Celtic patriots who are trying to restore the self-respect of Northhaven is Jasper Dean, who is engaged to the niece of Mayor Hardman of Southhaven. Millicent's fortune would be jeopardized should Dean's political program prevail. The lure of happiness with her and the luxury of Southhaven society life finally wear down his loyalty and he forsakes his life work. Moore's play is a thoughtful study in moral responsibility set against a political and social background, but it lacks gusto. It fails to assault our imagination. Its lifeblood pulsates feebly.[16]

[16] The previously written *The Strike at Arlingford* (1893) is also the story of a leader of men who renounces his principles for love and social advantage. As J. T. Grein observes, it is a drama " less of action than of psychological observation." It is by no means a social comedy, but it is full of implications of the life and manners of society.

Having inaugurated the Abbey Theatre movement so auspiciously, Miss Horniman sought to repeat her success in the Lancashire region of England. In 1908 she bought and remodeled the Gaiety Theatre in Manchester and put on a succession of short runs similar to those at the Court Theatre in London. She brought over Mr. Iden Payne from Dublin to direct the theatre, but hers was the vision and the initiative. It was her aim to give Manchester what she called a "Civilized Theatre," where a provincial city might enjoy the best of the English and foreign drama of the past as well as of the present. Having awakened a lively interest in the drama, she hoped then to build up by degrees a local school of playwrights who would reflect Lancashire life. The movement never achieved the homogeneity of a school, but should rather be called a concerted effort and an experiment. Although little felt outside the Manchester region, it brought into being an estimable peasant and middle-class drama, earnestly conceived, socially conscious, and abhorring everything artificial.

Outstanding in talent in this Manchester group was William Stanley Houghton, whose untimely death in 1913 left a dramatic career unfulfilled. Instinctively a rebel, he was also sufficiently an artist to acknowledge the discipline of his chosen art. As we should expect, Houghton's contribution to the comedy of manners is infused with the spirit of revolt. It concerns itself with ordinary people—not of London but of his own Lancashire country. His first two ventures in the field, *Independent Means* and *Marriages in the Making*, both of

1909, already give evidence of his gift for bringing his characters at once into intimate relation with his audience. Both have to do with suburban life as it falls under the scrutiny of an observant eye. In the former comedy, Edgar Forsyth comes from a well-to-do but ill-managed upper-middle-class home, where he has been trained for nothing except to wear the empty title of gentleman. When he marries Sidney, a spirited girl of advanced ideas, who insists on living her own life, a conflict of forces is inevitable. The play records the triumph of the wife, as it should, but grows rather thin in the last act. *Marriages in the Making* is almost devoid of plot, but once again we feel ourselves present in a smug suburban household, where the cant of "doing our duty" is counted unto them for righteousness. Houghton delights in his young people. Dolly Cartwright is twin-sister to the Sidney of the earlier comedy. Dolly, however, has this advantage—she discovered before, rather than after marriage, how priggish and conceited a badly reared young man can be.

The Younger Generation (1910) is the author's most successful play next to *Hindle Wakes*. Through it moves a sincerity that yet at no time impairs its comic complexion. Like *Misalliance* and *Milestones* it is a play about parents and children, and like his own preceding comedies, it inveighs against the bigotry that age so often breeds. The truth it pronounced that each generation must work out its own salvation was almost a platitude when the play was published. Arthur, Reggie, and Grace Kennion are forced into chronic fibbing by their parents' domination. It is the old story of love and intelligent sympathy not co-operating in the rearing of a family. After reprehending his children for lying, James Kennion is himself forced by them into a falsehood, in order that he may hold the moral victory he thinks he has gained. He and his more tolerant brother, Tom, who has never lost the viewpoint of youth, recall at once the two Mr. Wetherbys. Indeed Houghton reminds us of Hankin whenever he "takes a fall" out of the moral formalists of society. Houghton skilfully plays against each other the three generations, from staid grandmother to rebellious grandchildren; the old lady is as displeased with her son for his laxity as a parent as his children are for his own severity to them. The playwright does not attempt to settle the issues he has raised. He is perspicacious enough to see that the conflict between crabbed age and youth is as unending as it is inevitable. The radical of twenty becomes the reactionary of sixty when the years have taken their toll. In that fact rests the ironic, universal note of the play.

Partners (1911), an enlargement of *Fancy Free,* is Houghton's nearest approach to the true comedy of manners in its un-morality and complete surrender to the spirit of banter and badinage. It is an altogether delicious piece of funning about the exchange of flirtations between two married couples—a situation that would be most graceless were it not abandoned so utterly to the spirit of mirth. A critic said of it at the time, "It is a little gem, and it has all the elfin grace, the elusiveness, the unexpected turnings of Oscar Wilde." *The Hillarys* (1915) was completed by Harold Brighouse after Houghton's death. A class-proud country family, finding that the son has become smitten with the governess, try to substitute a bachelor uncle as her suitor. In the end she gives them both their *congé*. It is a more artificial contrivance than the earlier comedies.

Harold Brighouse also belongs to the drama of revolt. Although his plays about the Lancashire folk constitute but a small part of his total, they represent the best he has done. Social manners appear only as side lights on the middle-class provincial life which he so freshly depicts. *Odd Man Out* (1912) is an entertaining country-house comedy of modest attainments. Barbara has been reared by a dour, sanctimonious stepfather, who has brought her to think it her duty to marry a cousin of the same stripe. Her real father, a beloved vagabond, returns in time to confound the schemers and bestow upon her the man of her choice. *Garside's Career* (1914) is the story of a callow young Socialist, who gets elected to Parliament, is lured away by the glamor of society and almost makes a ruin of his career. His blatant self-esteem is Napoleonic. The play should be mentioned here only for the contrast between the manners of two social worlds which it affords—those of the working class and those of the aristocratic Mottram family. The latter are well presented. Lady Mottram is the typical haughty matron, but her son Freddie is individualized. He is just saved from foppishness by his rich sense of humor, which preserves his perspective on class distinctions.

In *Hobson's Choice* (New York, 1915, London, 1916) we gain an authentic picture of a hard-headed, practical

Lancashire family of the lower middle class. A domineering father sees his three daughters, whom he has tried to browbeat out of matrimony, leave him one by one to get married. In time he finds himself dependent on Maggie, the eldest, whose energy had been the secret of his business success. The play was deservedly popular for the genuineness of its characterization and the breeziness of its humor.

One other play by a Manchester playwright remains to be mentioned—*The Education of Mr. Surrage* (1912) by Allan Monkhouse, for many years on the editorial staff of the *Manchester Guardian.* Like the comedies of Brighouse it glimpses manners rather than pictures them. Mr. Surrage is a wealthy widower who has retired to his country estate. His children bring into his sedate little world a group of Bohemians who disturb most profoundly his conventional views of life. Though baffled, he endeavors to understand his guests, and in that attempt he finds the stimulation that rejuvenates his mind.

IX

A WORD IN GENERAL

WE have traced the comedy of manners from its brilliant exemplification in *The School for Scandal* down to the beginning of the Great War in 1914. Between Sheridan and Robertson we could discover only sporadic instances of its existence, and those were of the eighteenth-century tradition. With Robertson the type revived, but passed into the keeping of the middle class. At the close of the century we noted in Wilde and in certain of the plays of Jones, Pinero, and Carton an efflorescence of high comedy, in which the manners of the upper classes were treated without deprecation and without moral implication. In the opening years of our present century the form continued to maintain its identity between the drama of social ideas on the one hand and the very profuse but mediocre body of popular plays on the other.

As the awful pall of war shut down upon our dramatic landscape, we bring our study to a close. Many of the forces at work for a more enlightened drama were disintegrated by that catastrophe. The continuity of dramatic endeavor was irrevocably interrupted. The normal forms of comedy gave way to somber tragedy or hectic farce. Few of the older writers of comedy regained their stride after the war; some of the younger ones it blotted out, others like Sutro and Maugham continued to be prolific. In the main, however, we must entrust the comedy of upper- or middle-class manners to other hands. As heretofore, it appears in a variety of blends: in Frederick Lonsdale's *Aren't We All* and *The High Road* it runs true to form in its ironic and sophisticated inheritances from Wilde, Shaw, and Maugham; in A. A. Milne's *Mr. Pim Passes By* and *The Dover Road* it strays into whimsicality; in the *I'll Leave It to You, The Young Idea,* and *Hay Fever* of Noel Coward it becomes an ironic, ultra-modern comedy of bad manners; in Ashley Dukes's *The Man with a Load of Mischief* it is once again a costume play, but intellectual as well as romantic; in C. K. Munro's *At Mrs. Beam's* and *Storm* it becomes a realistic and yet fantastic photograph of petty, spiritually bankrupt middle-class lives; and in Eden Phillpotts' *St. George and the Dragons* it presents a *tranche de vie* of Dartmoor society from farmer to county aristocrat.

Let us conclude with a few observations:

I. It is the province of comedy in general to reflect the surface phases of life, the ever-changing modes and habits of society. Every decade of the nineteenth century in England has its own peculiar interest for the social historian, and yet in the comedy of that century we find no adequate, representative presentation of the social scene in town or country, in high life or in humble life. The city of London, a veritable microcosm of human society, was a constant challenge to the imagination, but its resources were scarcely tapped.

II. The comedy of manners in its present sense, as we defined it at the outset, does not flourish in English soil. John Palmer speaks of it as "the natural flower of the civilized life of leisured and clever people, as it reveals itself upon the surface." He says that it is a display, a detached commentary, rather than an identification of the author with his world. This the English comedy of manners has rarely achieved. The element of satire is too generally present, not as an intellectual exercise but as a moral corrective or an indictment of that which is unsocial in life. A social conscience supplants a social consciousness.

III. Audiences. The English temperament ill adjusts itself to the impersonal, intellectual type of comedy, which does not touch the heart or stir the soul. Congreve wrote in the rarefied atmosphere of abstract comedy, but Vanbrugh and Cibber were more truly English when they began to identify themselves with their characters and their action, and to tincture their comedies with feeling. The comedy of manners requires an audience that is morally and intellectually emancipated, so that it may laugh not only at the characters upon the stage but laugh at itself as well. "True comedy," as Ludwig Lewisohn affirms, "is a test both of the inner freedom of the mind and the outer freedom of the society in which men live." Only under these conditions can we surrender ourselves to the Comic Spirit and find in a play the universal solvent for all our illusions and disillusions.

John Palmer's remarks on this subject in the *Saturday Review*[1] are worthy of brief paraphrase and quotation. The dearth of a modern comedy comparable to that of Elizabethan and Restoration England may be laid at

[1] CXVII (1914), 334, 366.

the door of our intellectual humbuggery and cowardice. We refuse to accept virtue without sentiment and vice without indignation or squeamishness. Our comedies are emasculate because they are apologetic. "The modern attempt to present life in terms of a middle-class drawing-room is only comparable with the attempt to make Rabelais sweet and wholesome." We do not have in our theatres that free expression of ideas which is the concomitant of good manners and the *sine qua non* of polite comedy. "Free expression will come back into English comedy when free expression comes back into the drawing-rooms of our playgoing classes." Such an expression will avoid both pruriency and prudishness. We must have a middle-class utterance that is as unabashed as that found in the lowest and highest circles. "People must learn to live their comedies before they can expect to see them in the theatres."

IV. Playwrights. With the sole exception of Wilde those who have essayed the modern English comedy of manners do not write as one to the manner born, but perforce from hearsay.[2] That section of the upper class which delights in display and self-advertisement finds its way readily into social comedy, but it is not

[2] Wilde excepted again, England's titled class has contributed to the modern drama no comedy of manners of distinction. Lady Violet Greville has been already noted. Sir William Young's little volume of dramatic sketches, *Scenes from Society* (1890), is trivial. The *Borrowed Plumes* (1909) of Lady Randolph Churchill treats of a middle class which she knew only adventitiously instead of her own world which she knew intimately. Her political play, *The Bill* (1915), may be called a clever piece of writing, but its construction betrays an amateur's hand. In contradistinction, the experience of Sir Charles L. Young (died 1887) as an actor aided him in fitting his plays to stage usage, but he had nothing to say.

representative. The true British aristocrat of the old school does not get himself talked about. To be sure, the aristocracy is no longer veiled behind privilege; it is accessible through the channels of business and society, but such contacts are after all casual. Even if the writer for the theatre learns something of the London life of titled folk through gossip and the press, what does he know of them in their country homes, where they are at their intimate best and worst? The country house, playing as it does so large a part in the life of the well-born, has rarely been given faithful representation on the stage.

V. Actors. Those who impersonate characters from high life on the stage too often lack the good breeding which carries conviction. They may be correct in surface deportment, but they cannot simulate an unconscious ease and a patrician air. The attempt is superficial smartness merely.

VI. The comedy of manners will always persist as the expression of a small, select, unrepresentative group in society—an aristocracy of breeding and cultivation as well as of birth. As long as the English gentleman continues to live by an established code the comedy of manners will be written. His observance of that code will be reflected in its graces; his blind or affected veneration for the code will be mirrored in its absurdities. This type of comedy demands a unique and selective audience—one proud of its birthright, cultivated in the arts and graces of society, sophisticated and of restrained emotions. It wears a surface nonchalance but is intellectually honest.[3] It regards conversation as a fine art and cherishes its friends not so much for what they do as how they do it. It has tasted life in many cups and has found them all good. And finally, it is an audience in which women are respected for their intelligence. For such an audience Etherege and Congreve wrote, and today we are nearer the social conditions that will duplicate it than at any time since the eighteenth century. The comedy of manners occupies a small niche in the temple of Thespis, but its candle burns for its devotees with a hard and gem-like flame, without smoke and without the fragrance of incense.

[3] "Before a nation may produce fashionable comedy it must produce a class to whom polish is not an acquired but a natural attribute. It must produce a class, first and foremost, so certain of its traditions and position that it can laugh at itself, for save it can laugh at itself, it cannot persuade audiences to laugh with it." G. J. Nathan, *Art of the Night*, p. 25.

BIBLIOGRAPHY

History—Dramatic

Anonymous. " The Drama." *Fraser's Magazine,* XXIX (1844). 181–186.

Anonymous. " The Drama." *Blackwood's,* LXXIX (1856). 209–231.

Anonymous. " Dramatic Register for 1853." *Quarterly Review,* XCV (1854). 71–88.

Anonymous. " The New Drama." *Quarterly Review,* CLXXXII (1895). 399–428.

Anonymous. " The Present Aspect of the London Stage." *Temple Bar,* XL (1874). 470–477.

Anonymous. " The Present State of the English Stage." *Temple Bar,* XXXIII (1871). 456–468.

Anonymous. " The Stage and Its Prospects." *Fraser's Magazine,* XLI (1850). 69–75.

Anonymous. " State of the Acted Drama." *Fraser's Magazine,* XXXVIII (1848). 41–48.

Anonymous. " The State of the Stage." *Fraser's Magazine,* XVII (1838). 156–170.

Anonymous. *Gentleman's Magazine,* LXIX (1799). 3–5.

Archer, Wm. " Drama in the Doldrums." *Fortnightly Review,* LVIII (1892). 146–167.

Archer, Wm. *The Old Drama and the New.* London, 1923.

Archer, Wm. " The Theatrical Situation." *Fortnightly Review,* XCIV (1910). 736–750.

Barnes, J. H. " The Drama of Today." *Nineteenth Century,* LXIII (1908). 305–310.

Bates, K. L. and Godfrey, L. B. *English Drama: a Working Basis.* Boston, 1896.

Bernbaum, Ernest. *The Drama of Sensibility, 1696–1780.* Boston, 1915.

Boaden, James. *Memoirs of the Life of John Philip Kemble, Including a History of the Stage from the Time of Garrick to the Present Period,* 2 v. London, 1825.

Borsa, Mario. *The English Stage of Today.* London, 1908.

Boucicault, Dion. " Decline of the Drama." *North American Review,* CXXV (1877). 235–245.

Boyd, Ernest A. *The Contemporary Drama of Ireland.* Boston, 1917.

Buchanan, Robt. *Dramatic Notes, a Chronicle of the London Stage, 1879–1882.* London, 1883.

Cox, J. E. *The Rise of Sentimental Comedy.* Olney, Ill., 1926.

Dickinson, T. H. *Contemporary Drama of England.* Boston, 1922.

Dobrée, B. *Restoration Comedy, 1660–1720.* Oxford, 1924.

Filon, Augustin. *The English Stage, an Account of the Victorian Drama.* London, 1897.

Hankin, St. John. " Puritanism and the English Stage." *Fortnightly Review,* LXXXVI (1906). 1055–1064.

Harrison, Frederic. " The Revival of the Drama." *Forum,* XVI (1893). 184–194.

Henderson, Archibald. *The Changing Drama.* New York, 1914.

Herford, C. H. *A Sketch of the History of the English Drama in Its Social Aspects.* Cambridge (Eng.), 1881.

Krutch, J. W. *Comedy and Conscience after the Restoration.* New York, 1924. (Columbia University Studies in English and Comparative Literature, v. 33.)

Lewes, G. H. " Regeneration of the Drama." *Westminster Review,* XXXVII (1842). 38–51.

Lewisohn, Ludwig. *The Modern Drama.* New York, 1915.

Lynch, K. M. *Social Mode of Restoration Comedy.* New York, 1926. (Univ. of Mich. Publications of Language and Literature, v. 3.)

Malone, Andrew E. *The Irish Drama.* London, 1929.

Morgan, A. E. *Tendencies of Modern English Drama.* New York, 1924.

Nettleton, G. H. *English Drama of the Restoration and Eighteenth Century* New York, 1914.

Nicoll, Allardyce. *British Drama.* New York, 1925.

Nicoll, Allardyce. *A History of Early Eighteenth Century Drama, 1700–1750.* Cambridge (Eng.), 1925.

Nicoll, Allardyce. *A History of Late Eighteenth Century Drama, 1750–1800.* Cambridge (Eng.), 1927.

Nicoll, Allardyce. *Restoration Drama, 1660–1700.* Cambridge (Eng.), 1923.

North, C. " The Drama." *Blackwood's,* XVIII (1825). 240–246.

North, C. " On the Drama." *Blackwood's,* XI (1822). 440–448.

Palmer, John. *The Comedy of Manners.* London, 1913.

Palmer, John. *The Future of the Theatre.* London, 1913.

Perry, H. T. *The Comic Spirit in Restoration Drama.* New Haven, London, 1925.

" Philo-Dramaticus." " On the Present State of the Stage." *Blackwood's,* XVII (1825). 727–731.

Pollock, Walter. " A Glance at the Stage." *National Review,* V (1885). 646–651.

Poole, John. " Processions." *London Magazine,* VI (1822). 37–48.

Proelss, Robt. *Geschichte des Neueren Dramas,* 3 v. Leipzig, 1881–3.

Schelling, F. E. *English Drama.* London, 1914.

Scott, Clement. *The Drama of Yesterday and Today,* 2 v. London, 1899.

Stahl, Ernst Leopold. *Das Englische Theater im 19 Jahrhundert.* München, Berlin, 1914.

Stauffer, Ruth M. *The Progress of Drama through the Centuries.* New York, 1927.

Stuart, Donald C. *The Development of Dramatic Art.* New York, 1928.

Thorndike, Ashley H. *English Comedy.* New York, 1929.

Tree, H. B. " Some Aspects of the Drama of Today." *North American Review,* CLXIV (1897). 66–74.

Waterhouse, Osborn. "The Development of English Sentimental Comedy in the Eighteenth Century." *Anglia,* XXX (1907). 137–172.

Watson, E. B. *Sheridan to Robertson.* Cambridge, Mass., 1926.

Wedmore, Fred'k. "Position of the Drama in England." *Nineteenth Century,* XLIV (1898). 224–233.

Weygandt, Cornelius. *Irish Plays and Playwrights.* Boston, 1913.

Wyndham, Charles. "Modern Tendencies of Comedy." *North American Review,* CXLIX (1889). 607–615.

Wynne, Arnold. *The Growth of English Drama.* Oxford, 1914.

History—Theatrical

Anonymous. "Dramatic Reform—Classification of Theatres." *Edinburgh Review,* LXXVIII (1843). 382–401.

Anonymous. "Music-Halls versus the Drama." *Cornhill,* XV (1867). 119–128.

Baker, H. B. *History of the London Stage and Its Famous Players, 1576–1903.* London, 1904.

Barker, Harley Granville. *The Exemplary Theatre.* London, 1922.

Broadbent, R. J. *Annals of the Liverpool Stage from the Earliest Period to the Present Time.* Liverpool, 1908.

Broughton, F. C. "Modern Audiences." *Theatre* (Lond.), I, n. s. (1878). 36–38.

Bunn, Alfred. *The Stage, Both Before and Behind the Curtain,* 2 v. London, 1840.

Cheney, Sheldon. *The Theatre. Three Thousand Years of Drama, Acting and Stagecraft.* London, New York, 1929.

Doran, John. *Annals of the English Stage,* 3 v. New York, London, 1888.

Doran, John. *In and About Drury Lane,* 2 v. London, 1881.

Fitzgerald, Percy. *A New History of the Stage from the Restoration to the Liberty of the Theatres in Connection with the Patent Houses.* London, 1882.

Fowell, F. and Palmer, F. *The Censorship in England.* London, 1913.

G. M. G. *The Stage Censor: an Historical Sketch, 1544–1907.* London, 1908.

Hamilton, Cicely and Baylis, Lilian. *The Old Vic.* New York, n. d.

Hastings, Chas. *The Theatre: Its Development in France and England.* London, 1901.

Hollingshead, John. *Gaiety Chronicles.* London, 1898.

Howe, P. P. *The Repertory Theatre: a Record and a Criticism.* London, 1910.

The Incorporated Stage Society—Ten Years, 1899 to 1909. London, 1909.

Knight, Joseph. *History of the English Stage during the Reign of Victoria.* London, 1901.

MacCarthy, Desmond. *The Court Theatre, 1904–1907.* London, 1907.

Maude, Cyril. *The Haymarket Theatre, Some Records and Reminiscences.* London, 1903.

Nicholson, Watson. *The Struggle for a Free Stage in London.* Boston, New York, 1906.

Nicoll, Allardyce. *The Development of the Theatre; a Study of Theatrical Art from the Beginnings to the Present Day.* London, 1927.

Oliver, D. E. *The English Stage: Its Origin and Modern Developments.* London, 1912.

Pollock, Lady. "Attitude of Audiences." *Theatre* (Lond.), I, n. s. (1880). 81–83.

Sharp, R. F. *A Short History of the English Stage from Its Beginnings to the Summer of the Year 1908.* London, 1909.

Stoker, Bram. "The Censorship of Stage Plays." *Nineteenth Century,* LXVI (1909). 975–989.

Vernon, Frank. *The Twentieth Century Theatre.* Boston, New York [1924].

Wedmore, Fred'k. "The Theatrical Revival." *Nineteenth Century,* XIII (1883). 217–228.

Wyndham, Henry Saxe. *Annals of Covent Garden Theatre from 1732 to 1897,* 2 v. London, 1906.

MEMOIRS AND REMINISCENCES OF ACTORS, PLAYWRIGHTS, MANAGERS, ETC.

Adolphus, John. *Memoirs of John Bannister,* 2 v. London, 1839.

Archer, Frank. *An Actor's Notebooks.* London, n. d.

Bancroft, Sir S. B. *Empty Chairs.* London, 1925.

Bancroft, Marie and Squire. *Recollections of Sixty Years.* London, New York, 1909.

Barnes, J. H. *Forty Years on the Stage.* New York, 1915.

[Barrington, Rutland.] *Rutland Barrington—by Himself, a Record of Thirty-five Years' Experience on the English Stage.* London, 1908.

Bettany, Lewis, ed. *Edward Jerningham and His Friends. A Series of Eighteenth Century Letters.* New York, 1919.

Boucicault, Dion. "Debut of a Dramatist." *North American Review,* CXLVIII (1889). 454–463.

Boucicault, Dion. "Early Days of a Dramatist." *North American Review,* CXLVIII (1889). 584–593.

Brookfield, C. H. E. *Random Reminiscences.* London, 1902.

Burnand, Sir F. C. *Records and Reminiscences, Personal and General,* 2 v. London, 1904.

Calvert, Adelaide H. *Sixty-eight Years on the Stage.* London, 1911.

Carr, Alice Vansittart. *Mrs. J. Comyns Carr's Reminiscences.* London, 1925.

Coleman, John. *Fifty Years of an Actor's Life,* 2 v. New York, 1904.

Coleman, John. *Players and Playwrights I Have Known: a Review of the English Stage from 1840 to 1880,* 2 v. London, 1888.

Cornwallis-West, Mrs. George. *Reminiscences of Lady Randolph Churchill.* New York, 1908.

Cumberland, Richard. *Memoirs of Richard Cumberland.* New York, 1806, London, 1807.

Desmond, Shaw. *London Nights in the Gay Nineties.* New York, 1928.

Fitzgerald, Percy H. *Memoirs of an Author,* 2 v. London, 1895.

Forbes-Robertson, Sir Johnston. *A Player under Three Reigns.* London, 1925.

Greville, Lady Violet. *Vignettes of Memory.* London, n. d.

Hall, Samuel C. *Retrospect of a Long Life.* New York, 1883.

Hare, John. "Reminiscences and Reflections." *Strand,* XXXV, XXXVI (1908).

Hawtrey, Chas. *The Truth at Last.* Boston, 1924.

Hibbert, H. G. *Fifty Years of a Londoner's Life.* London, 1916.

Hibbert, H. G. *A Playgoer's Memories.* London, 1920.

[Holcroft, Thos.] *Memoirs of the Late Thomas Holcroft, Written by Himself and Continued to the Time of his Death.* . . . London, 1852.

Hollingshead, John. *My Lifetime.* London, 1895.

James, Henry. *The Middle Years.* New York, 1917.

Jupp, J. *The Gaiety Stage Door. Thirty Years' Reminiscences of the Theatre.* London, 1923.

Langtry, Lillie. *The Days I Knew.* London, 1925.

Lennox, Lord William Pitt. *Celebrities I Have Known, with Episodes Political, Social, Sporting and Theatrical,* 4 v. London, 1876.

Mathews, Mrs. A. J. *Memoirs of Charles Mathews, Comedian,* 4 v. Philadelphia, 1838–39.

[Maude, Cyril.] *Behind the Scenes with Cyril Maude, by Himself.* London, 1927.

Maude, Cyril. *Lest I Forget, Being the Reminiscences of Social and Dramatic Life in England and America.* New York, 1928.

Millward, Jesse. *Myself and Others.* London, 1923.

Moore, Eva. *Exits and Entrances.* New York, 1923.

Newton, Henry C. *Cues and Curtain Calls.* London, 1927.

[O'Keefe, John.] *Recollections of the Life of John O'Keefe, Written by Himself,* 2 v. London, 1826.

[Oxberry, Wm.] *Oxberry's Dramatic Biography and Histrionic Anecdotes,* 6 v. London, 1825–26.

Pearce, C. E. *The Jolly Duchess. Harriott Mellon, Afterwards Mrs. Coutts and the Duchess of St. Albans. A Sixty Years' Gossipping Record of the Stage and Society (1777 to 1837)*. New York [1915].

Planché, J. R. *Recollections and Reflections.* London, 1872.

Pollock, Sir Frederick, ed. *Macready's Reminiscences, and Selections from His Diaries and Letters.* New York, 1875.

[Reynolds, Frederick.] *The Life and Times of Frederick Reynolds, Written by Himself,* 2 v. London, 1826.

Robins, Edward. *Echoes of the Playhouse, Reminiscences of Some Past Glories of the English Stage.* New York, 1895.

Ryley, S. W. *The Itinerant; or, Memoirs of an Actor,* 2 v. London, 1817–27. New York, 1810.

Scott, Mrs. Clement. *Old Days in Bohemian London.* New York, n. d.

Sims, G. R. *My Life: Sixty Years' Recollection of Bohemian London.* London, 1916.

Skinner, Otis. *Footlights and Spotlights, Recollections of My Life on the Stage.* Indianapolis, 1924.

Sothern, E. H. *The Melancholy Tale of Me.* New York, 1916.

Stirling, Edward. *Old Drury Lane: Fifty Years' Recollections of an Author, Actor and Manager,* 2 v. London, 1881.

Stoddard, R. H., ed. *Personal Reminiscences.* New York, 1874.

Tweedie, Mrs. Alec. *Behind the Footlights.* London, 1904.

Vandenhoff, George. *Leaves from an Actor's Notebook.* New York, 1860.

Vincent, W. T. *Recollections of Fred Leslie.* London, 1894.

Ward, Genevieve and Whiteing, Richard. *Both Sides of the Curtain.* London, 1918.

Warde, Frederick. *Fifty Years of Make-believe.* New York, 1920.

Watson, Alfred E. T. *A Sporting and Dramatic Career.* London, 1918.

Winter, Wm. *Other Days, Being Chronicles and Memories of the Stage.* New York, 1908.

Winter, Wm. *Shadows of the Stage,* 3 v. New York, 1893–95.

Winter, Wm. *Vagrant Memories, Being Further Recollections of Other Days.* New York, 1915.

Wood, W. B. *Personal Recollections of the Stage, Embracing Notices of Actors, Authors and Auditors, During a Period of Forty Years.* Philadelphia, 1855.

[Yates, Edmund H.] *Edmund Yates: His Recollections and Experiences,* 2 v. London, 1884.

Biography and Criticism of Actors

Ainger, Alfred. *Lectures and Essays,* 2 v. London, 1905.

Allen, Percy. *The Stage Life of Mrs. Stirling.* New York, n. d.

Anderson, J. R. *An Actor's Life.* London, 1902.

Archer, Wm., ed. *Eminent Actor Series.* London, New York, 1891.

Beerbohm, Max. *Herbert Beerbohm Tree.* London, 1920.

Broadley, A. M. and Melville, Lewis. *The Beautiful Lady Craven.* New York, 1914.

[Cibber, Colley.] *An Apology for the Life of Mr. Colley Cibber, ...* London, 1740. (With Notes and Supplement by Robert W. Lowe. London, 1889.)

Cole, J. W. *Life and Theatrical Times of Charles Kean, Including a Summary of the English Stage for the Last Fifty Years, . . .* 2 v. London, 1859.

Cran, Mrs. George. *Herbert Beerbohm Tree.* New York, 1907.

Fyles, Franklin. *The Theatre and Its People.* New York, 1900.

Fyvie, John. *Comedy Queens of the Georgian Era.* London, 1906.

The Georgian Era: Memoirs of Most Eminent Persons Who Have Flourished in Great Britain . . . George I–George IV, 4 v. London, 1832.

Goddard, Arthur. *Players of the Period,* 2 v. London, 1891.

Jerrold, Clare. *The Story of Dorothy Jordan.* New York, 1914.

Lamb, Chas. "The Old Actors." *London Magazine,* V (1822). 305–311.

McCarthy, Justin. *Portraits of the Sixties.* New York, 1903.

Marston, J. W. *Our Recent Actors: Being Recollections Critical, and in Many Instances Personal,* 2 v. London, 1888.

Mathews, Mrs. [Anne]. *Life and Correspondence of Charles Mathews, the Elder, Comedian.* London, 1860.

Matthews, J. B. and Hutton, Lawrence. *Actors and Actresses of Great Britain and the United States, from the Days of David Garrick to the Present Time,* 5 v. New York, 1886.

[Munden, T. S.] *Memoirs of Joseph Shepherd Munden, by His Son.* London, 1846.

Pascoe, C. E., ed. *The Dramatic List.* London, 1879.

Peake, Rich. B. *Memoirs of the Colman Family.* London, 1841.

Pearce, C. E. *Madame Vestris and Her Times.* New York, 1923.

Pemberton, T. E. *John Hare, Comedian.* London, 1895.

Pemberton, T. E. *The Kendals.* London, 1900.

Pemberton, T. E. *Memoir of Edward Askew Sothern (1830–1889).* London, 1889.

Pemberton, T. E. *Sir Charles Wyndham, a Biography.* London, 1904.

Phelps, W. May and Robertson, John Forbes. *The Life and Life Work of Samuel Phelps.* London, 1886.

Raymond, George. *Memoirs of Robert William Elliston, Comedian,* 2 v. London, 1846.

Russell, W. C. *Representative Actors. . . .* London, n. d.

Shore, Florence T. *Sir Charles Wyndham.* London, New York, 1908.

Smythe, Arthur J. *The Life of William Terriss, Actor.* Westminster, 1898.

Strang, Lewis C. *Players and Plays of the Last Quarter Century,* 2 v. Boston, 1902–03.

Wemyss, F. C. *Theatrical Biography of Eminent Actors and Authors.* New York, n. d.

Whitton, Joseph. *Wags of the Stage.* Philadelphia, 1902.

Whyte, Frederic. *Actors of the Century.* London, 1898.

Biography and Criticism of Playwrights

Anonymous. " Right Hon. Richard Brinsley Sheridan." *Gentleman's Magazine,* LXXXVI (1816). 81–86, 177–182.

Andrews, Charlton. *The Drama Today.* Philadelphia, 1913.
Archer, Wm. *English Dramatists of Today.* London, 1882.
Archer, Wm. *Real Conversations.* London, 1904.
Armstrong, C. F. *Shakespeare to Shaw.* London, 1913.
Benjamin, P. "Sheridan Knowles." *North American Review,* XL (1835). 141–150.
Brown, Edith A. *W. S. Gilbert.* London, 1907.
Cooke, Wm. *Memoirs of the Life and Writings of Samuel Foote,* 3 v. London, 1805.
Cunliffe, J. W. *Modern English Playwrights.* London, New York, 1927.
Dark, Sidney and Grey, Rowland. *W. S. Gilbert: His Life and Letters.* London, 1923.
Dukes, Ashley. *Modern Dramatists.* Chicago, 1912.
Dukes, Ashley. *The Youngest Drama, Studies of Fifty Dramatists.* Chicago, 1924.
Edgar, Pelham. *Henry James, Man and Author.* Boston, New York, 1927.
Fitzgerald, Percy H. *The Savoy Opera and the Savoyards.* London, 1894.
Fitzgerald, Percy H. *Samuel Foote: a Biography.* London, 1910.
Fitzgerald, Percy H. *The Sheridans,* 2 v. London, n. d.
Fitzgerald, S. J. A. *Dickens and the Drama.* London, 1910.
Foot, Jessé. *The Life of Arthur Murphy.* London, 1811.
Friswell, J. H. *T. W. Robertson.* London, 1870. (Modern Men of Letters.)
Fyfe, H. *Arthur Wing Pinero, Playwright.* London, 1902.
Godwin, A. H. *Gilbert and Sullivan. A Critical Appreciation of the Savoy Opera.* London, 1926.
Goldberg, Isaac. *The Story of Gilbert and Sullivan.* New York, 1928.
Hale, jr., E. E. *Dramatists of Today.* New York, 1905.
Hamelius, P. *A. W. Pinero u. das Englische Drama der Jetztzeit.* Brüssel, 1900.
Harris, Frank. *Contemporary Portraits,* ser. 1. New York, 1916.

Hazlitt, Wm. "The Life of Thomas Holcroft." Collected Works, II. 1–280. London, 1902.

Henderson, Archibald. *European Dramatists.* Cincinnati, 1914.

Hind, C. L. *Authors and I.* New York, 1921.

Hind, C. L. *More Authors and I.* New York, 1922.

Hopkins, R. T. *Oscar Wilde, a Study of the Man and His Work.* London, 1913.

Howe, P. P. *Dramatic Portraits.* London, 1913.

Hughes, Thos. "In Memoriam, Tom Taylor." *Living Age,* CXLVI (1880). 802–805.

Ingleby, L. C. *Oscar Wilde, a Study.* London, 1907.

Jay, Harriett. *Robert Buchanan, Some Account of His Life, His Life-Work and His Literary Friendships.* London, 1903.

Jerrold, W. Blanchard. *Life and Literary Remains of Douglas Jerrold.* London, Boston, 1859.

Jerrold, Walter. *Douglas Jerrold, Dramatist and Wit,* 2 v. London, 1914.

Kenilworth, W. W. *A Study of Oscar Wilde.* New York, 1912.

Kennedy, J. M. *English Literature, 1880–1905.* London, 1912.

Littlewood, S. R. *Mrs. Inchbald and Her Circle.* London, 1921.

[Lytton, Earl.] *Life of Edward Bulwer, First Lord Lytton, by His Grandson, the Earl of Lytton,* 2 v. London, 1913.

Lytton, Henry A. *The Secrets of a Savoyard.* London, 1922.

Mais, S. P. B. *Some Modern Authors.* New York, 1923.

Melville, Lewis. *William Makepeace Thackeray, a Biography,* 2 v. London, 1910.

[Meredith, W. M.] *Letters of George Meredith, Collected and Edited by His Son,* 2 v. New York, 1912.

Monkhouse, Allan. *Books and Plays.* London, 1894.

Moore, George. "Our Dramatists and Their Literature." *Fortnightly Review,* LII (1889). 620–632.

Murray, Henry. *Robert Buchanan, a Critical Appreciation.* London, 1901.

Pemberton, T. E. *Charles Dickens and the Stage.* London, 1888.

Pemberton, T. E. *The Life and Writings of T. W. Robertson.* London, 1893.

Phelps, W. L. *Essays on Modern Dramatists.* New York, 1921.

Pinero, Arthur W. *Robert Louis Stevenson as a Dramatist.* New York, 1914. (Columbia University Dramatic Museum Publications, ser. 1, v. 4.)

" Q " [Thomas Purnell]. *Dramatists of the Present Day.* London, 1871.

Ransome, Arthur. *The Life of Oscar Wilde, a Critical Study.* London, 1912.

[Richards, J. M.] *Life of John Oliver Hobbes, Told in Her Correspondence with Numerous Friends. . . .* New York, 1911.

[Robertson, T. W.] *The Principal Dramatic Works of T. W. Robertson. With Memoir by His Son,* 2 v. London, 1889.

Sanders, L. C. *Life of Richard Brinsley Sheridan.* London, n. d.

Scott, Dixon. *Men of Letters.* New York, 1923.

Sherard, R. H. *Oscar Wilde.* London, 1906.

Sherard, R. H. *The Real Oscar Wilde.* London, 1915.

Sherman, Stuart P. *Critical Woodcuts.* New York, London, 1926.

Sichel, Walter. *Sheridan from New and Original Material . . .,* 2 v. London, 1909.

Stoecker, Willibald. " Pinero's Dramen: Studien ueber Motive, Charaktere und Technik." *Anglia,* XXXV (1912). 1–79.

Sutton, Graham. *Some Contemporary Dramatists.* London, 1924.

Symons, Arthur. *Studies in Prose and Verse.* London, 1910.

Teichmann, Hans. *Henry Arthur Jones's Dramen.* Giessen, 1913.

Walbrook, H. M. *Gilbert and Sullivan Opera: a History and a Comment.* London, 1922.

Walsh, Townsend. *The Career of Dion Boucicault.* New York, 1915. (Publications of Dunlap Society, ser. 3, v. 1.)

Williams, Harold. *Modern English Writers.* New York, 1919.

Williams, S. T. *Richard Cumberland, His Life and Dramatic Works.* New Haven, 1917.

Dramatic Essays and Criticism

Agate, J. E. *Buzz, Buzz! Essays of the Theatre.* London, 1917.

Agate, J. E. *The Contemporary Theatre, 1923.* London, 1924.

Anonymous. " Animadversions on the Moral Tendency of *The School for Scandal.*" *Gentleman's Magazine,* XLVIII (1778). 57–59.

Anonymous. " Beauties of the Living Dramatists." *London Magazine,* V (1822). 27, 137, 253, 362, 436.

Archer, Wm. *About the Theatre.* London, 1886.

Archer, Wm. and Lowe, W. E., ed. *Dramatic Essays,* 3 v. London [1894–96].

Archer, Wm. " Stage and Literature." *Fortnightly Review,* LVII (1892). 219–232.

Arnold, Matthew. *Letters of an Old Playgoer.* New York, 1919. (Columbia University Dramatic Museum Publications, ser. 4, v. 4.)

Austin, Alfred. " Divorce between Literature and Stage." *National Review,* II (1884). 680–694.

Bancroft, Squire. " Dramatic Thoughts: Retrospective—Anticipative." *Fortnightly Review,* LXXXIII (1905). 933–945.

Barnes, J. H. " An Actor's Views on Plays and Play-writing." *Nineteenth Century,* LXIV (1908). 461–468.

Beerbohm, Max. *Around Theatres.* London, 1924.

Buchanan, Rob't. *A Look Round Literature.* London, 1887.

Buchanan, Rob't. " Modern Drama and Its Minor Critics." *Contemporary Review,* LVI (1889). 908–925.

Chandler, F. W. *Aspects of Modern Drama.* New York, 1922.

Cook, Dutton. *A Book of the Play,* 2 v., 2d ed. London, 1876.

Cook, Dutton. *Hours with the Players.* London, 1883.

Cook, Dutton. *Nights at the Play.* London, 1883.

Courtney, W. L. *Old Saws and Modern Instances.* London, 1919.

Crawford, B. V. " High Comedy in Terms of Restoration Practice." *Philological Quarterly,* VIII (1929). 339–347.

Cumberland, Gerald. *Set Down in Malice.* New York, 1919.

Darbyshire, Alfred. *The Art of the Victorian Stage.* London, 1907.

Darlington, W. A. *Literature in the Theatre and Other Essays.* London, 1925.

Darlington, W. A. *Through the Fourth Wall.* New York, n. d.

Eaton, W. P. *Plays and Players, Leaves from a Critic's Scrapbook.* Cincinnati, 1916.

Goldman, Emma. *The Social Significance of Modern Drama.* Boston, 1914.

Goldsmith, Oliver. "Sentimental Comedy." *Miscellaneous Works,* IV. 457–461. London, 1812.

Grein, J. T. *Dramatic Criticism,* 5 v. London, 1899–1905.

Grundy, Sydney. *The Play of the Future by a Playwright of the Past.* London, 1914.

Hamilton, Clayton. *Conversations on Contemporary Drama.* New York, 1924.

Hankin, St. John. *Dramatic Works,* Vol. III. New York, 1912.

Hanley, Peter. *A Jubilee of Playgoing.* London, 1887.

Hazlitt, Wm. *A View of the English Stage; or, a Series of Dramatic Criticisms.* London, 1818. (Vol. VIII, Collected Works.)

Hunt, Leigh. *Critical Essays on the Performers of the London Theatres, Including General Observations on the Practice and Genius of the Stage.* London, 1807.

Irving, H. B. *Occasional Papers, Dramatic and Historical.* Boston, 1907.

Jones, H. A. "Cornerstones of Modern Drama." *Fortnightly Review,* LXXXVI (1906). 1084–1094.

Jones, H. A. *The Foundations of a National Drama.* New York, London, 1913.

Jones, H. A. "Literature and the Modern Drama." *Atlantic Monthly,* XCVIII (1906). 796–807.

Jones, H. A. *The Renascence of the English Drama.* London, 1895.

Knight, Joseph. *Theatrical Notes.* London, 1893.

Matthews, Brander. *Playwrights on Playmaking and Other Studies of the Stage.* New York, 1923.

Meredith, George. *An Essay on Comedy and the Uses of the Comic Spirit.* New York, 1897.

Montague, C. E. *Dramatic Values.* London, 1911.

Moore, George. *Impressions and Opinions.* New York, 1891.

Moore, J. B. *Comic and Realistic in English Drama.* Chicago, 1925.

Morley, Henry. *The Journal of a London Playgoer from 1851 to 1886.* London, 1891.

Morris, Mowbray. *Essays in Theatrical Criticism.* London, 1882.

Nathan, G. J. *Art of the Night.* New York, 1928.

Nicoll, Allardyce. *An Introduction to Dramatic Theory.* New York, 1924.

Palmer, John. "Comedy and Cant." *Saturday Review,* CXVII (1914). 334.

Palmer, John. "Comedy Again and Cant." *Saturday Review,* CXVII (1914). 366.

Pollock, Channing. *Footlights, Fore and Aft.* Boston, 1911.

Ruhl, A. B. *Second Nights; People and Ideas of the Theatre Today.* New York, 1914.

Russell, Sir Edward R. *The Theatre and Things Said About It.* Liverpool, 1911.

Scott, Clement. *From "The Bells" to "King Arthur."* London, 1897.

Shaw, G. B. *Dramatic Opinions and Essays,* 2 v. London, 1907.

Simpson, J. P. "Manners on the Stage." *Theatre* (Lond.), III, n. s. (1879). 270–273.

S[pence], E. F. *Our Stage and its Critics.* London, 1910.

Taylor, Tom. "Some Thoughts on the English Stage." *Every Saturday,* VII (1869). 193–198.

Tree, H. B. *Thoughts and After-thoughts.* London, New York, 1913.

Walbrook, H. M. *Nights at the Play.* London, 1911.

Walkley, A. B. *The Drama and Life.* London, 1907.

Walkley, A. B. *Dramatic Criticism.* London, 1903.
Walkley, A. B. *Pastiche and Prejudice.* New York, 1921.
Walkley, A. B. *Playhouse Impressions.* London, 1892.
Walkley, A. B. *Still More Prejudices.* New York, 1925.
Wyndham, Horace. *A Magnificent Mummer.* London, 1909.

Social Background

Arnold, Walter. *The Life and Death of the Sublime Society of Beefsteaks.* London, 1871.
Barker, Harley Granville, ed. *The Eighteen Seventies. Essays by Fellows of the Royal Society of Literature.* Cambridge (Eng.), New York, 1929.
Beer, Thomas. *The Mauve Decade.* New York, 1926.
Besant, Sir Walter. *London in the Eighteenth Century.* London, 1902.
Botsford, J. B. *English Society in the Eighteenth Century.* New York, 1924.
Boulton, Wm. B. *The Amusements of Old London,* 2 v. London, 1901.
Burdett, Osbert. *The Beardsley Period.* New York, 1925.
Egan, Pierce. *Life in London.* London, 1821.
Egan, Pierce. *The True History of Tom and Jerry.* London, n. d.
Escott, T. H. S. *Social Transformations of the Victorian Age. A Survey of Court and Country.* London, 1897.
Escott, T. H. S. *Society in the Country House.* London, 1907.
Escott, T. H. S. *Society in London.* London, 1886.
Fitzgerald, Percy H. *Life and Times of William IV, Including a View of Social Life and Manners during His Reign,* 2 v. London, 1884.
Fitzgerald, Percy H. *Life of George the Fourth, Including His Letters and Opinions with a View of the Men, Manners, and Politics of His Reign.* London, 1881.
Goede, C. A. G. *A Foreigner's Opinion of England.* Boston, 1822.
Inge, Wm. R. *The Victorian Age.* Cambridge (Eng.), 1922.

Jackson, Frederick John Foakes. *Social Life in England, 1750–1850.* New York, 1916.

Jackson, Holbrook. *The Eighteen Nineties.* New York, 1913.

Le Gallienne, Rich. *The Romantic Nineties.* Garden City, N. Y., 1925.

Lennox, Lord William Pitt. *Fashion Then and Now. . . .* London, 1878.

Molloy, J. F. *Victoria Regina: Her Court and Her Subjects from Her Accession to the Death of the Prince-Consort,* 2 v. New York, 1908.

Murray, E. C. G. *Sidelights on English Society.* London, 1883.

Nevill, Ralph. *The World of Fashion, 1837–1922.* New York, 1924.

Parker, George. *A View of Society and Manners in High and Low Life,* 2 v. London, 1781.

" Paston, George " [Emily Morse Symonds]. *Sidelights on the Georgian Period.* London, 1902.

Quiller-Couch, Arthur. *Studies in Literature,* 3 v. New York, 1922–1929.

Stephen, Sir Leslie. *English Literature and Society in the Eighteenth Century.* London, 1904.

Synge, M. B. *A Short History of Social Life in England.* London, 1906.

Timbs, John F. S. A. *Clubs and Club Life in London.* London, 1872.

Traill, H. D. and Mann, J. S. *Social England,* 6 v. London, New York, 1904.

Turberville, A. S. *English Men and Manners in the Eighteenth Century.* Oxford, 1926.

Wyndham, Horace. *The Nineteen Hundreds.* London, 1923.

Yates, Edmund H. *Fifty Years of London Life.* New York, 1885.

Bibliography and Reference

Adams, W. D. *A Dictionary of the Drama. . . .* London, 1904.

Baker, David E. *Biographia Dramatica, . . . ,* 3 v. London,

1812.

Baker, G. H. *List of Books Chiefly on the Drama and Literary Criticism.* New York, 1897. (Columbia University Publications.)

Boase, Frederic. *Modern English Biography,* 3 v. London, 1892–1901. (Supplement, 1908–1912.)

Boston Public Library. *Catalogue of Allen A. Brown Collection of Books Relating to the Stage.* Boston, 1919.

Cant, Monna. " Bibliography of English Drama from 1890 to 1920." *Library Association Record,* Feb., 1922.

Carson, Lionel, ed. *Stage Year Book.* London, 1908–1927.

Catalogue of a Collection of Books Relating to the Drama, the English and American Stage, Dramatic Memoirs, etc. New York, n. d. G. C. Leavitt & Co., Auctioneers.

Clarence, Reginald. *" The Stage " Cyclopedia. A Bibliography of Plays, ...* London, 1909.

Faxon, F. W. *Dramatic Index.* Boston, 1909 ff.

French, Samuel. *Catalogue of Plays, ...* New York, 1930.

French, Samuel & Son. *International Descriptive Catalogue of Plays and Dramatic Works.* New York, n. d.

[Genest, John.] *Some Account of the English Stage, from the Restoration in 1660 to 1830,* 10 v. Bath, 1832.

Leach, H. S. *Union List of Collections of English Drama in American Libraries.* Princeton, 1916.

Lowe, R. W. *A Bibliographical Account of English Theatrical Literature.* London, 1888.

Lowndes, Wm. T. *Bibliographer's Manual of English Literature,* 5 v. in 10. London, 1857–1864.

Newberry Library. *Materials for the Study of the English Drama (excluding Shakespeare): a Selected List of Books in the Newberry Library.* Chicago, 1912.

Northup, C. S. *A Register of Bibliographies of the English Language and Literature.* New Haven, 1925.

Parker, John. *Who's Who in the Theatre: a Biographical Record of the Contemporary Stage,* 6th edition. London, 1930.

Pence, J. H., compiler. *The Magazine and the Drama, an Index.* New York, 1896. (Publications of Dunlap Society, ser. 2, v. 2.)

Plarr, Victor G. *Men and Women of the Time, a Dictionary of Contemporaries,* 14th edition. London, 1895.

Thespian Dictionary. . . . London, 1805.

United States Copyright Offices. *Dramatic Compositions; Signatures Catalogue of Copyright Dramas.* U. S. Government Printing Office, Washington, 1915.

INDEX